Chapters 1-6 Story by
Chapters 1,5,6 Art by **En**
Chapters 2-4 Art by

No Dominion Story by **[**
No Dominion Art by **Mich**

MW00805312

Cover by **Jacen Burrows**

Chapter Breaks by
**Jacen Burrows, Raulo Caceres,
Ron Adrian, Christian Zanier**

Cover Gallery by **German Nobile**

Lettering by **Kurt Hathaway**

God is Dead created by
Jonathan Hickman

William Christensen editor-in-chief

Mark Seifert creative director

Jim Kuhoric managing editor

Ariana Osborne production assistant

w w w . a v a t a r p r e s s . c o m
www.twitter.com/avatarpress
www.facebook.com/avatarpresscomics

God is Dead **Volume Eight**
May 2016. Published by Avatar Press, Inc.,
515 N. Century Blvd. Rantoul, IL 61866. ©2016 Avatar
Press, Inc. God is Dead and all related properties TM
& ©2016 Jonathan Hickman and Avatar Press, Inc. All
characters as depicted in this story are over the age of
18. The stories, characters, and institutions mentioned
in this magazine are entirely fictional. Printed in Canada.

ONE

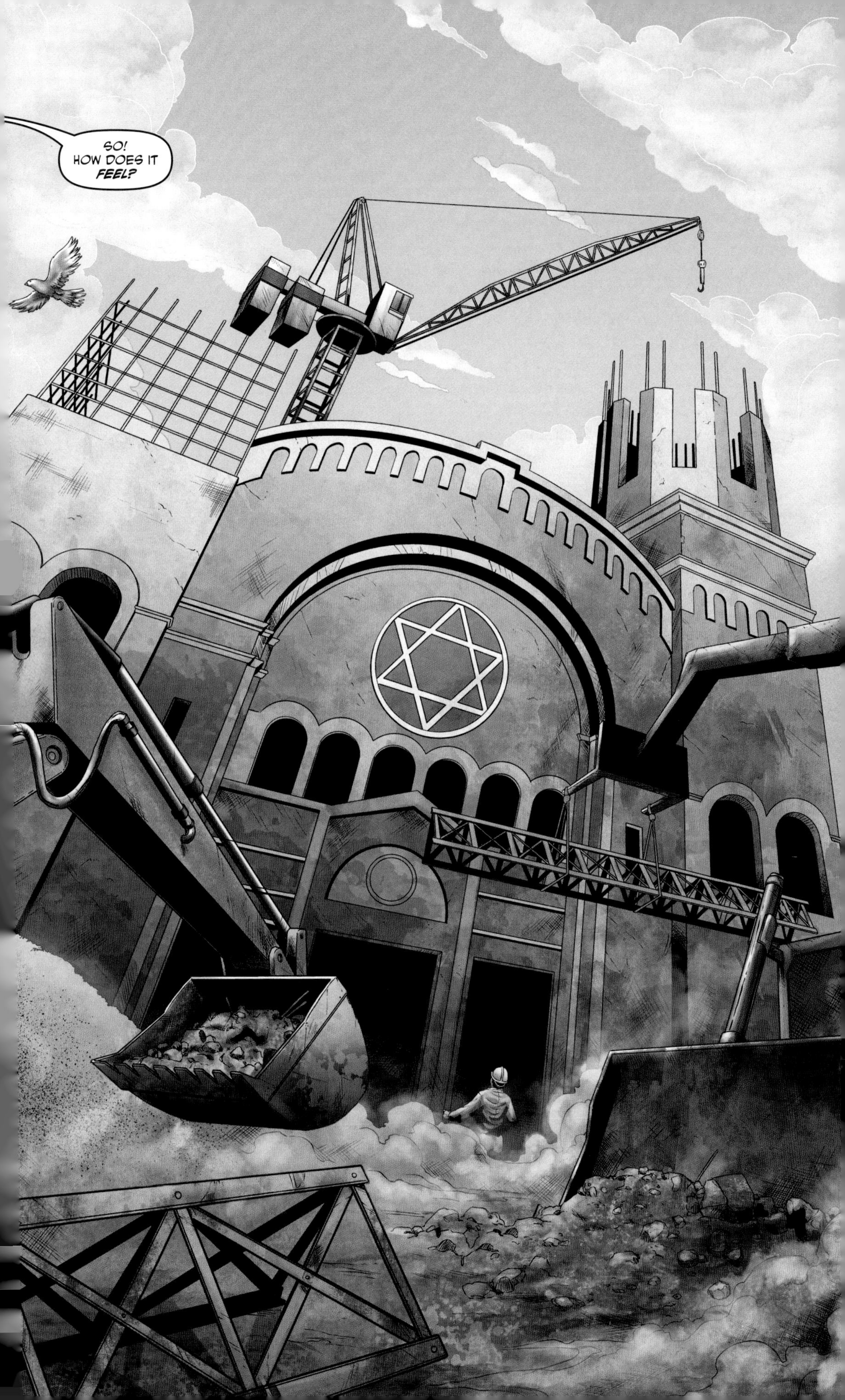
SO! HOW DOES IT *FEEL?*

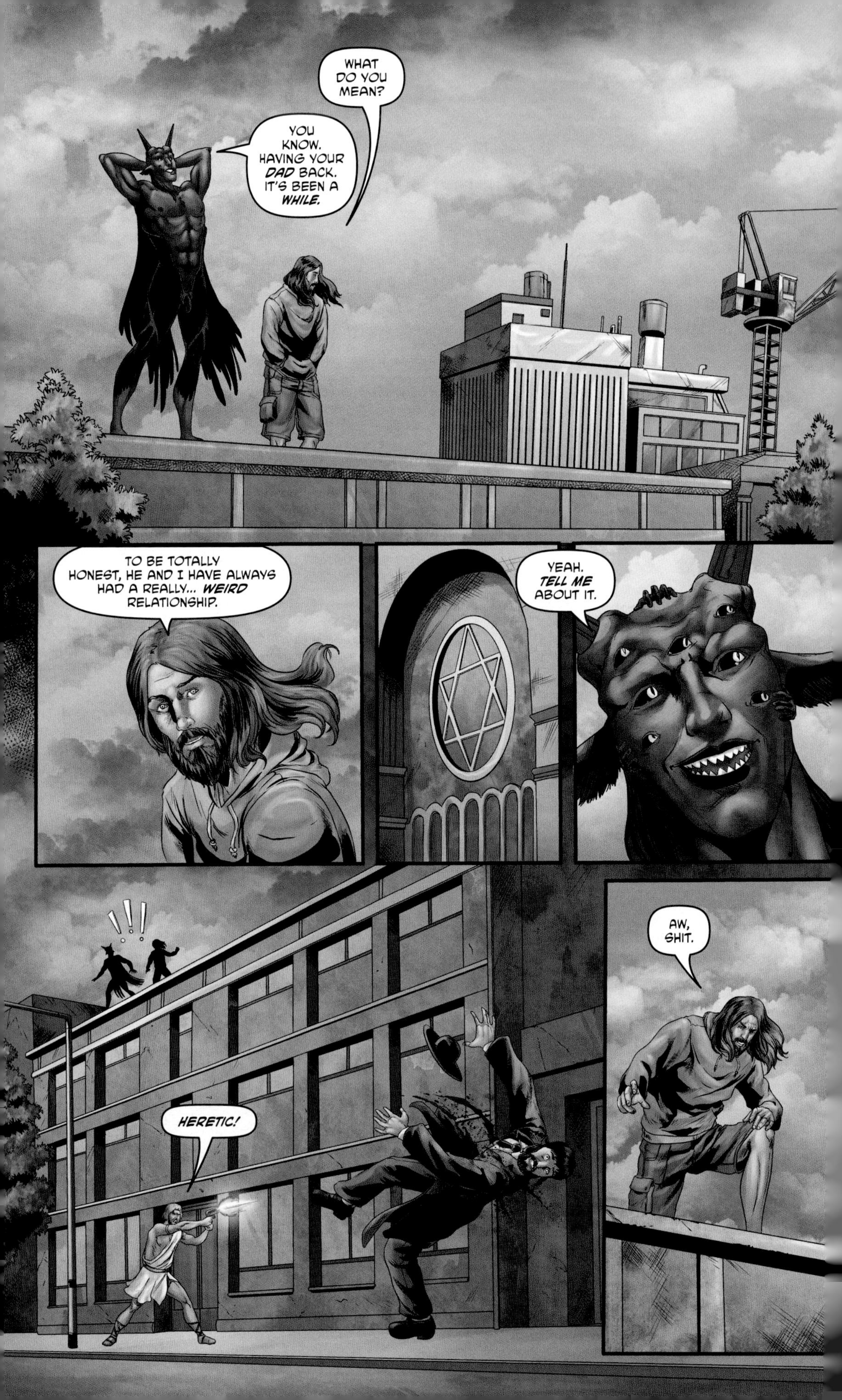
WHAT DO YOU MEAN?
YOU KNOW. HAVING YOUR *DAD* BACK. IT'S BEEN A *WHILE.*
TO BE TOTALLY HONEST, HE AND I HAVE ALWAYS HAD A REALLY... *WEIRD* RELATIONSHIP.
YEAH. *TELL ME* ABOUT IT.
!!!
HERETIC!
AW, SHIT.

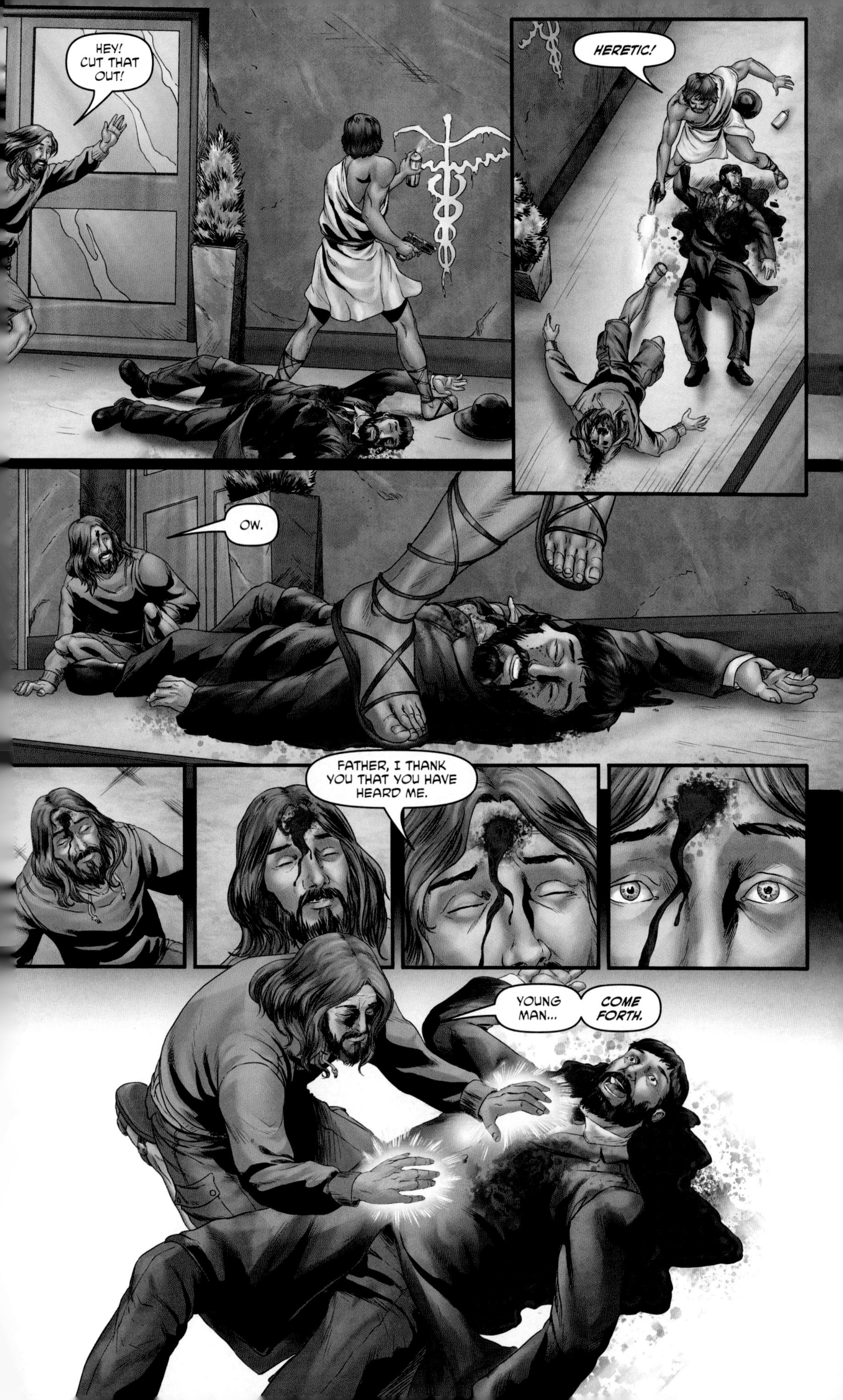
HEY! CUT THAT OUT!
HERETIC!
OW.
FATHER, I THANK YOU THAT YOU HAVE HEARD ME.
YOUNG MAN...
COME FORTH.

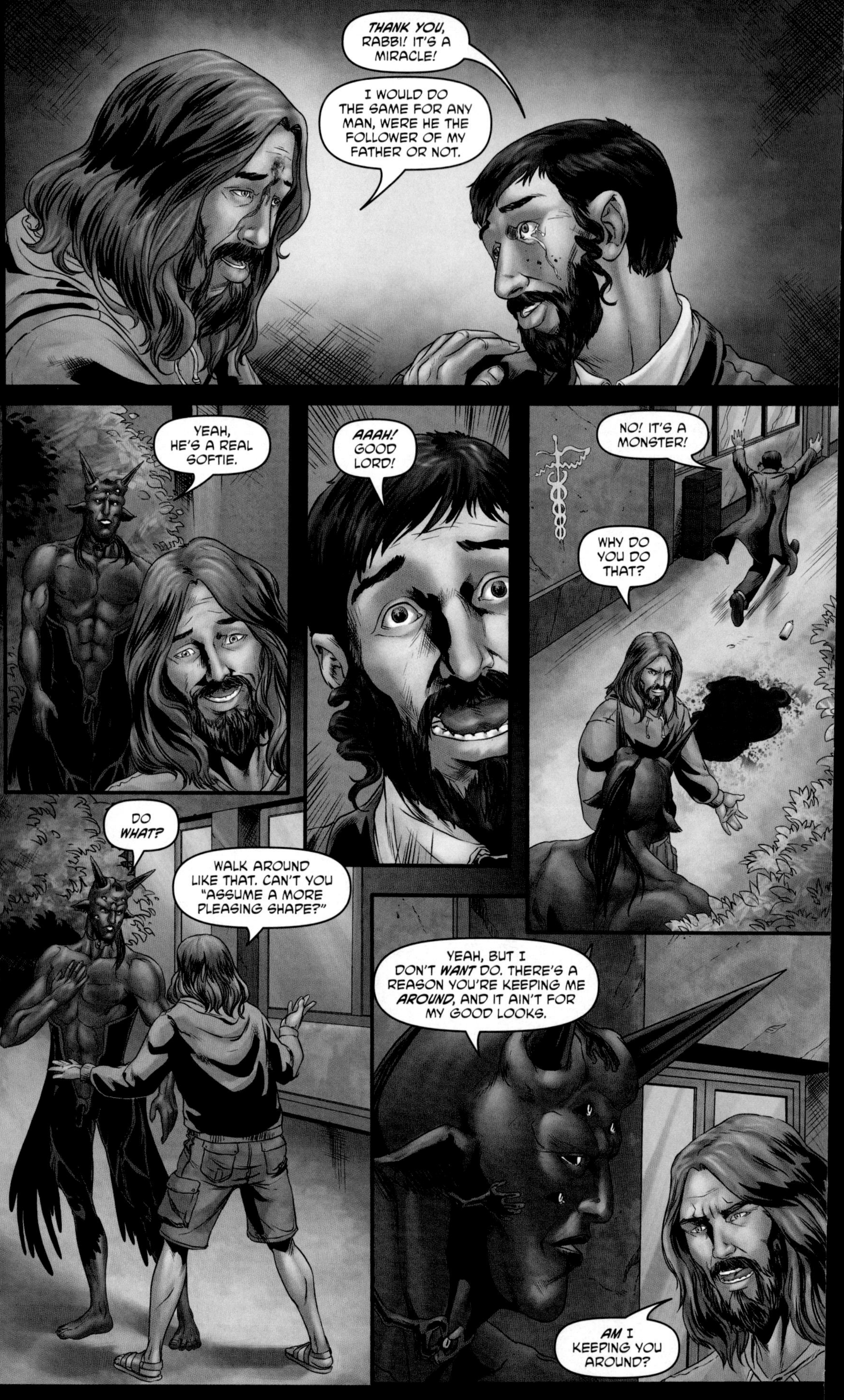
THANK YOU, RABBI! IT'S A MIRACLE!
I WOULD DO THE SAME FOR ANY MAN, WERE HE THE FOLLOWER OF MY FATHER OR NOT.
YEAH, HE'S A REAL SOFTIE.
AAAH! GOOD LORD!
NO! IT'S A MONSTER!
WHY DO YOU DO THAT?
DO WHAT?
WALK AROUND LIKE THAT. CAN'T YOU "ASSUME A MORE PLEASING SHAPE?"
YEAH, BUT I DON'T WANT DO. THERE'S A REASON YOU'RE KEEPING ME AROUND, AND IT AIN'T FOR MY GOOD LOOKS.
AM I KEEPING YOU AROUND?

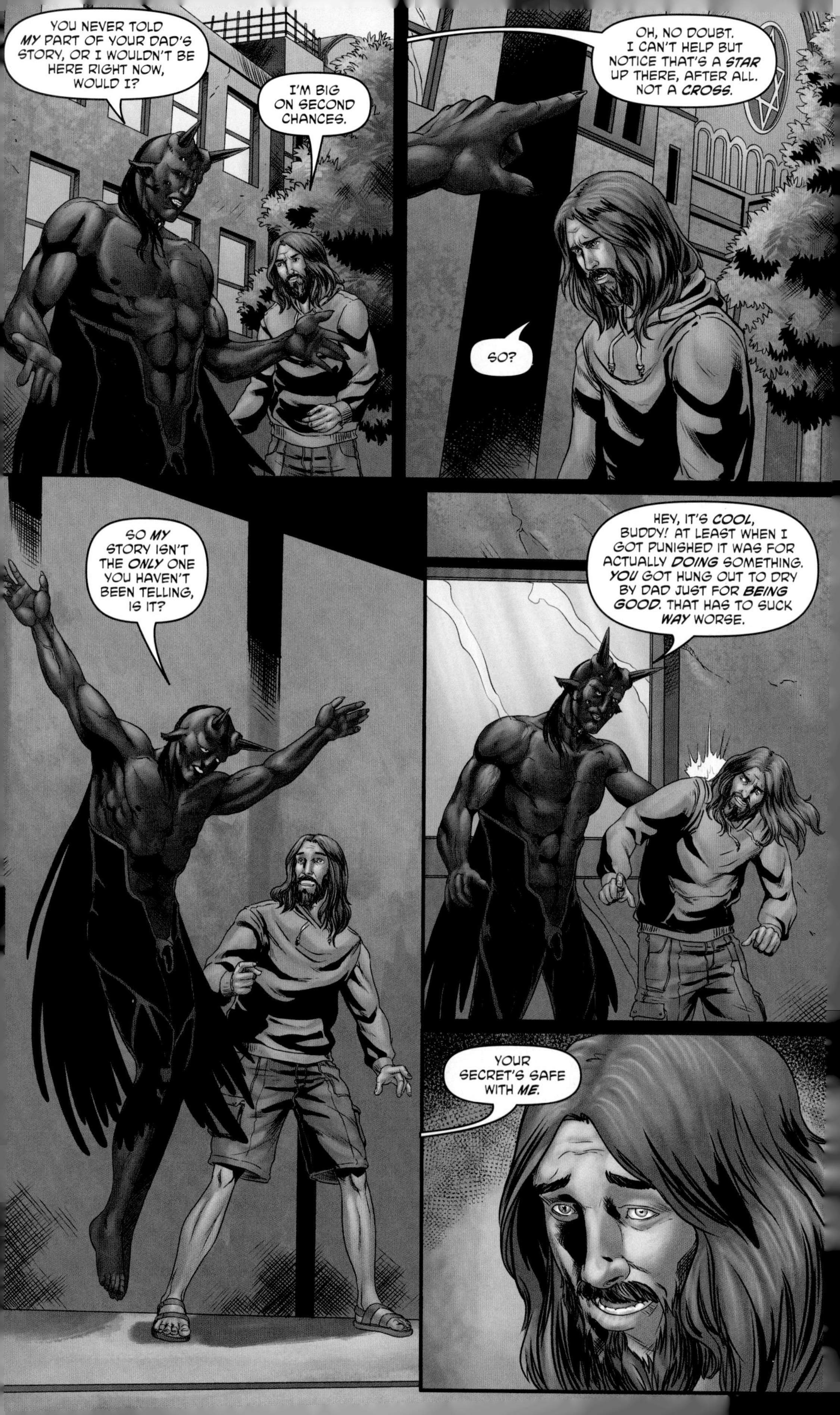
YOU NEVER TOLD MY PART OF YOUR DAD'S STORY, OR I WOULDN'T BE HERE RIGHT NOW, WOULD I?
I'M BIG ON SECOND CHANCES.
OH, NO DOUBT. I CAN'T HELP BUT NOTICE THAT'S A STAR UP THERE, AFTER ALL. NOT A CROSS.
SO?
SO MY STORY ISN'T THE ONLY ONE YOU HAVEN'T BEEN TELLING, IS IT?
HEY, IT'S COOL, BUDDY! AT LEAST WHEN I GOT PUNISHED IT WAS FOR ACTUALLY DOING SOMETHING. YOU GOT HUNG OUT TO DRY BY DAD JUST FOR BEING GOOD. THAT HAS TO SUCK WAY WORSE.
YOUR SECRET'S SAFE WITH ME.

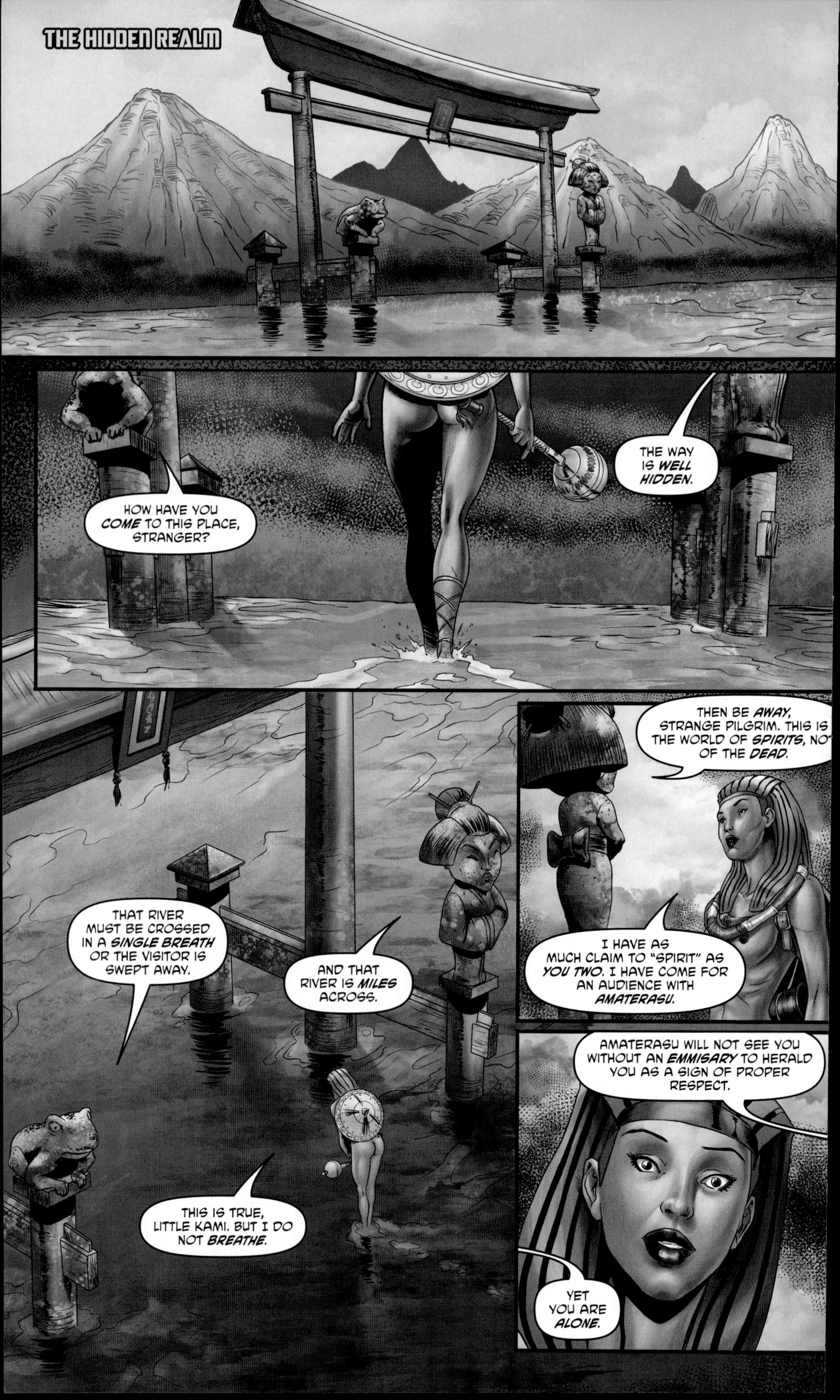
THE HIDDEN REALM
HOW HAVE YOU COME TO THIS PLACE, STRANGER?
THE WAY IS WELL HIDDEN.
THEN BE AWAY, STRANGE PILGRIM. THIS IS THE WORLD OF SPIRITS, NOT OF THE DEAD.
I HAVE AS MUCH CLAIM TO "SPIRIT" AS YOU TWO. I HAVE COME FOR AN AUDIENCE WITH AMATERASU.
AMATERASU WILL NOT SEE YOU WITHOUT AN EMMISARY TO HERALD YOU AS A SIGN OF PROPER RESPECT.
YET YOU ARE ALONE.
THAT RIVER MUST BE CROSSED IN A SINGLE BREATH OR THE VISITOR IS SWEPT AWAY.
AND THAT RIVER IS MILES ACROSS.
THIS IS TRUE, LITTLE KAMI. BUT I DO NOT BREATHE.

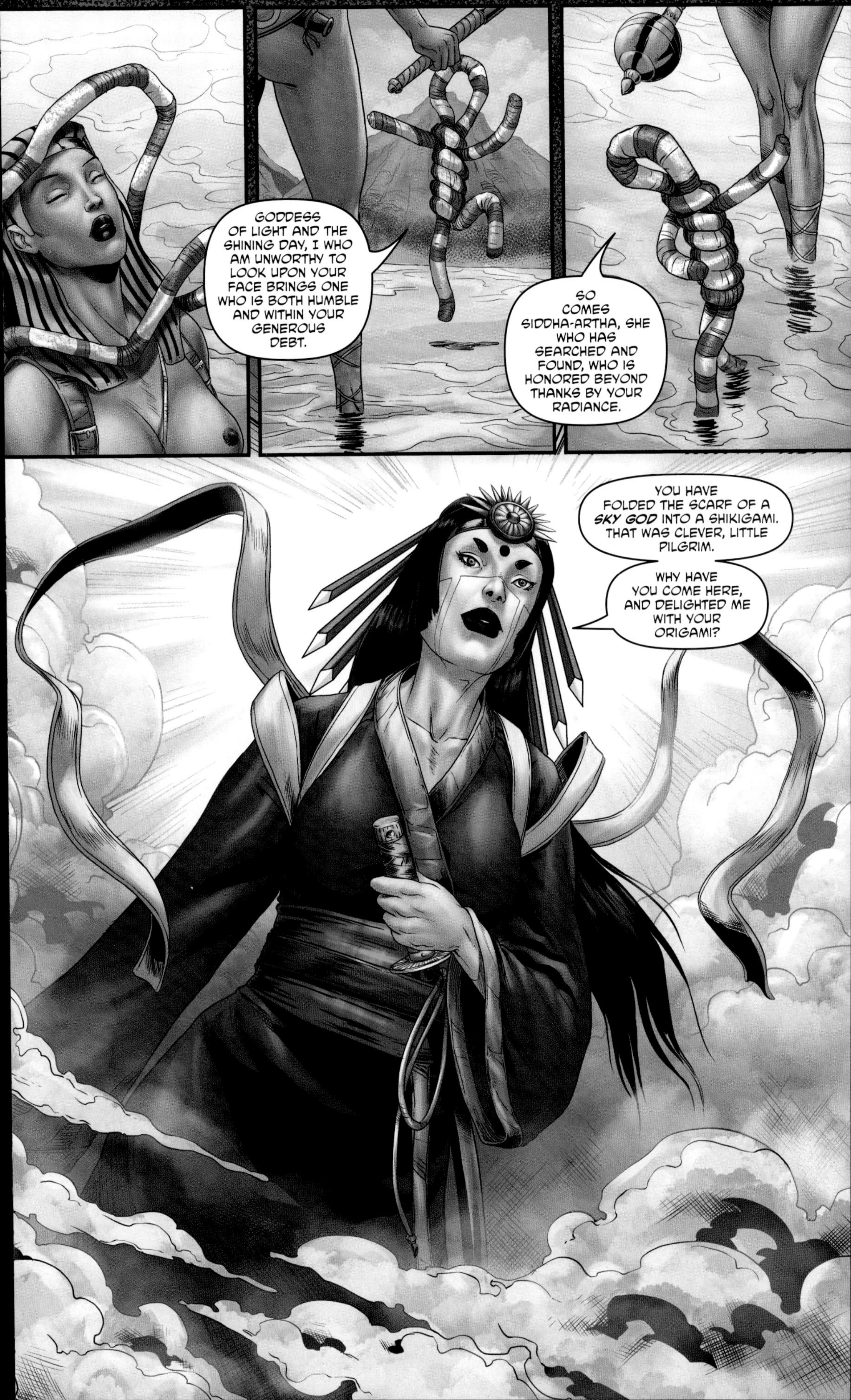
GODDESS OF LIGHT AND THE SHINING DAY, I WHO AM UNWORTHY TO LOOK UPON YOUR FACE BRINGS ONE WHO IS BOTH HUMBLE AND WITHIN YOUR GENEROUS DEBT.
SO COMES SIDDHA-ARTHA, SHE WHO HAS SEARCHED AND FOUND, WHO IS HONORED BEYOND THANKS BY YOUR RADIANCE.
YOU HAVE FOLDED THE SCARF OF A *SKY GOD* INTO A SHIKIGAMI. THAT WAS CLEVER, LITTLE PILGRIM.
WHY HAVE YOU COME HERE, AND DELIGHTED ME WITH YOUR ORIGAMI?

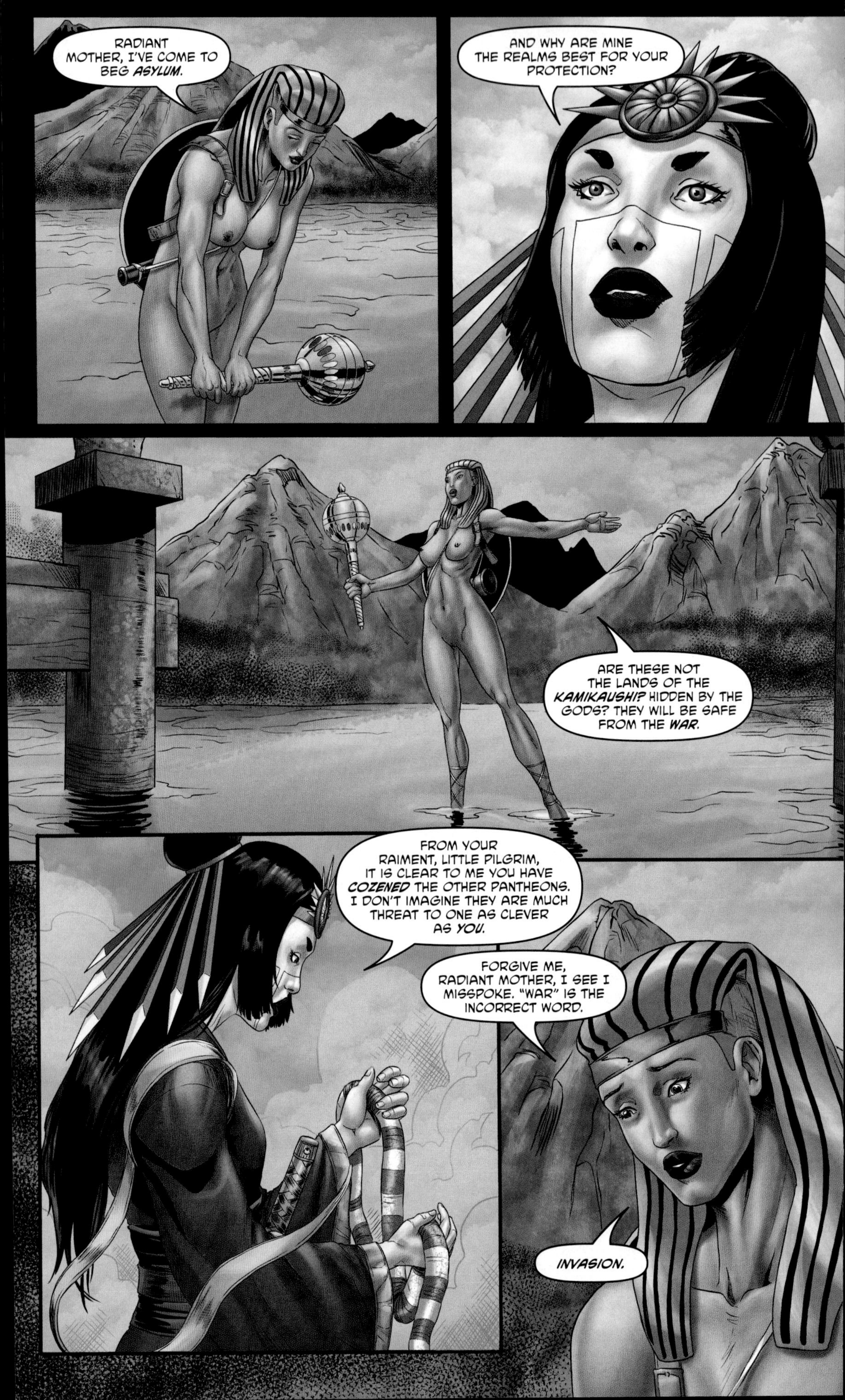
RADIANT MOTHER, I'VE COME TO BEG *ASYLUM*.
AND WHY ARE MINE THE REALMS BEST FOR YOUR PROTECTION?
ARE THESE NOT THE LANDS OF THE *KAMIKAUSHI?* HIDDEN BY THE GODS? THEY WILL BE SAFE FROM THE *WAR*.
FROM YOUR RAIMENT, LITTLE PILGRIM, IT IS CLEAR TO ME YOU HAVE *COZENED* THE OTHER PANTHEONS. I DON'T IMAGINE THEY ARE MUCH THREAT TO ONE AS CLEVER AS *YOU*.
FORGIVE ME, RADIANT MOTHER, I SEE I MISSPOKE. "WAR" IS THE INCORRECT WORD.
INVASION.

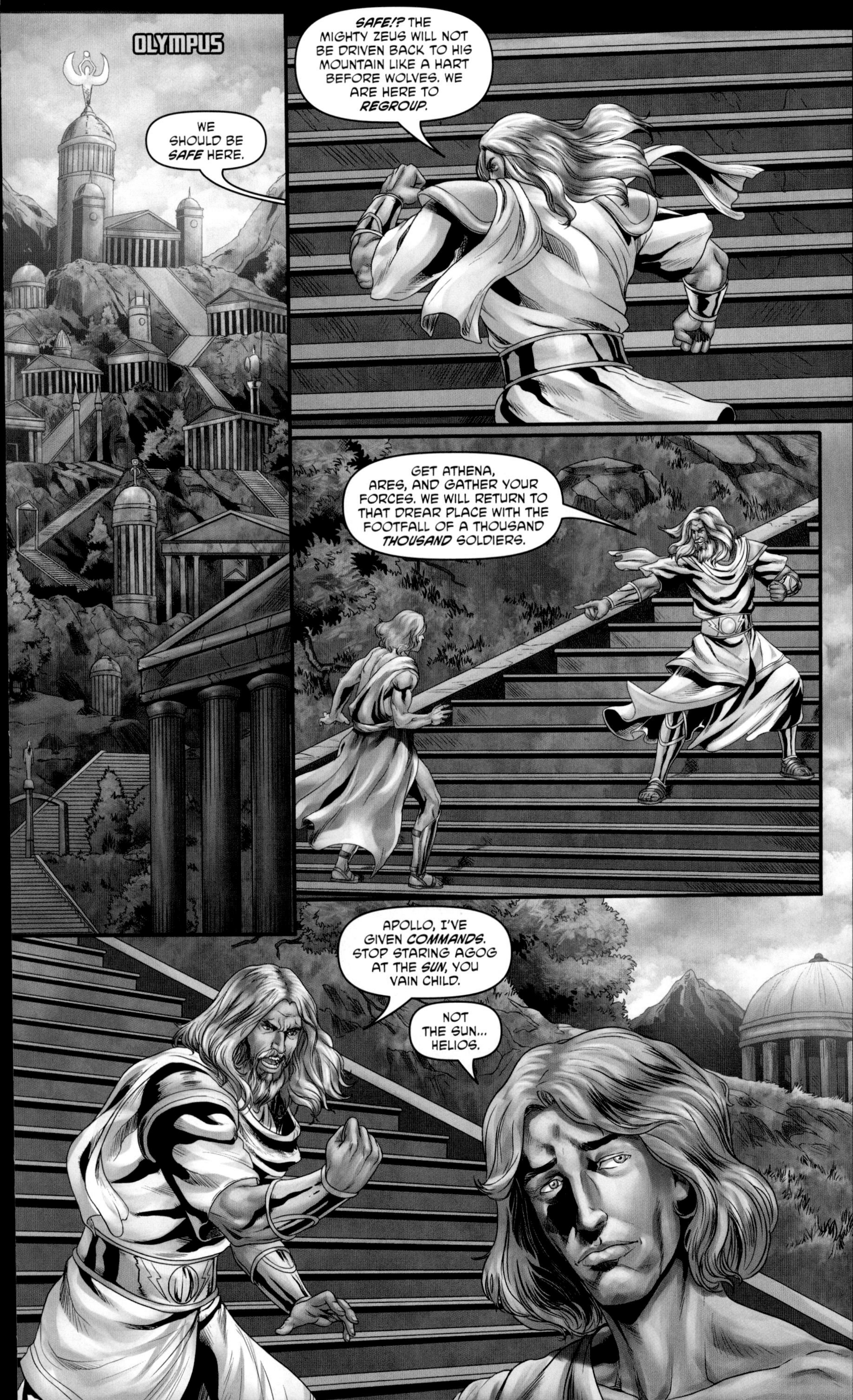
OLYMPUS
WE SHOULD BE SAFE HERE.
SAFE!? THE MIGHTY ZEUS WILL NOT BE DRIVEN BACK TO HIS MOUNTAIN LIKE A HART BEFORE WOLVES. WE ARE HERE TO REGROUP.
GET ATHENA, ARES, AND GATHER YOUR FORCES. WE WILL RETURN TO THAT DREAR PLACE WITH THE FOOTFALL OF A THOUSAND THOUSAND SOLDIERS.
APOLLO, I'VE GIVEN COMMANDS. STOP STARING AGOG AT THE SUN, YOU VAIN CHILD.
NOT THE SUN... HELIOS.

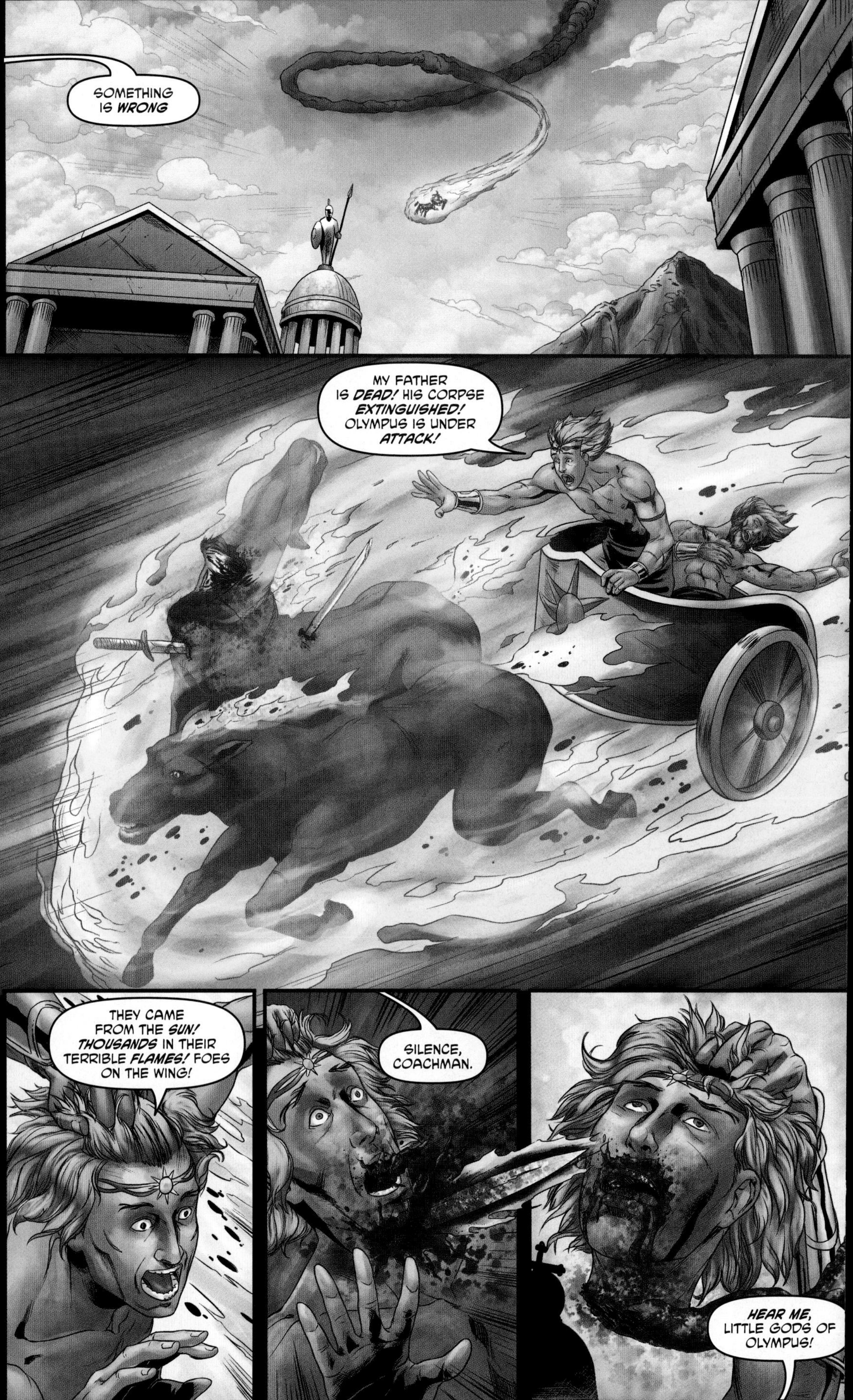
SOMETHING IS WRONG
MY FATHER IS DEAD! HIS CORPSE EXTINGUISHED! OLYMPUS IS UNDER ATTACK!
THEY CAME FROM THE SUN! THOUSANDS IN THEIR TERRIBLE FLAMES! FOES ON THE WING!
SILENCE, COACHMAN.
HEAR ME, LITTLE GODS OF OLYMPUS!

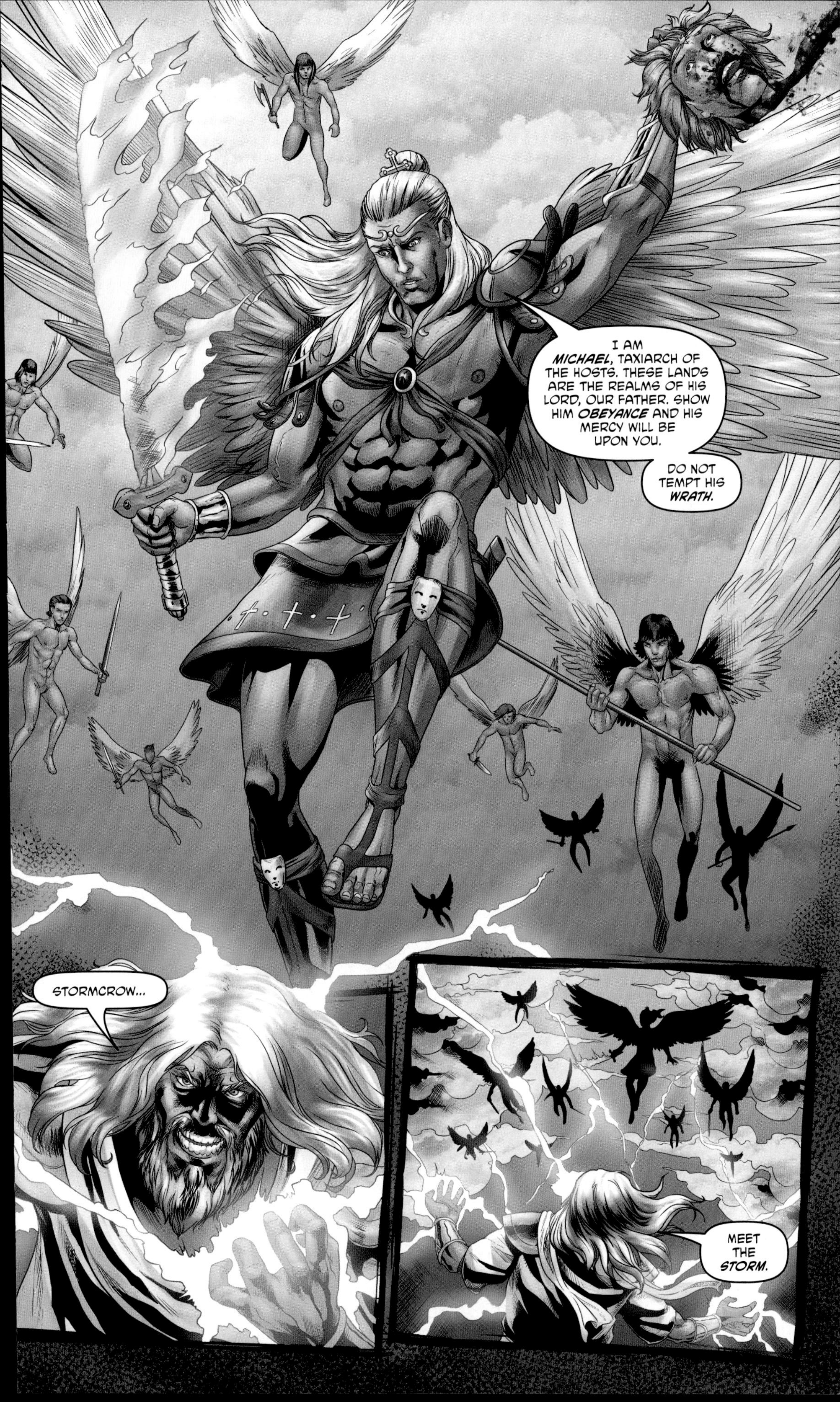

I AM *MICHAEL*, TAXIARCH OF THE HOSTS. THESE LANDS ARE THE REALMS OF HIS LORD, OUR FATHER. SHOW HIM *OBEYANCE* AND HIS MERCY WILL BE UPON YOU.
DO NOT TEMPT HIS *WRATH*.
STORMCROW...
MEET THE *STORM*.

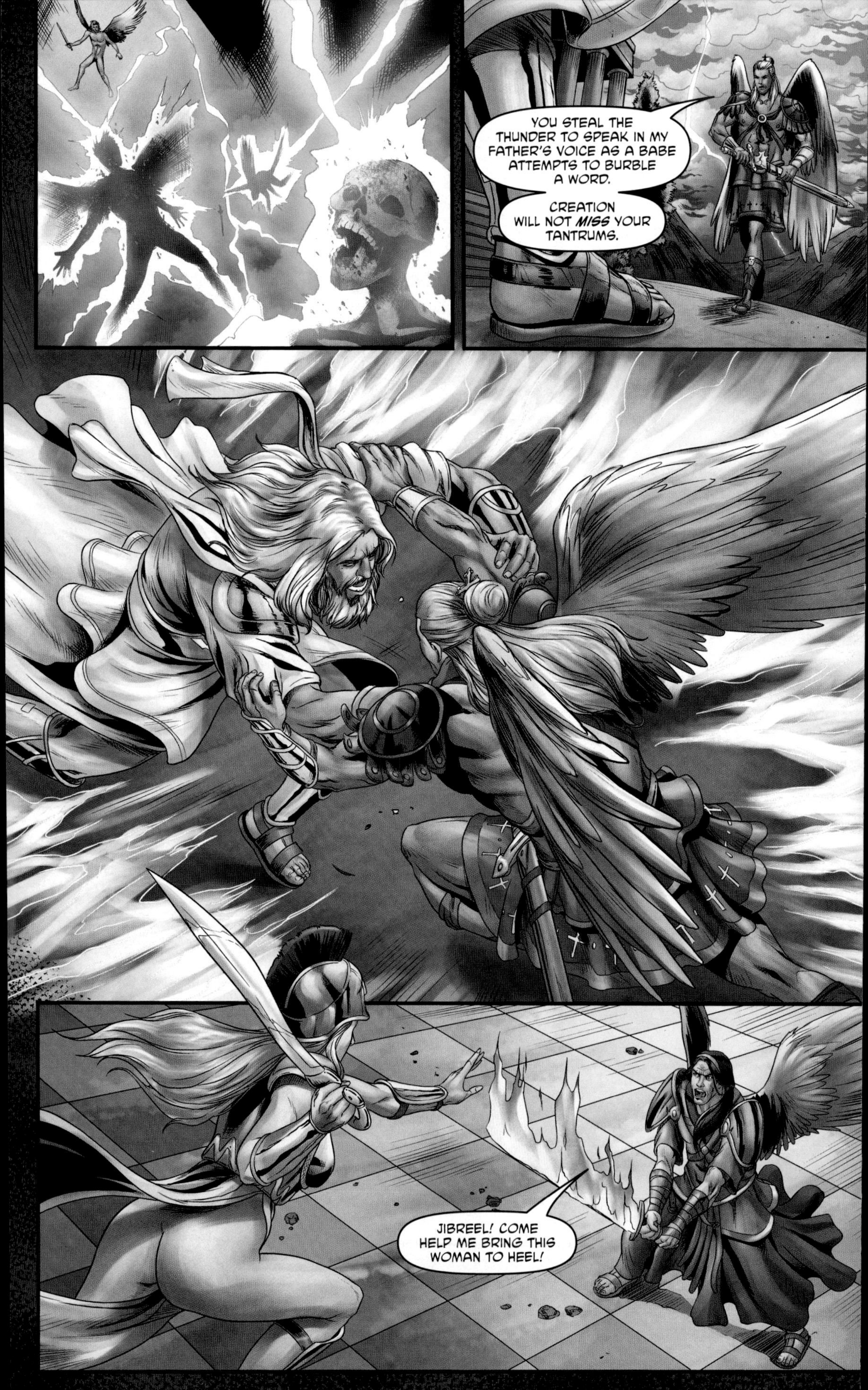
YOU STEAL THE THUNDER TO SPEAK IN MY FATHER'S VOICE AS A BABE ATTEMPTS TO BURBLE A WORD.
CREATION WILL NOT *MISS* YOUR TANTRUMS.
JIBREEL! COME HELP ME BRING THIS WOMAN TO HEEL!

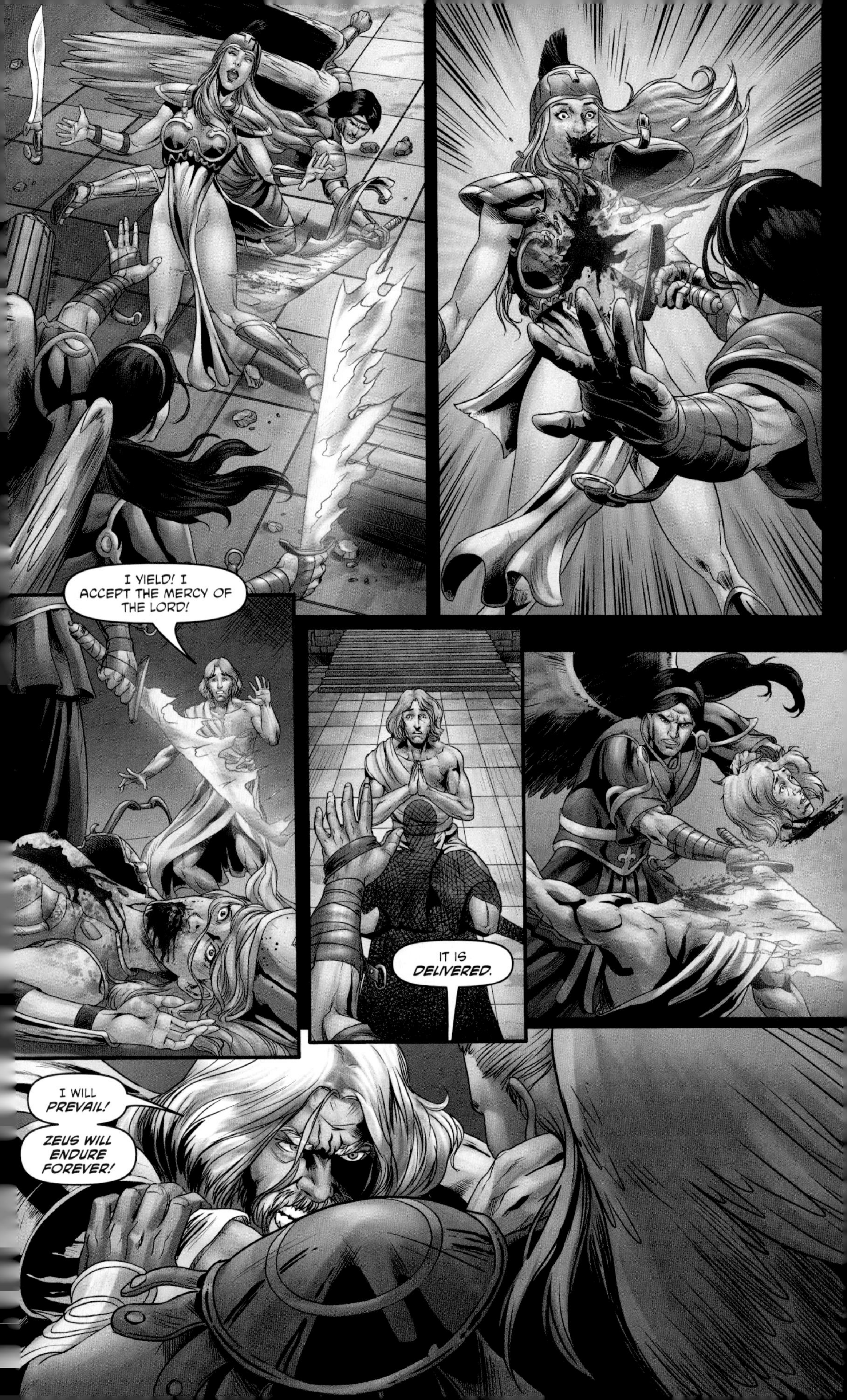
I YIELD! I ACCEPT THE MERCY OF THE LORD!
IT IS *DELIVERED.*
I WILL *PREVAIL!*
ZEUS WILL ENDURE FOREVER!

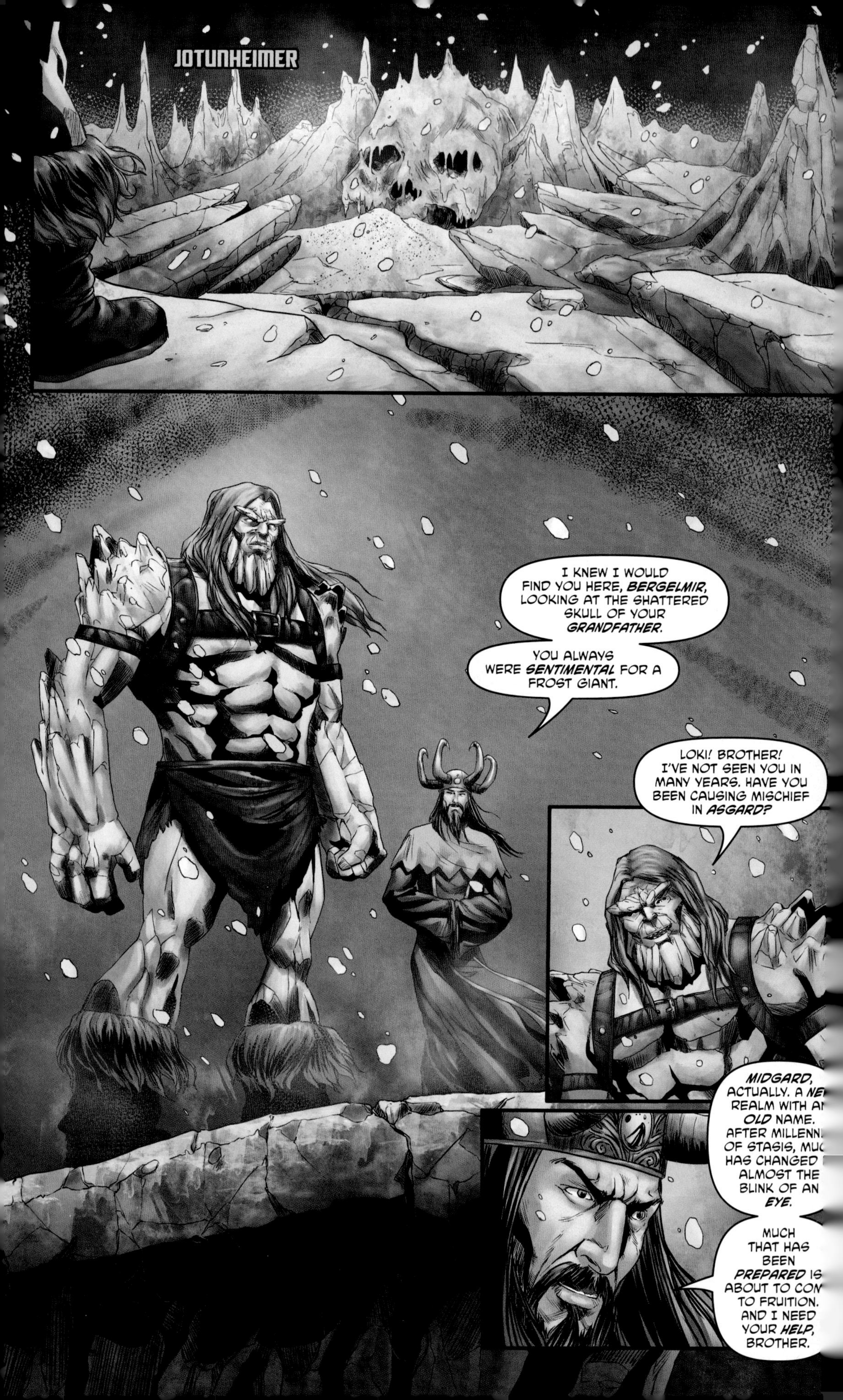
JOTUNHEIMER
I KNEW I WOULD FIND YOU HERE, BERGELMIR, LOOKING AT THE SHATTERED SKULL OF YOUR GRANDFATHER.
YOU ALWAYS WERE SENTIMENTAL FOR A FROST GIANT.
LOKI! BROTHER! I'VE NOT SEEN YOU IN MANY YEARS. HAVE YOU BEEN CAUSING MISCHIEF IN ASGARD?
MIDGARD, ACTUALLY. A NE REALM WITH A OLD NAME. AFTER MILLENN OF STASIS, MUC HAS CHANGED ALMOST THE BLINK OF AN EYE.
MUCH THAT HAS BEEN PREPARED IS ABOUT TO COM TO FRUITION. AND I NEED YOUR HELP, BROTHER.

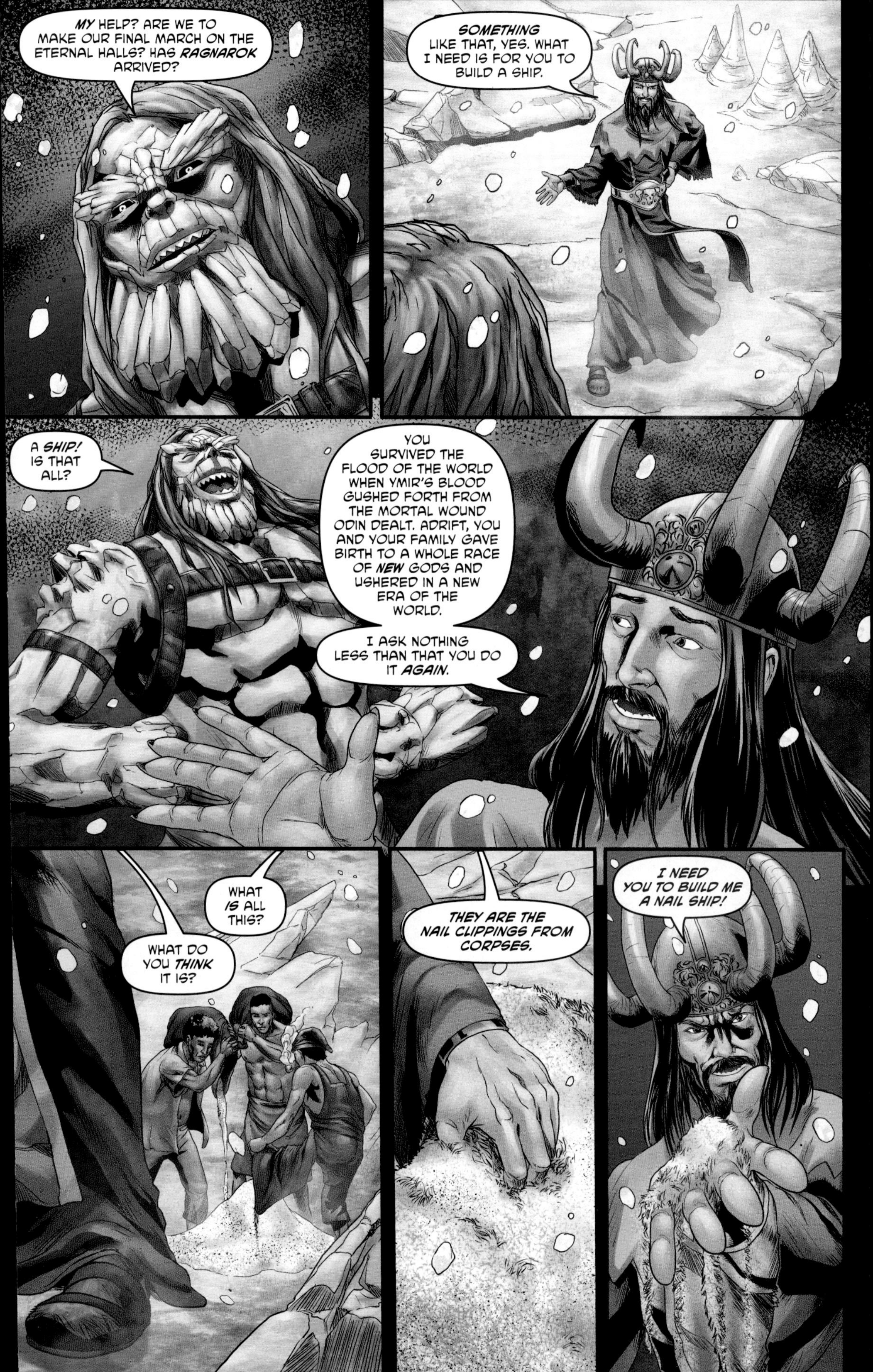
MY HELP? ARE WE TO MAKE OUR FINAL MARCH ON THE ETERNAL HALLS? HAS RAGNAROK ARRIVED?
SOMETHING LIKE THAT, YES. WHAT I NEED IS FOR YOU TO BUILD A SHIP.
A SHIP! IS THAT ALL?
YOU SURVIVED THE FLOOD OF THE WORLD WHEN YMIR'S BLOOD GUSHED FORTH FROM THE MORTAL WOUND ODIN DEALT. ADRIFT, YOU AND YOUR FAMILY GAVE BIRTH TO A WHOLE RACE OF NEW GODS AND USHERED IN A NEW ERA OF THE WORLD.
I ASK NOTHING LESS THAN THAT YOU DO IT AGAIN.
WHAT IS ALL THIS?
WHAT DO YOU THINK IT IS?
THEY ARE THE NAIL CLIPPINGS FROM CORPSES.
I NEED YOU TO BUILD ME A NAIL SHIP!

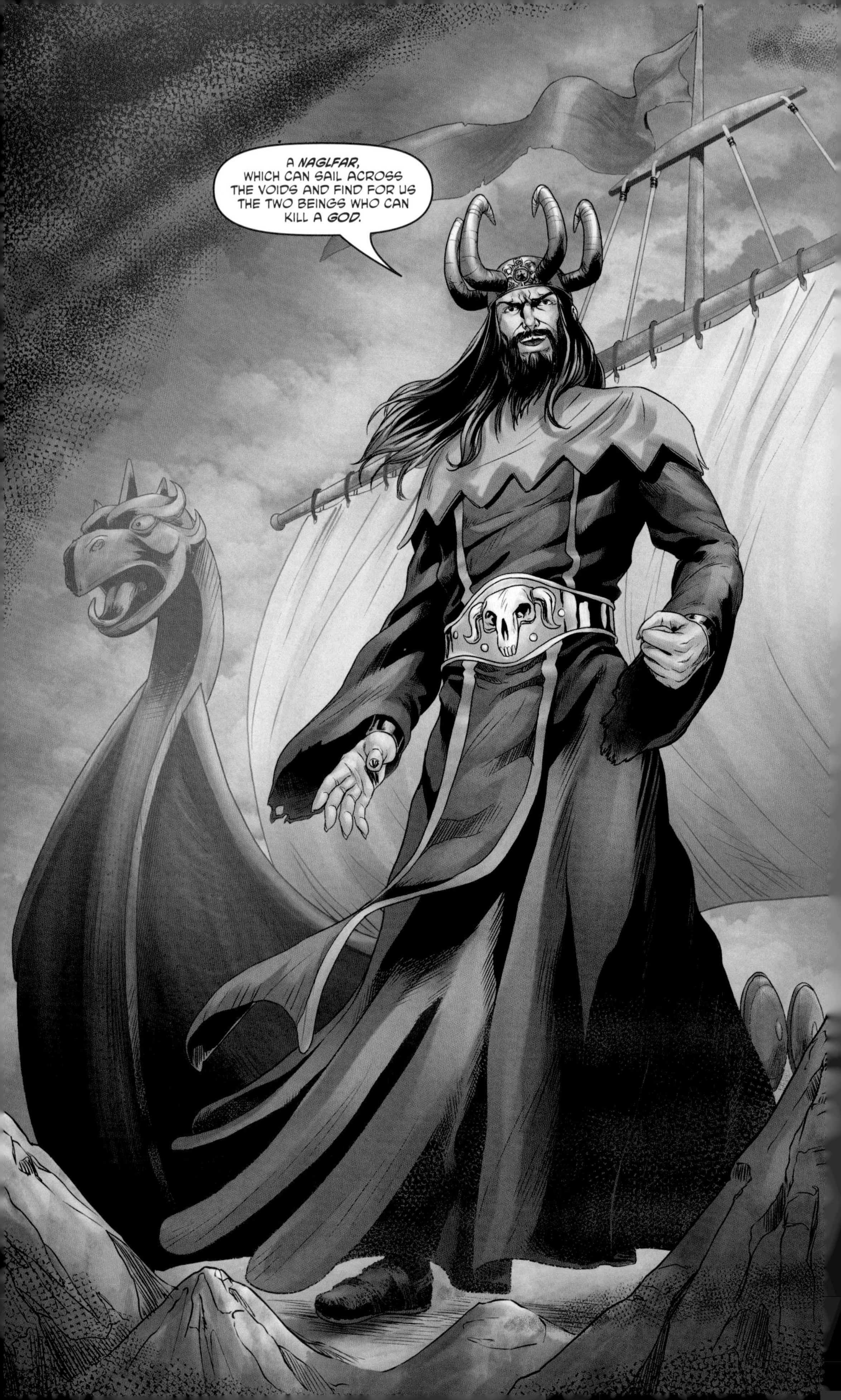
A NAGLFAR, WHICH CAN SAIL ACROSS THE VOIDS AND FIND FOR US THE TWO BEINGS WHO CAN KILL A GOD.

TWO

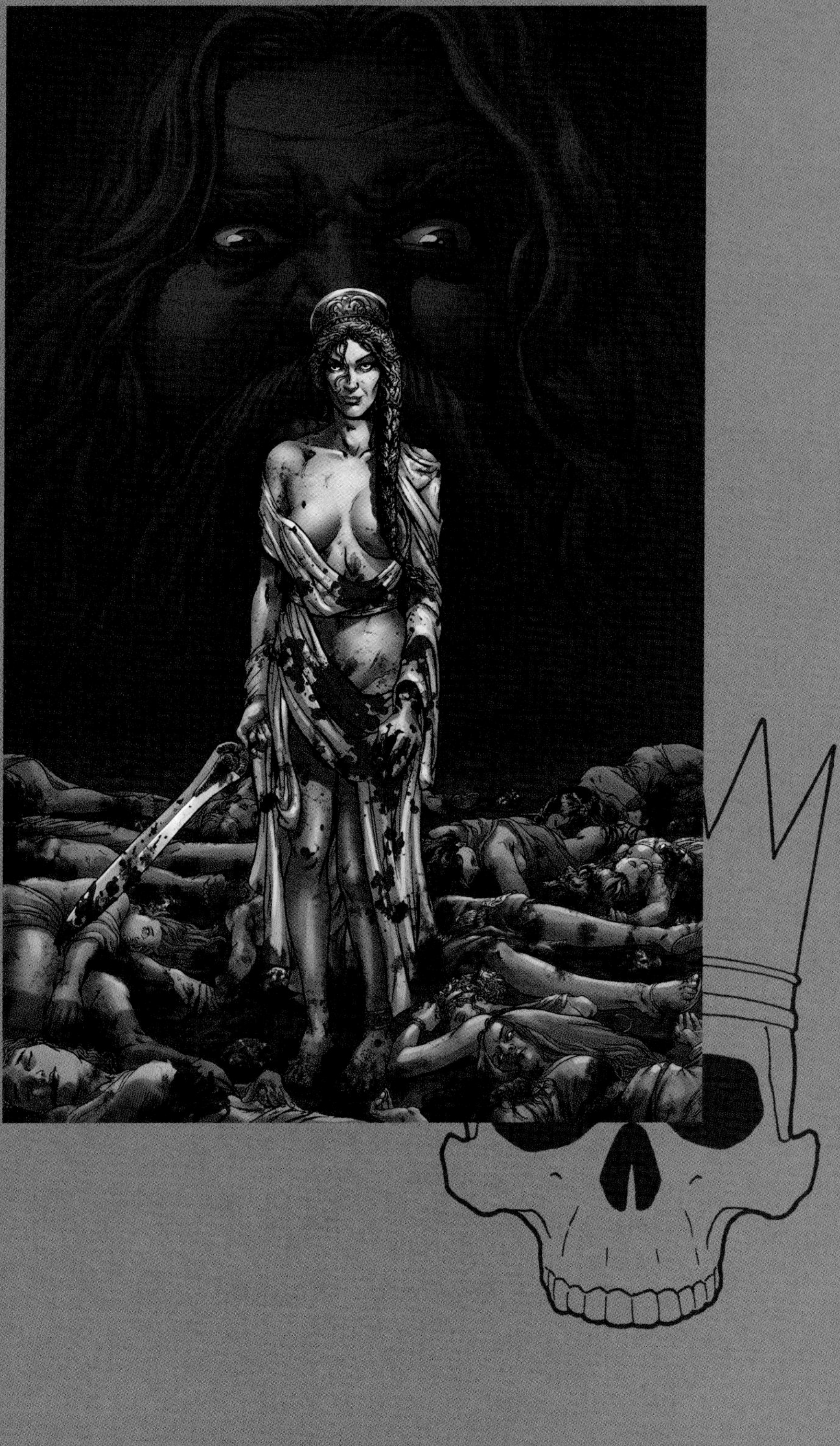

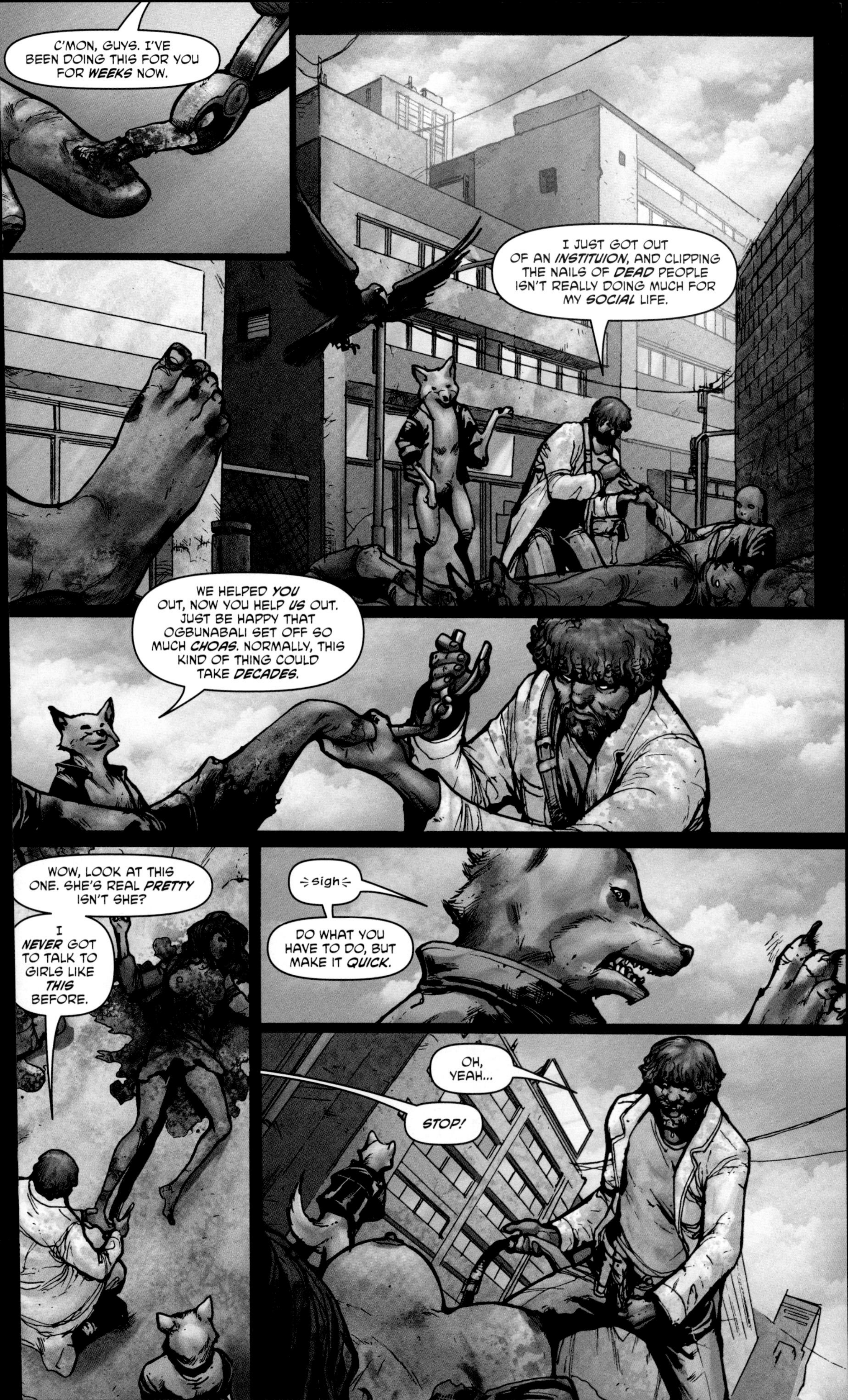
C'MON, GUYS. I'VE BEEN DOING THIS FOR YOU FOR WEEKS NOW.
I JUST GOT OUT OF AN INSTITUION, AND CLIPPING THE NAILS OF DEAD PEOPLE ISN'T REALLY DOING MUCH FOR MY SOCIAL LIFE.
WE HELPED YOU OUT, NOW YOU HELP US OUT. JUST BE HAPPY THAT OGBUNABALI SET OFF SO MUCH CHOAS. NORMALLY, THIS KIND OF THING COULD TAKE DECADES.
WOW, LOOK AT THIS ONE. SHE'S REAL PRETTY ISN'T SHE?
I NEVER GOT TO TALK TO GIRLS LIKE THIS BEFORE.
sigh
DO WHAT YOU HAVE TO DO, BUT MAKE IT QUICK.
OH, YEAH...
STOP!

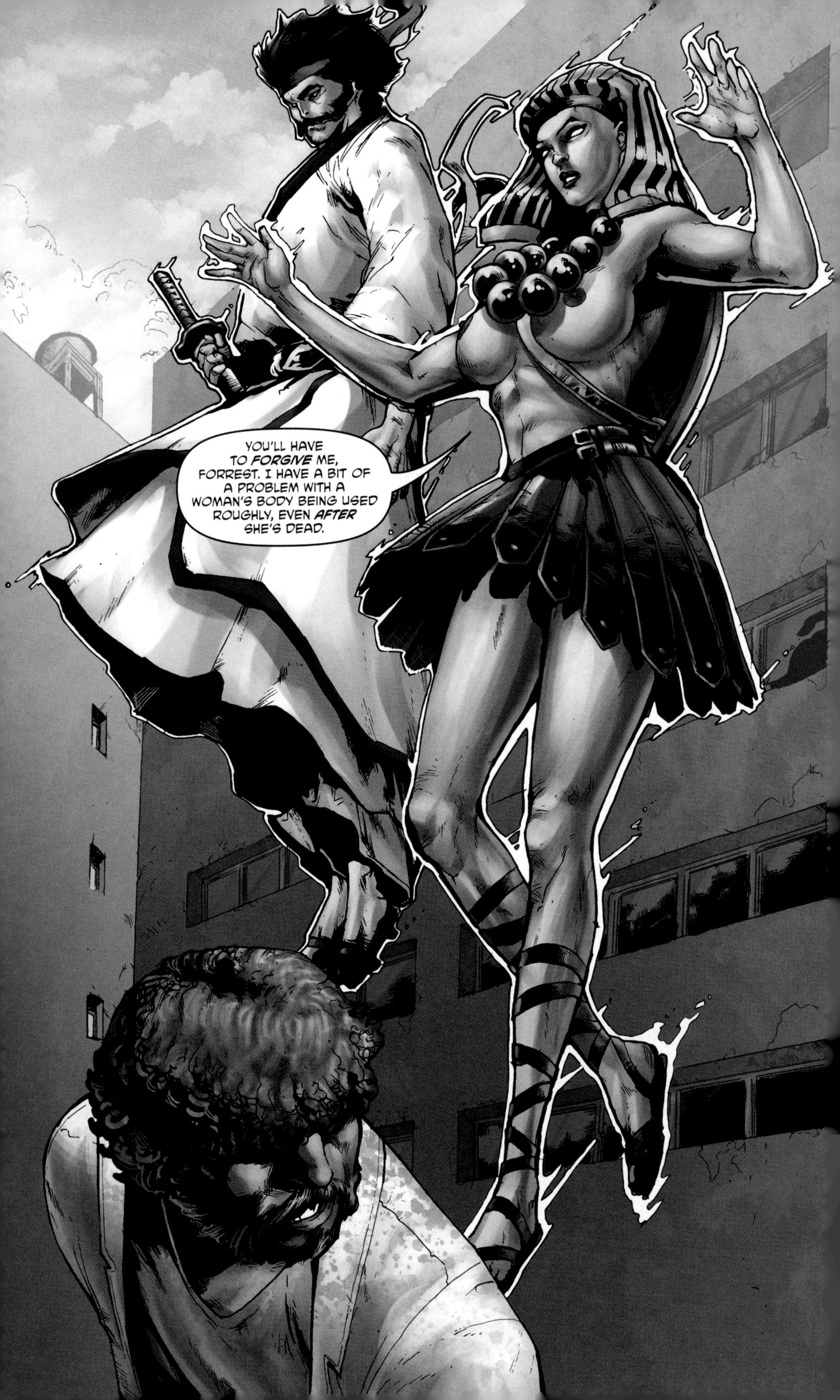
YOU'LL HAVE TO *FORGIVE* ME, FORREST. I HAVE A BIT OF A PROBLEM WITH A WOMAN'S BODY BEING USED ROUGHLY, EVEN *AFTER* SHE'S DEAD.

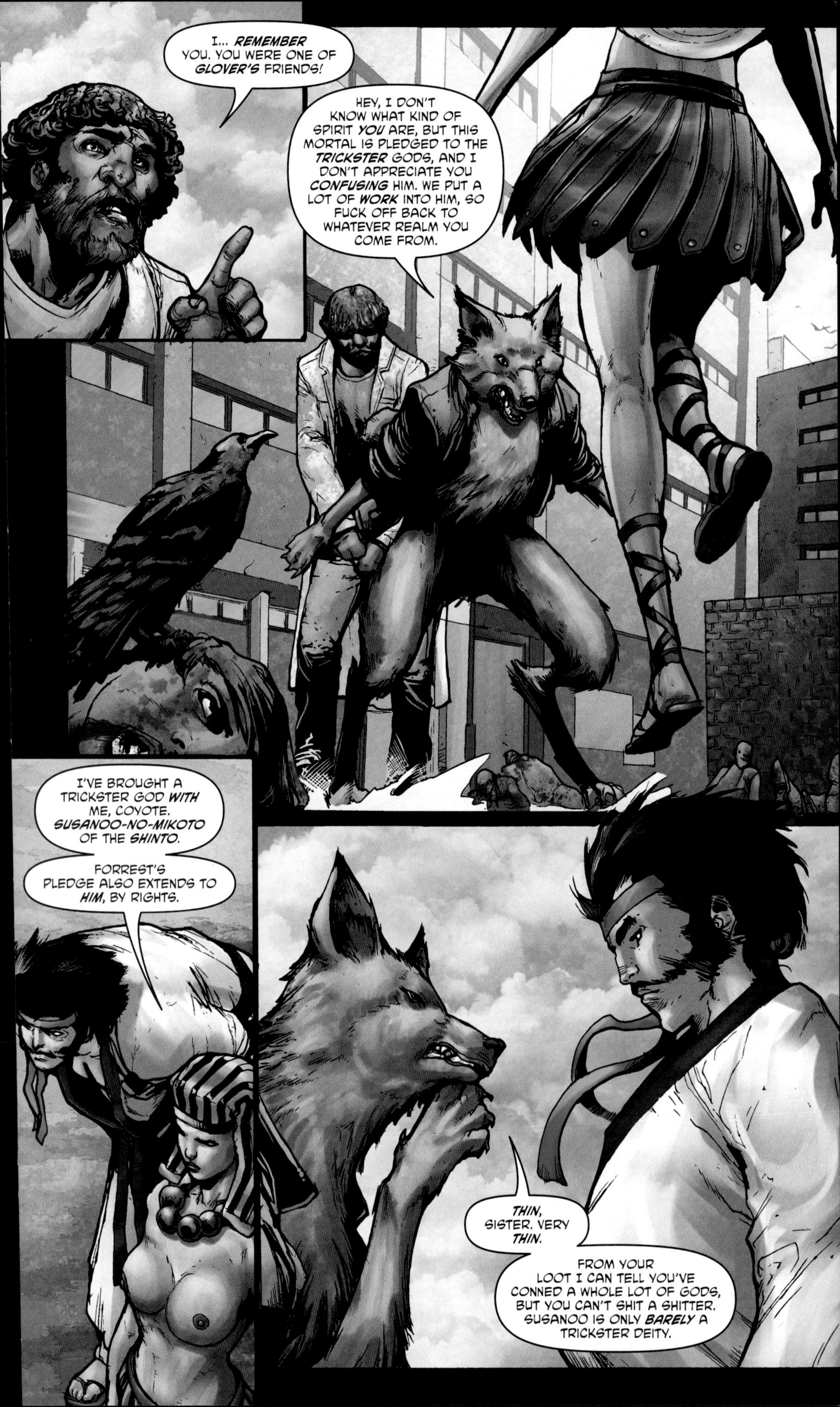
I... REMEMBER YOU. YOU WERE ONE OF GLOVER'S FRIENDS!
HEY, I DON'T KNOW WHAT KIND OF SPIRIT YOU ARE, BUT THIS MORTAL IS PLEDGED TO THE TRICKSTER GODS, AND I DON'T APPRECIATE YOU CONFUSING HIM. WE PUT A LOT OF WORK INTO HIM, SO FUCK OFF BACK TO WHATEVER REALM YOU COME FROM.
I'VE BROUGHT A TRICKSTER GOD WITH ME, COYOTE. SUSANOO-NO-MIKOTO OF THE SHINTO.
FORREST'S PLEDGE ALSO EXTENDS TO HIM, BY RIGHTS.
THIN, SISTER. VERY THIN.
FROM YOUR LOOT I CAN TELL YOU'VE CONNED A WHOLE LOT OF GODS, BUT YOU CAN'T SHIT A SHITTER. SUSANOO IS ONLY BARELY A TRICKSTER DEITY.

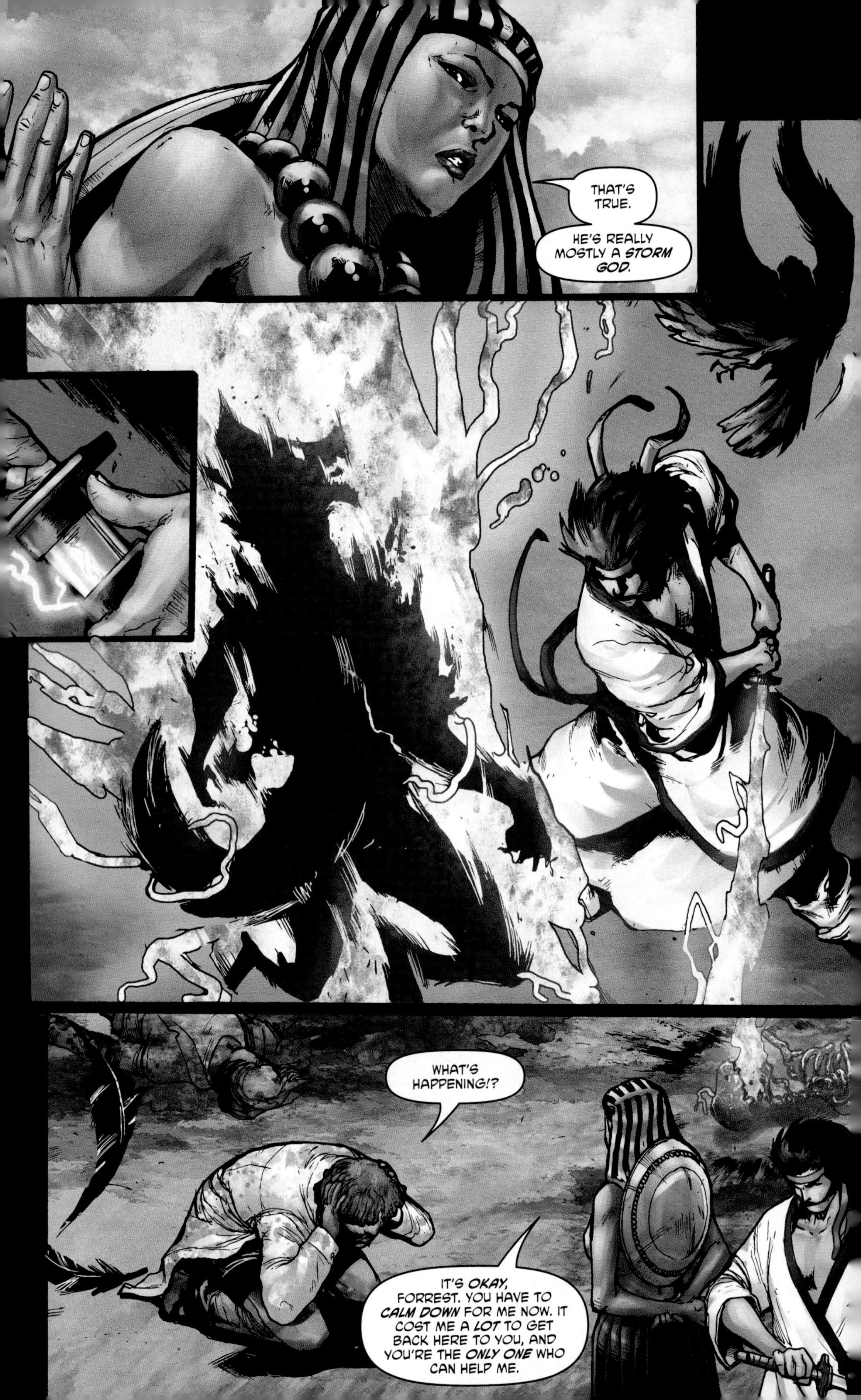
THAT'S TRUE.
HE'S REALLY MOSTLY A *STORM GOD*.
WHAT'S HAPPENING!?
IT'S *OKAY*, FORREST. YOU HAVE TO *CALM DOWN* FOR ME NOW. IT COST ME A *LOT* TO GET BACK HERE TO YOU, AND YOU'RE THE *ONLY ONE* WHO CAN HELP ME.

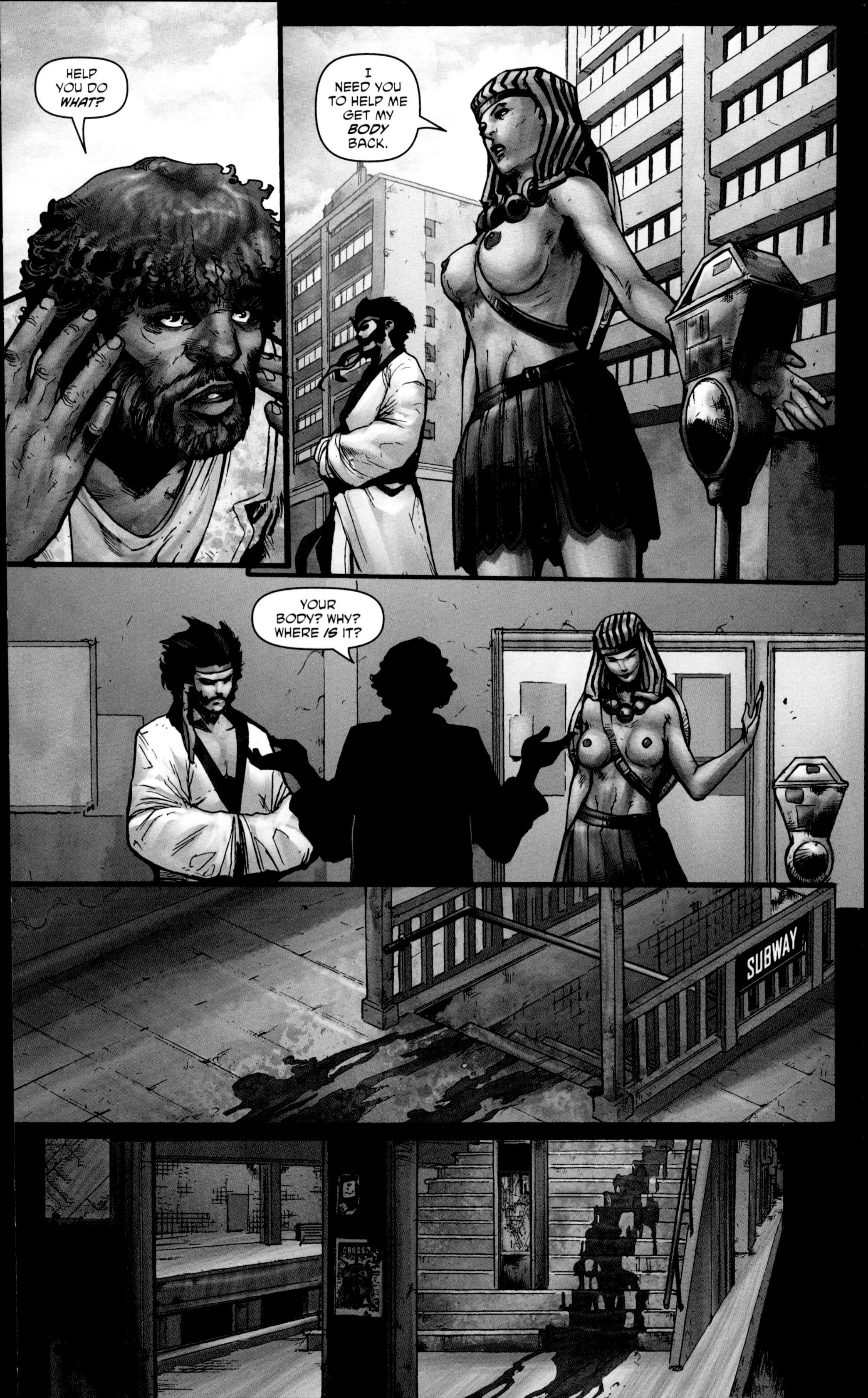
HELP YOU DO *WHAT?*
I NEED YOU TO HELP ME GET MY *BODY* BACK.
YOUR BODY? WHY? WHERE *IS* IT?
SUBWAY
CROSS?

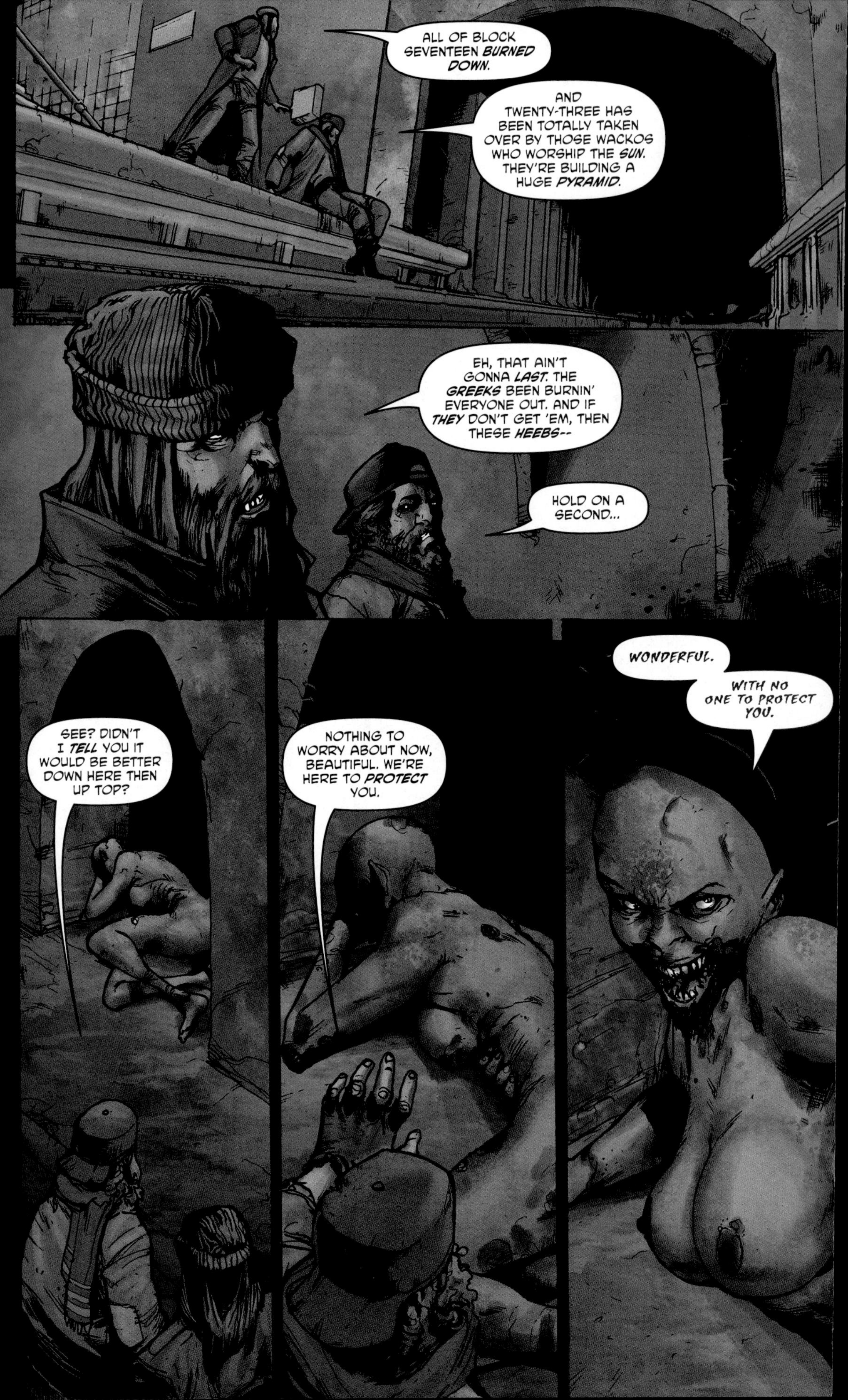

ALL OF BLOCK SEVENTEEN BURNED DOWN.
AND TWENTY-THREE HAS BEEN TOTALLY TAKEN OVER BY THOSE WACKOS WHO WORSHIP THE SUN. THEY'RE BUILDING A HUGE PYRAMID.
EH, THAT AIN'T GONNA LAST. THE GREEKS BEEN BURNIN' EVERYONE OUT. AND IF THEY DON'T GET 'EM, THEN THESE HEEBS--
HOLD ON A SECOND...
SEE? DIDN'T I TELL YOU IT WOULD BE BETTER DOWN HERE THEN UP TOP?
NOTHING TO WORRY ABOUT NOW, BEAUTIFUL. WE'RE HERE TO PROTECT YOU.
WONDERFUL.
WITH NO ONE TO PROTECT YOU.

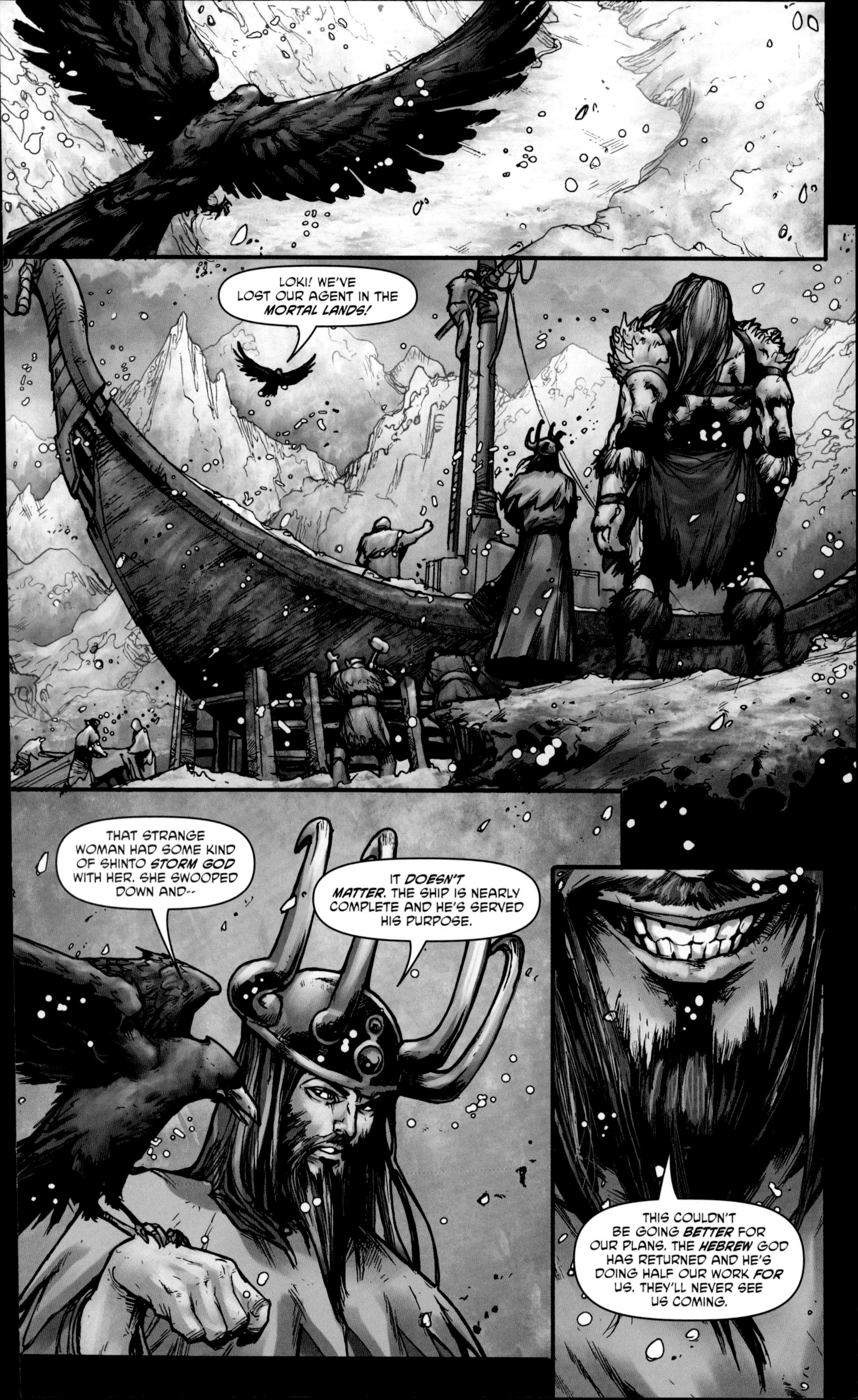
LOKI! WE'VE LOST OUR AGENT IN THE MORTAL LANDS!
THAT STRANGE WOMAN HAD SOME KIND OF SHINTO STORM GOD WITH HER. SHE SWOOPED DOWN AND--
IT DOESN'T MATTER. THE SHIP IS NEARLY COMPLETE AND HE'S SERVED HIS PURPOSE.
THIS COULDN'T BE GOING BETTER FOR OUR PLANS. THE HEBREW GOD HAS RETURNED AND HE'S DOING HALF OUR WORK FOR US. THEY'LL NEVER SEE US COMING.

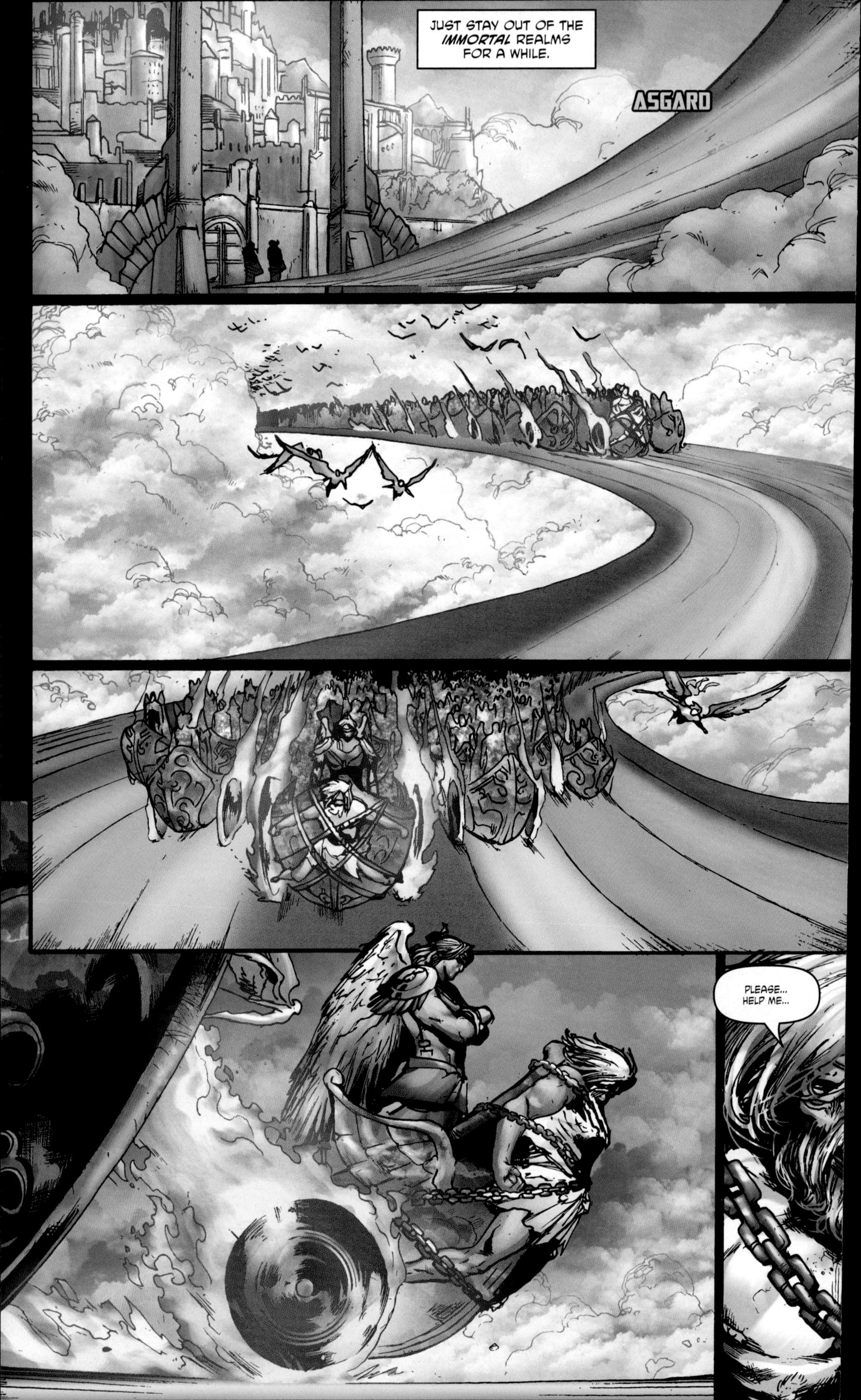
JUST STAY OUT OF THE *IMMORTAL* REALMS FOR A WHILE.
ASGARD
PLEASE... HELP ME...

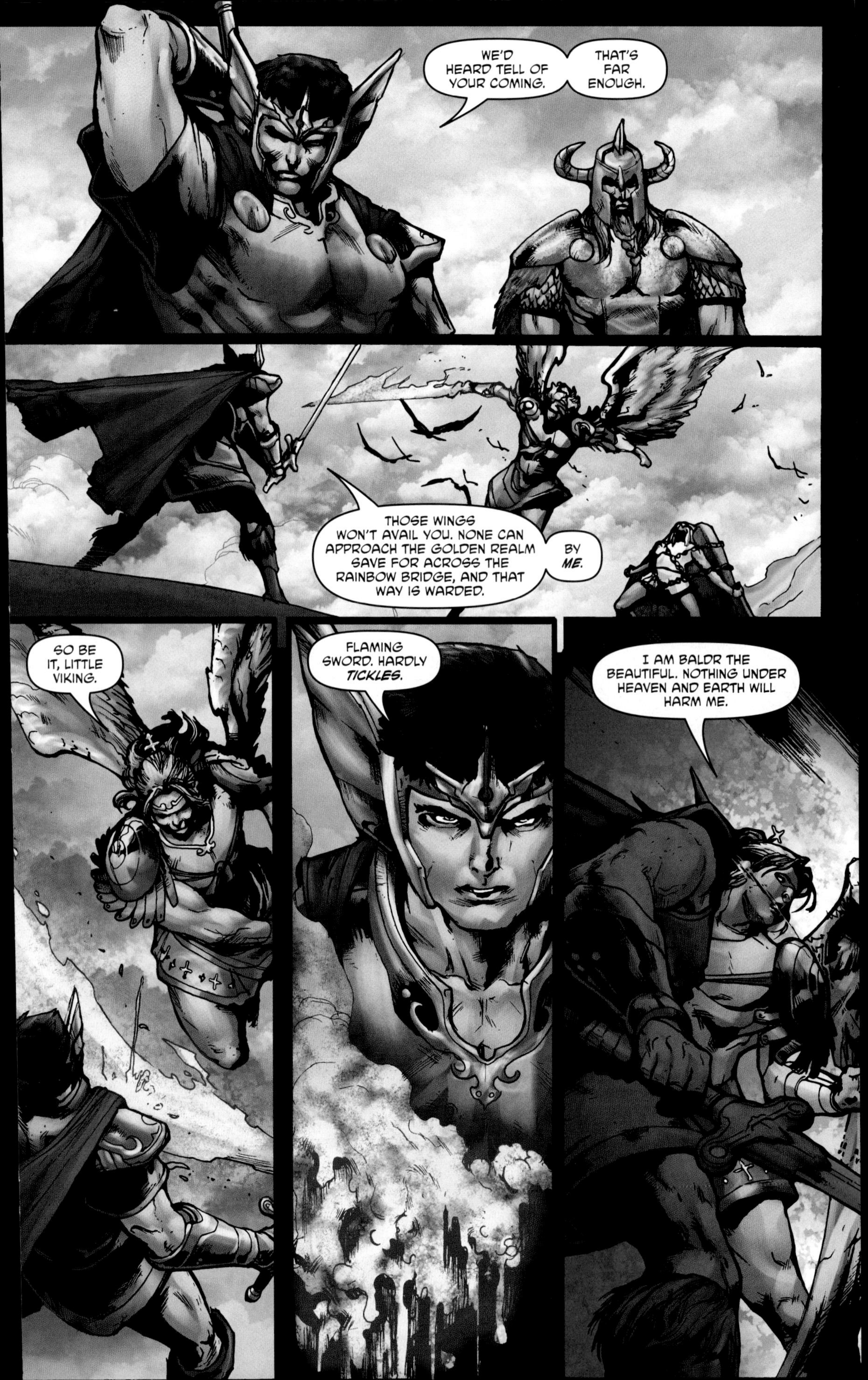
WE'D HEARD TELL OF YOUR COMING.
THAT'S FAR ENOUGH.
THOSE WINGS WON'T AVAIL YOU. NONE CAN APPROACH THE GOLDEN REALM SAVE FOR ACROSS THE RAINBOW BRIDGE, AND THAT WAY IS WARDED.
BY *ME*.
SO BE IT, LITTLE VIKING.
FLAMING SWORD. HARDLY *TICKLES*.
I AM BALDR THE BEAUTIFUL. NOTHING UNDER HEAVEN AND EARTH WILL HARM ME.

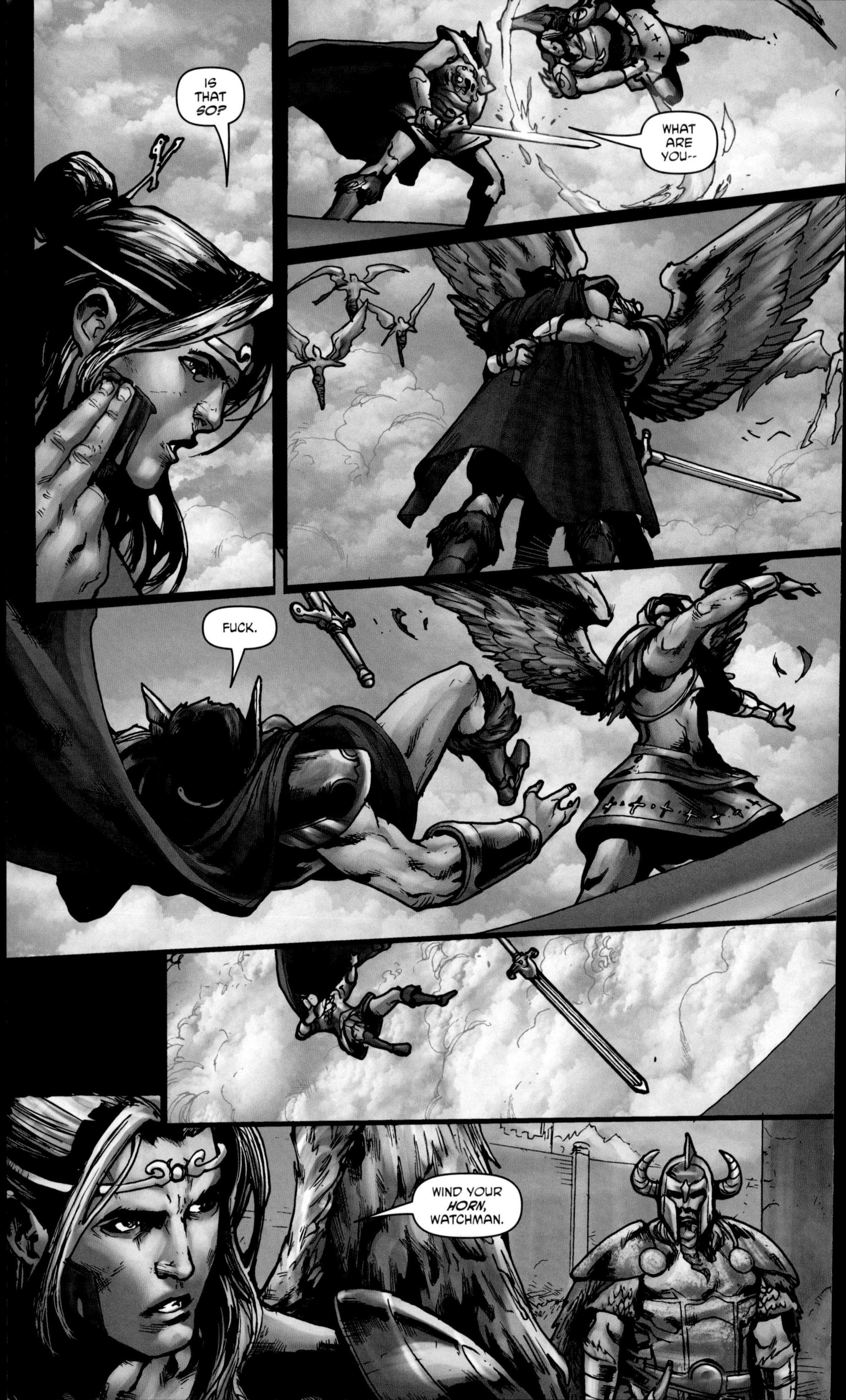
IS THAT SO?
WHAT ARE YOU--
FUCK.
WIND YOUR HORN, WATCHMAN.

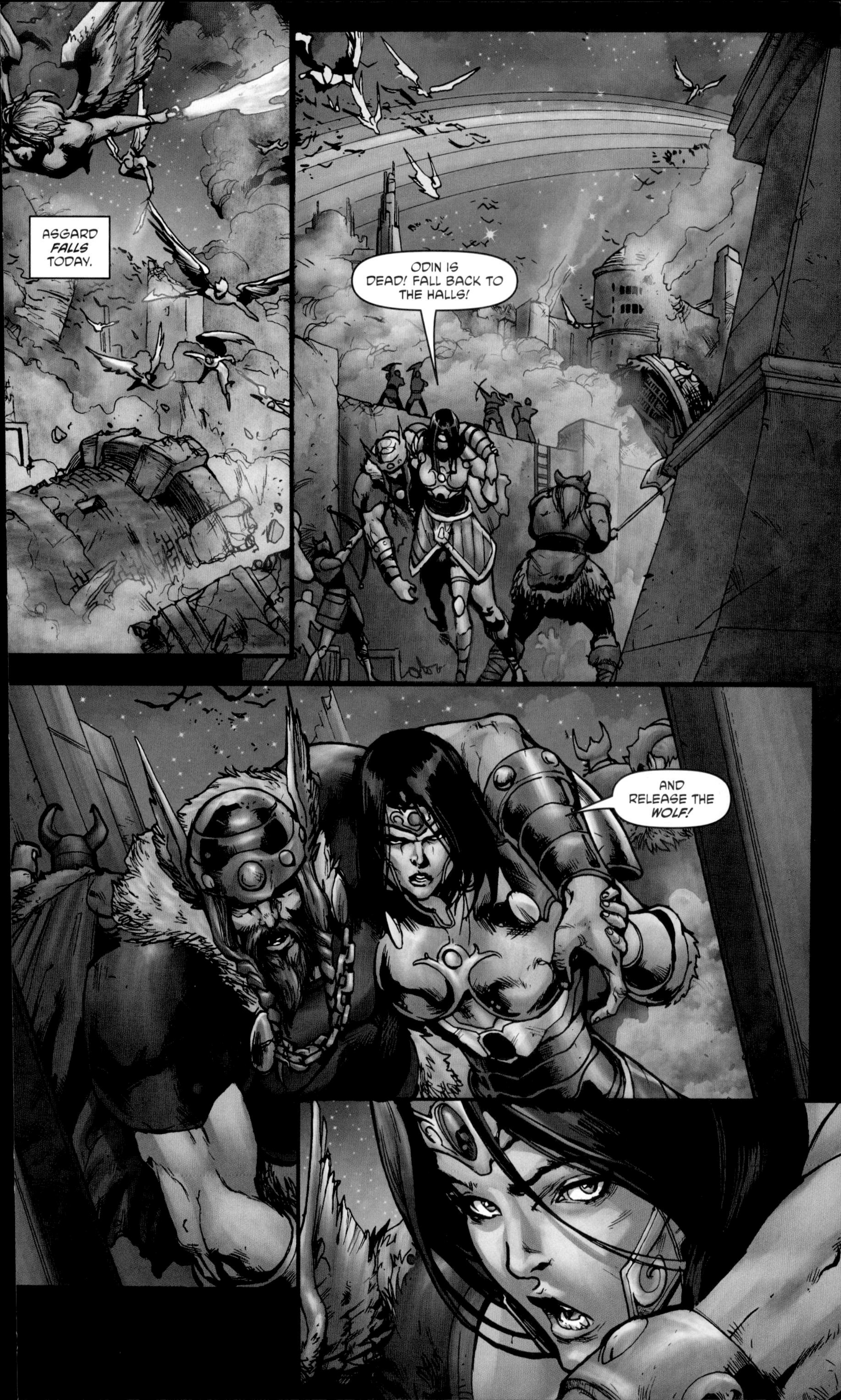
ASGARD *FALLS* TODAY.
ODIN IS DEAD! FALL BACK TO THE HALLS!
AND RELEASE THE *WOLF!*

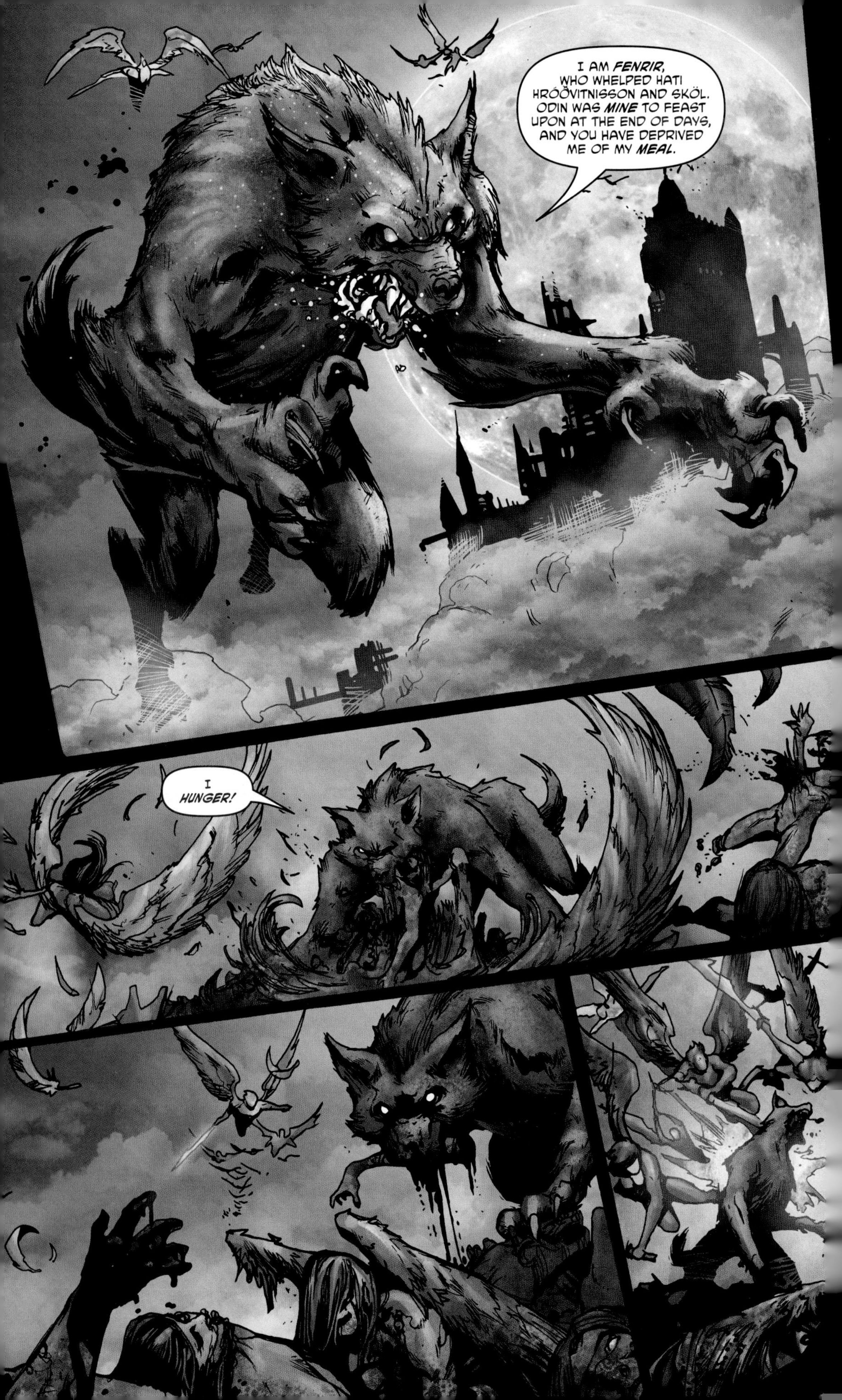
I AM *FENRIR*, WHO WHELPED HATI HRÓǑVITNISSON AND SKÖL. ODIN WAS *MINE* TO FEAST UPON AT THE END OF DAYS, AND YOU HAVE DEPRIVED ME OF MY *MEAL*.
I *HUNGER!*

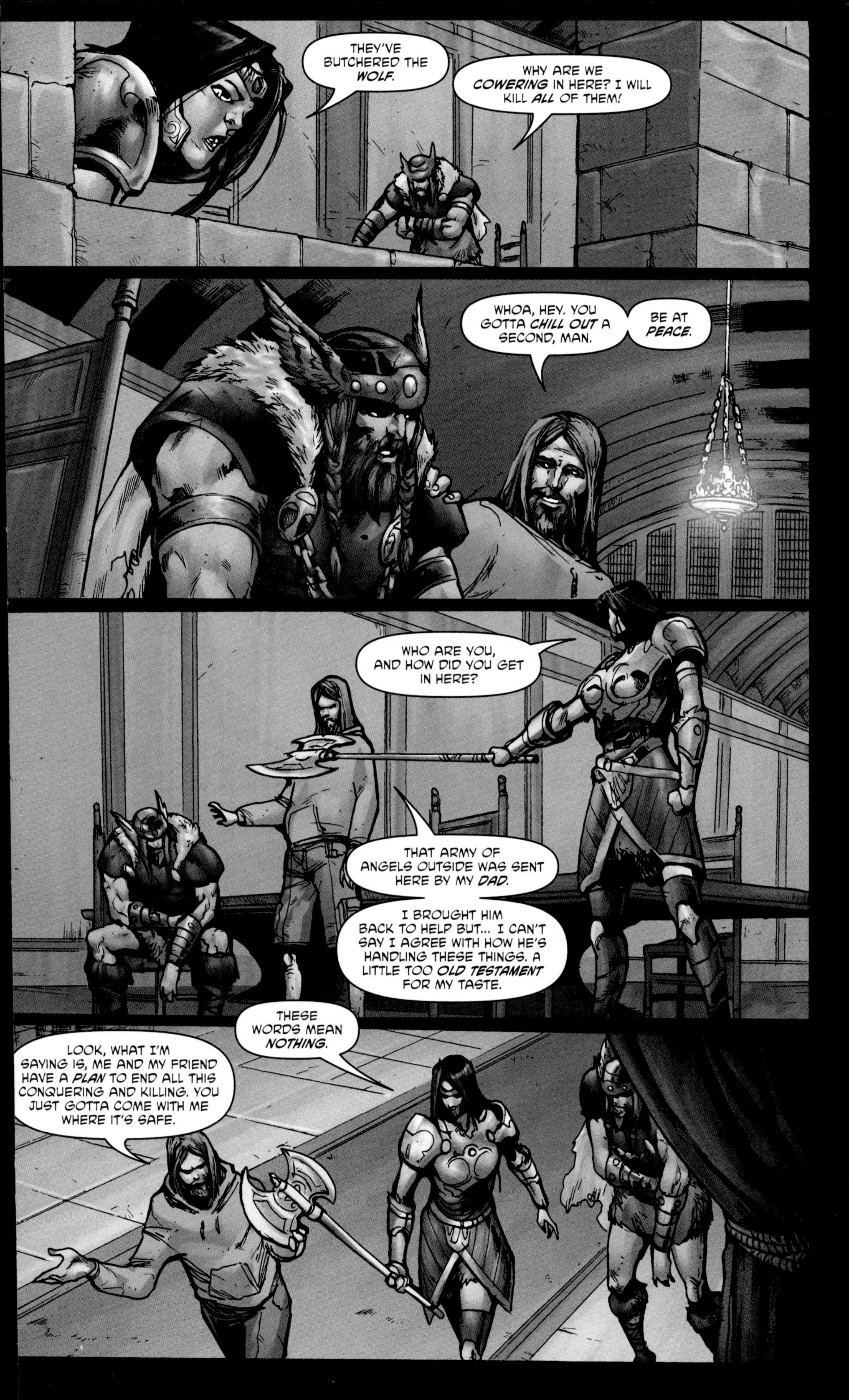
THEY'VE BUTCHERED THE WOLF.
WHY ARE WE COWERING IN HERE? I WILL KILL ALL OF THEM!
WHOA, HEY. YOU GOTTA CHILL OUT A SECOND, MAN.
BE AT PEACE.
WHO ARE YOU, AND HOW DID YOU GET IN HERE?
THAT ARMY OF ANGELS OUTSIDE WAS SENT HERE BY MY DAD.
I BROUGHT HIM BACK TO HELP BUT... I CAN'T SAY I AGREE WITH HOW HE'S HANDLING THESE THINGS. A LITTLE TOO OLD TESTAMENT FOR MY TASTE.
LOOK, WHAT I'M SAYING IS, ME AND MY FRIEND HAVE A PLAN TO END ALL THIS CONQUERING AND KILLING. YOU JUST GOTTA COME WITH ME WHERE IT'S SAFE.
THESE WORDS MEAN NOTHING.

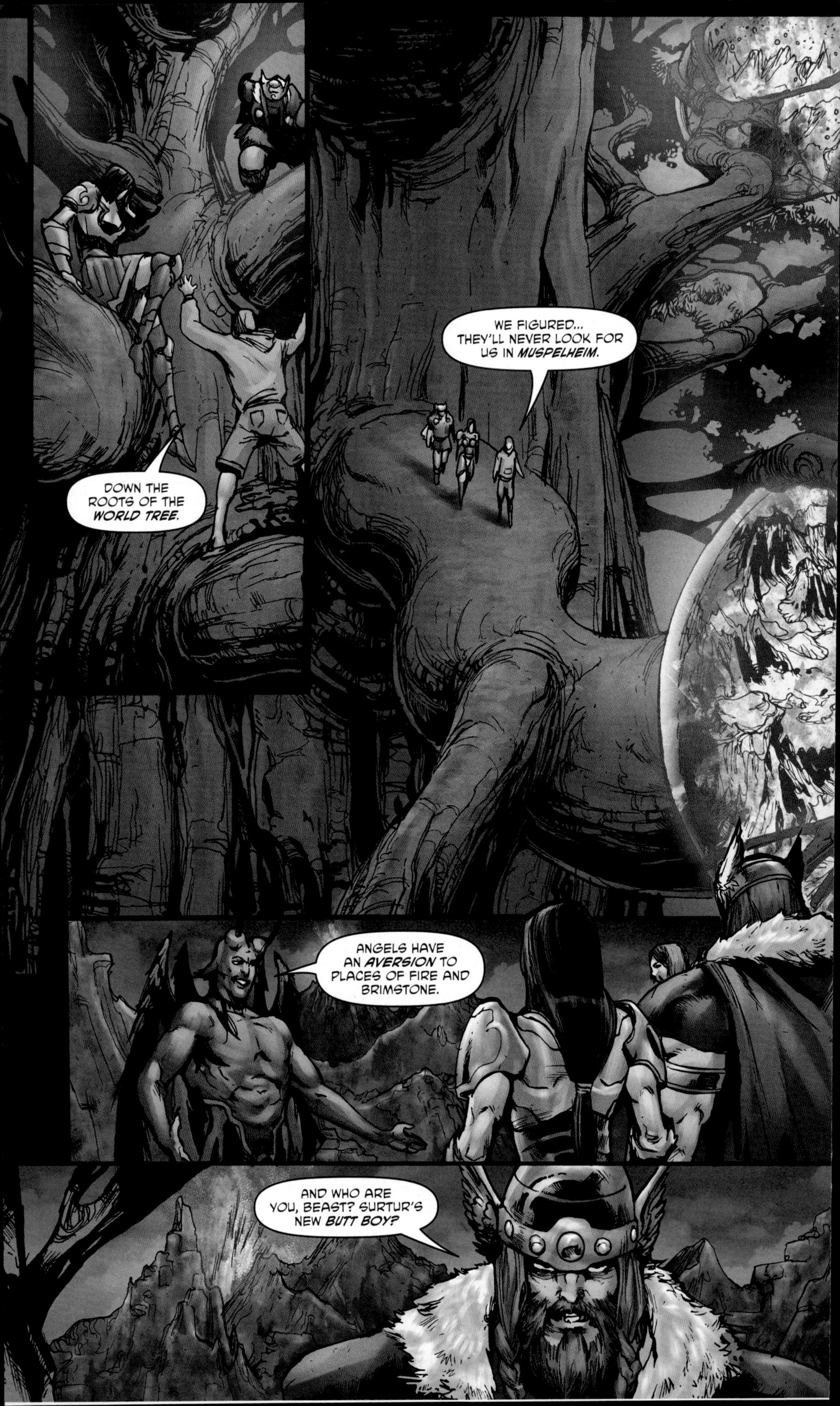
DOWN THE ROOTS OF THE *WORLD TREE*.
WE FIGURED... THEY'LL NEVER LOOK FOR US IN *MUSPELHEIM*.
ANGELS HAVE AN *AVERSION* TO PLACES OF FIRE AND BRIMSTONE.
AND WHO ARE YOU, BEAST? SURTUR'S NEW *BUTT BOY?*

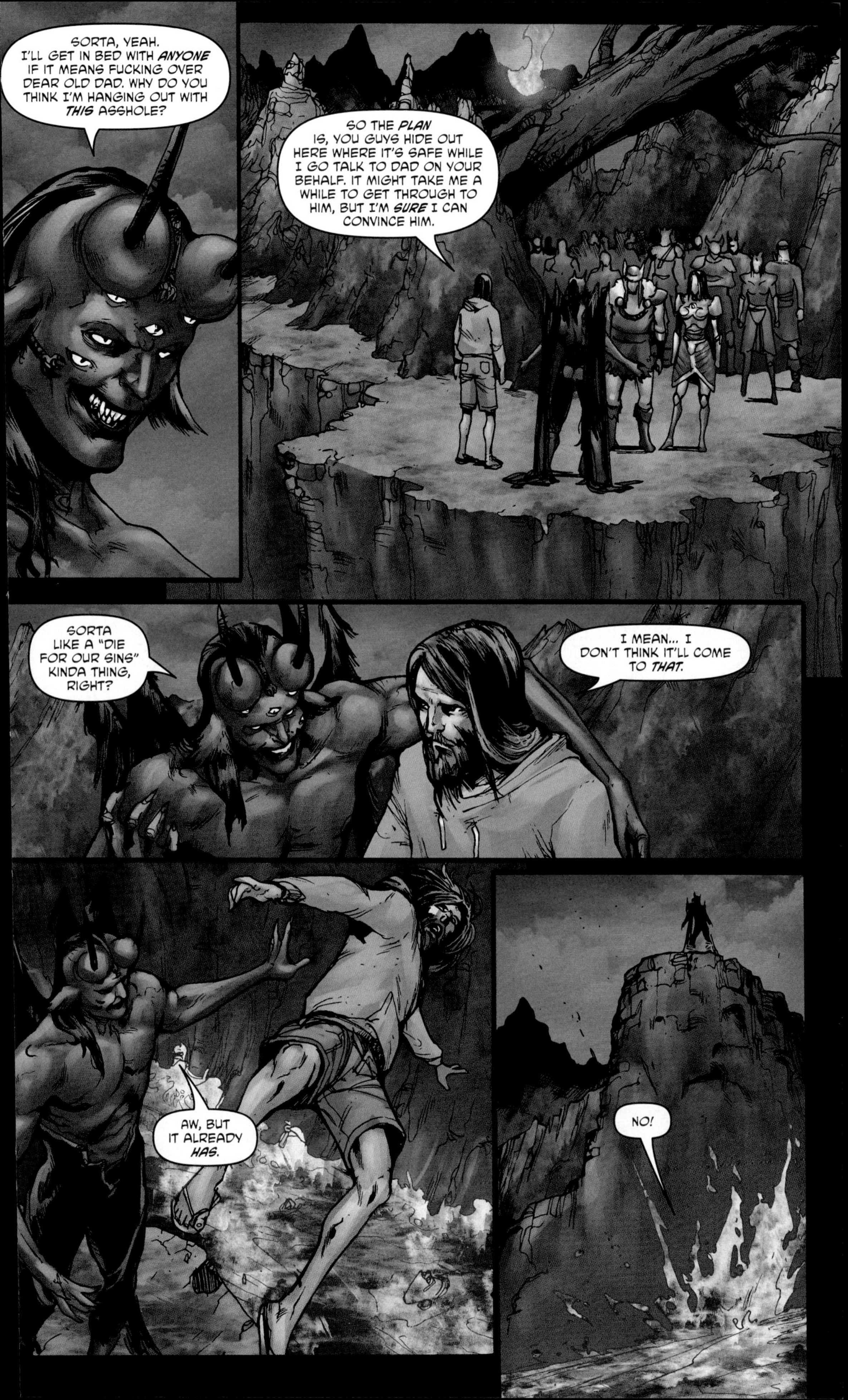
SORTA, YEAH. I'LL GET IN BED WITH ANYONE IF IT MEANS FUCKING OVER DEAR OLD DAD. WHY DO YOU THINK I'M HANGING OUT WITH THIS ASSHOLE?
SO THE PLAN IS, YOU GUYS HIDE OUT HERE WHERE IT'S SAFE WHILE I GO TALK TO DAD ON YOUR BEHALF. IT MIGHT TAKE ME A WHILE TO GET THROUGH TO HIM, BUT I'M SURE I CAN CONVINCE HIM.
SORTA LIKE A "DIE FOR OUR SINS" KINDA THING, RIGHT?
I MEAN... I DON'T THINK IT'LL COME TO THAT.
AW, BUT IT ALREADY HAS.
NO!

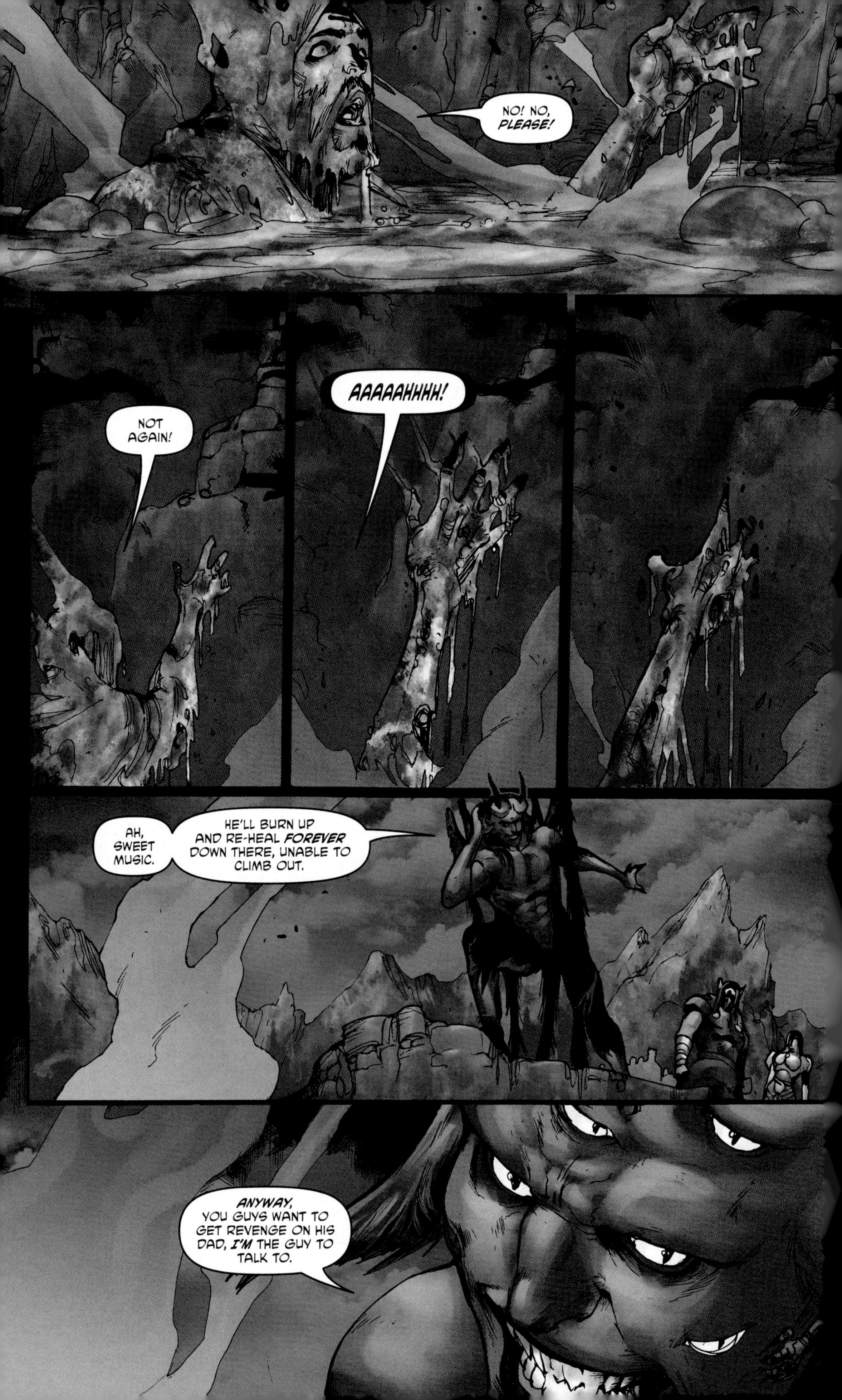
NO! NO, *PLEASE!*
NOT AGAIN!
AAAAAHHHH!
AH, SWEET MUSIC.
HE'LL BURN UP AND RE-HEAL *FOREVER* DOWN THERE, UNABLE TO CLIMB OUT.
ANYWAY, YOU GUYS WANT TO GET REVENGE ON HIS DAD, *I'M* THE GUY TO TALK TO.

THREE

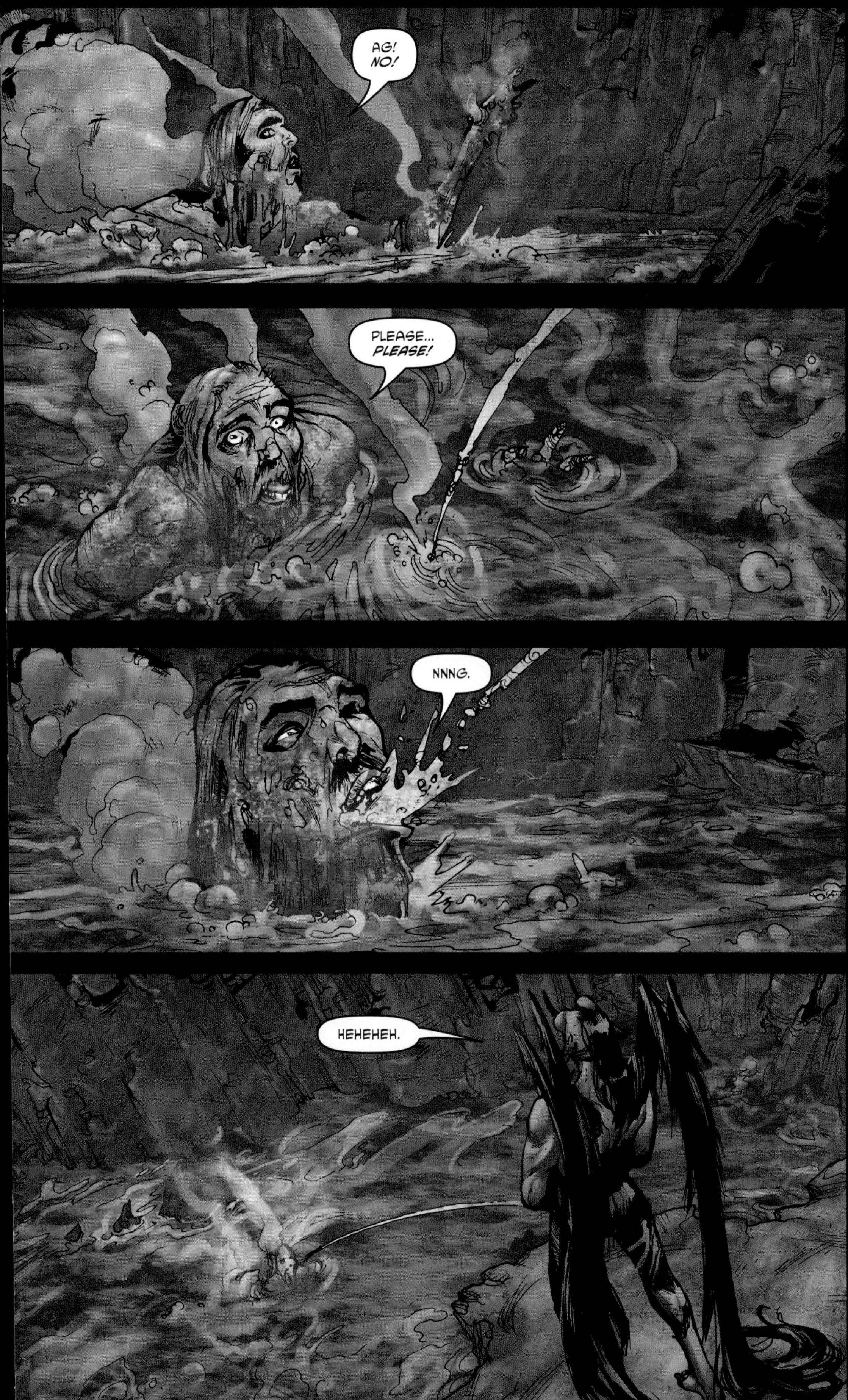
AG! NO!
PLEASE... PLEASE!
NNNG.
HEHEHEH.

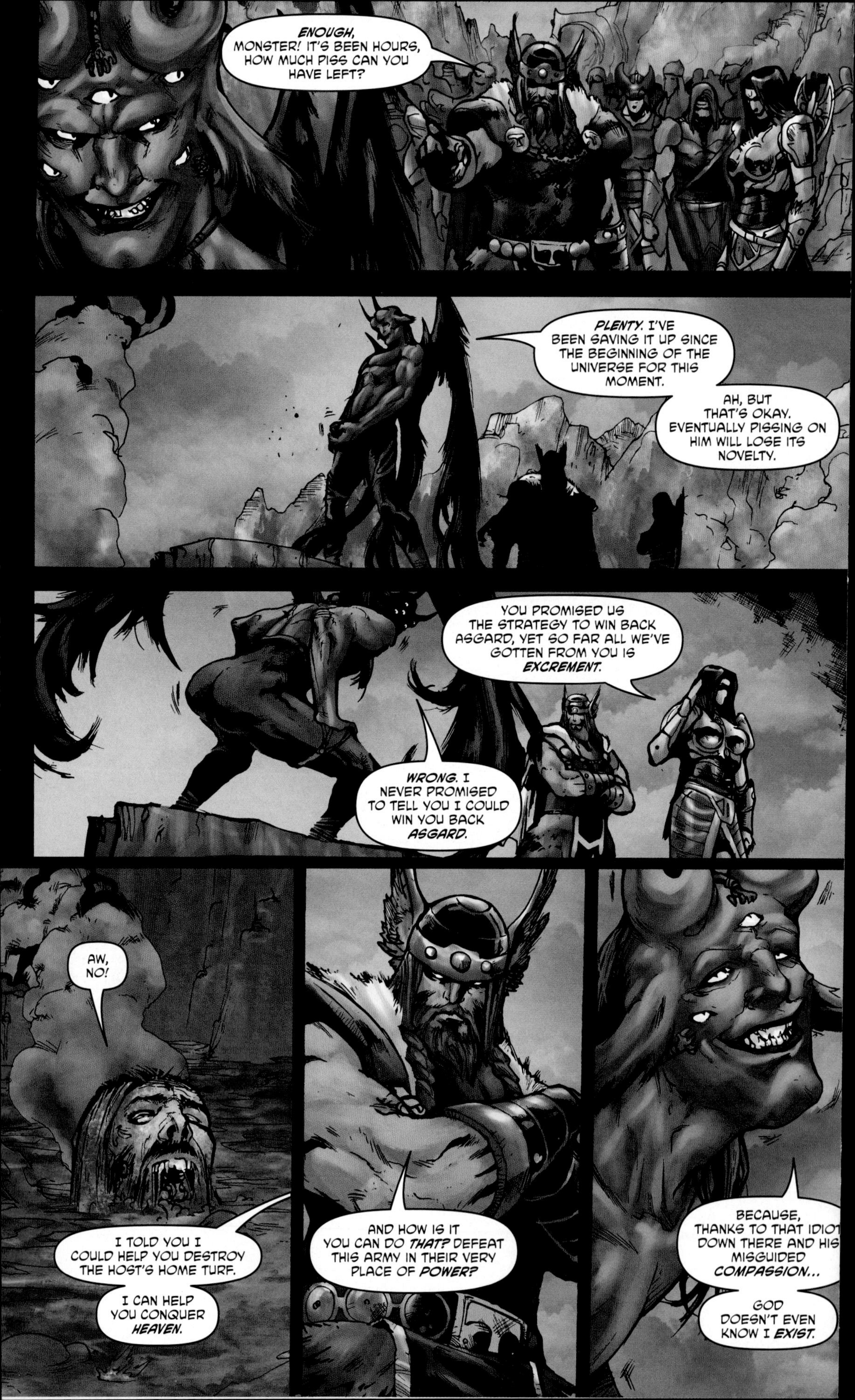
ENOUGH, MONSTER! IT'S BEEN HOURS, HOW MUCH PISS CAN YOU HAVE LEFT?
PLENTY. I'VE BEEN SAVING IT UP SINCE THE BEGINNING OF THE UNIVERSE FOR THIS MOMENT.
AH, BUT THAT'S OKAY. EVENTUALLY PISSING ON HIM WILL LOSE ITS NOVELTY.
YOU PROMISED US THE STRATEGY TO WIN BACK ASGARD, YET SO FAR ALL WE'VE GOTTEN FROM YOU IS EXCREMENT.
WRONG. I NEVER PROMISED TO TELL YOU I COULD WIN YOU BACK ASGARD.
AW, NO!
I TOLD YOU I COULD HELP YOU DESTROY THE HOST'S HOME TURF.
I CAN HELP YOU CONQUER HEAVEN.
AND HOW IS IT YOU CAN DO THAT? DEFEAT THIS ARMY IN THEIR VERY PLACE OF POWER?
BECAUSE, THANKS TO THAT IDIOT DOWN THERE AND HIS MISGUIDED COMPASSION...
GOD DOESN'T EVEN KNOW I EXIST.

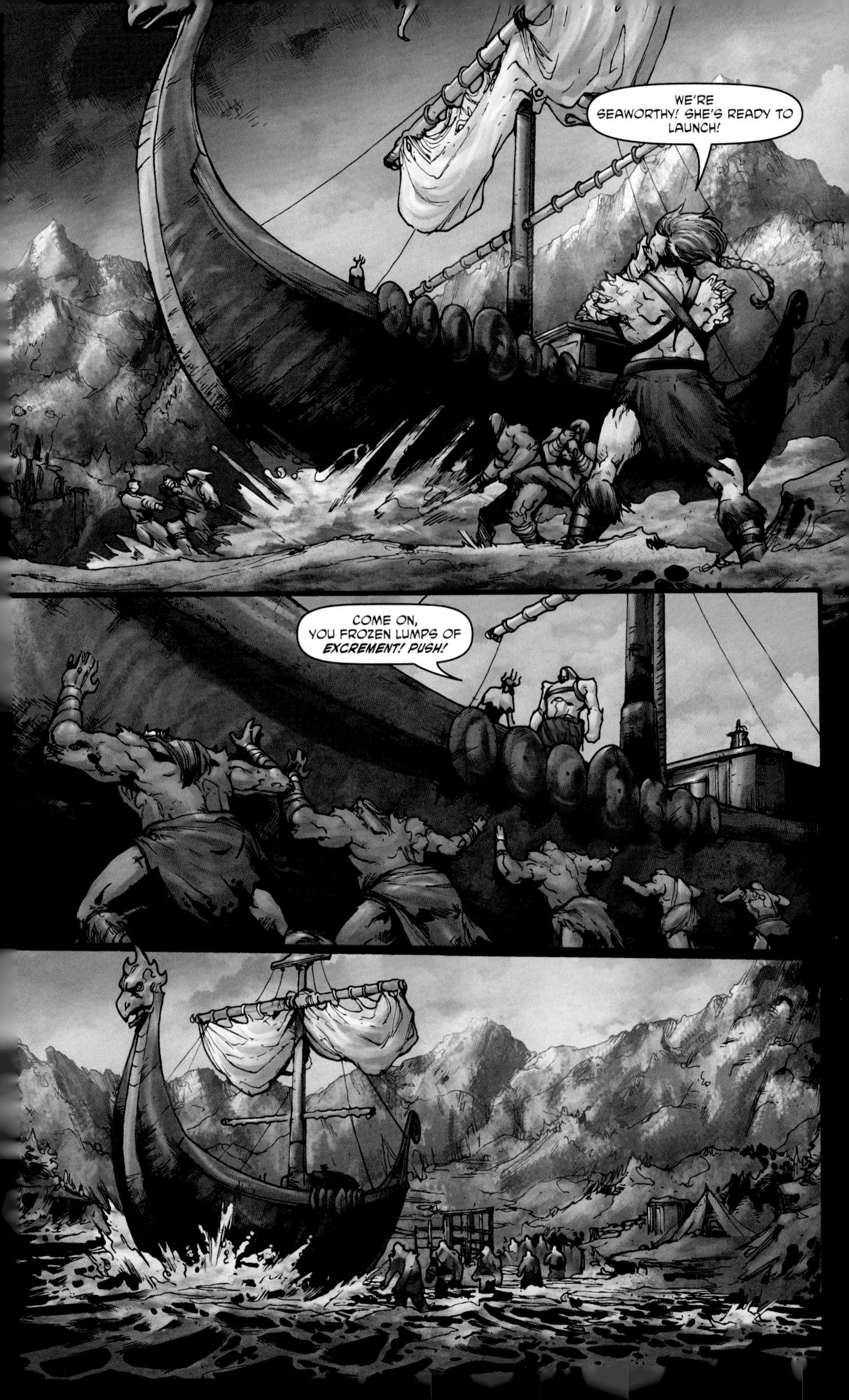
WE'RE SEAWORTHY! SHE'S READY TO LAUNCH!
COME ON, YOU FROZEN LUMPS OF *EXCREMENT! PUSH!*

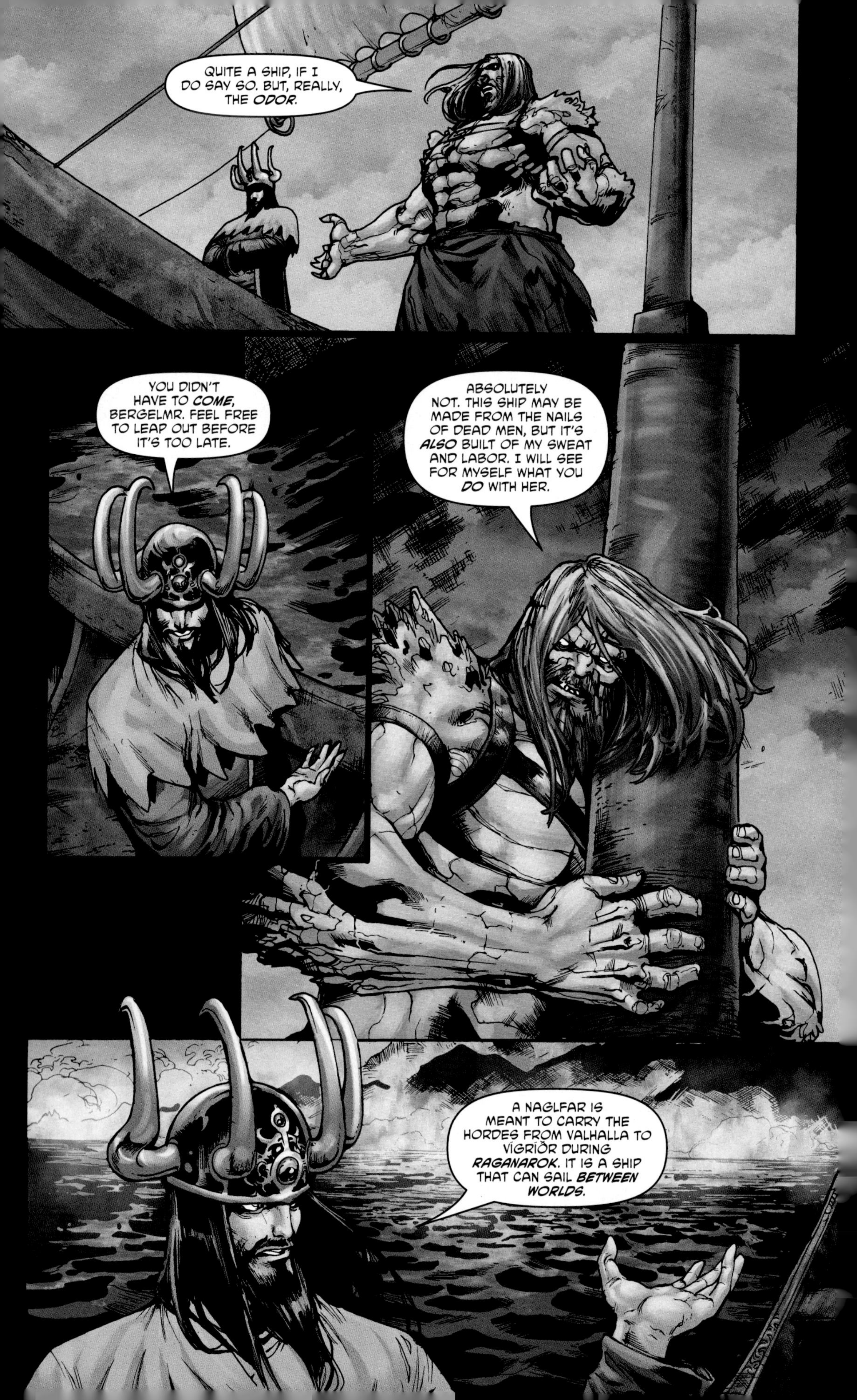
QUITE A SHIP, IF I DO SAY SO. BUT, REALLY, THE *ODOR*.
YOU DIDN'T HAVE TO *COME*, BERGELMR. FEEL FREE TO LEAP OUT BEFORE IT'S TOO LATE.
ABSOLUTELY NOT. THIS SHIP MAY BE MADE FROM THE NAILS OF DEAD MEN, BUT IT'S *ALSO* BUILT OF MY SWEAT AND LABOR. I WILL SEE FOR MYSELF WHAT YOU *DO* WITH HER.
A NAGLFAR IS MEANT TO CARRY THE HORDES FROM VALHALLA TO VÍGRÍÐR DURING *RAGANAROK*. IT IS A SHIP THAT CAN SAIL *BETWEEN WORLDS*.

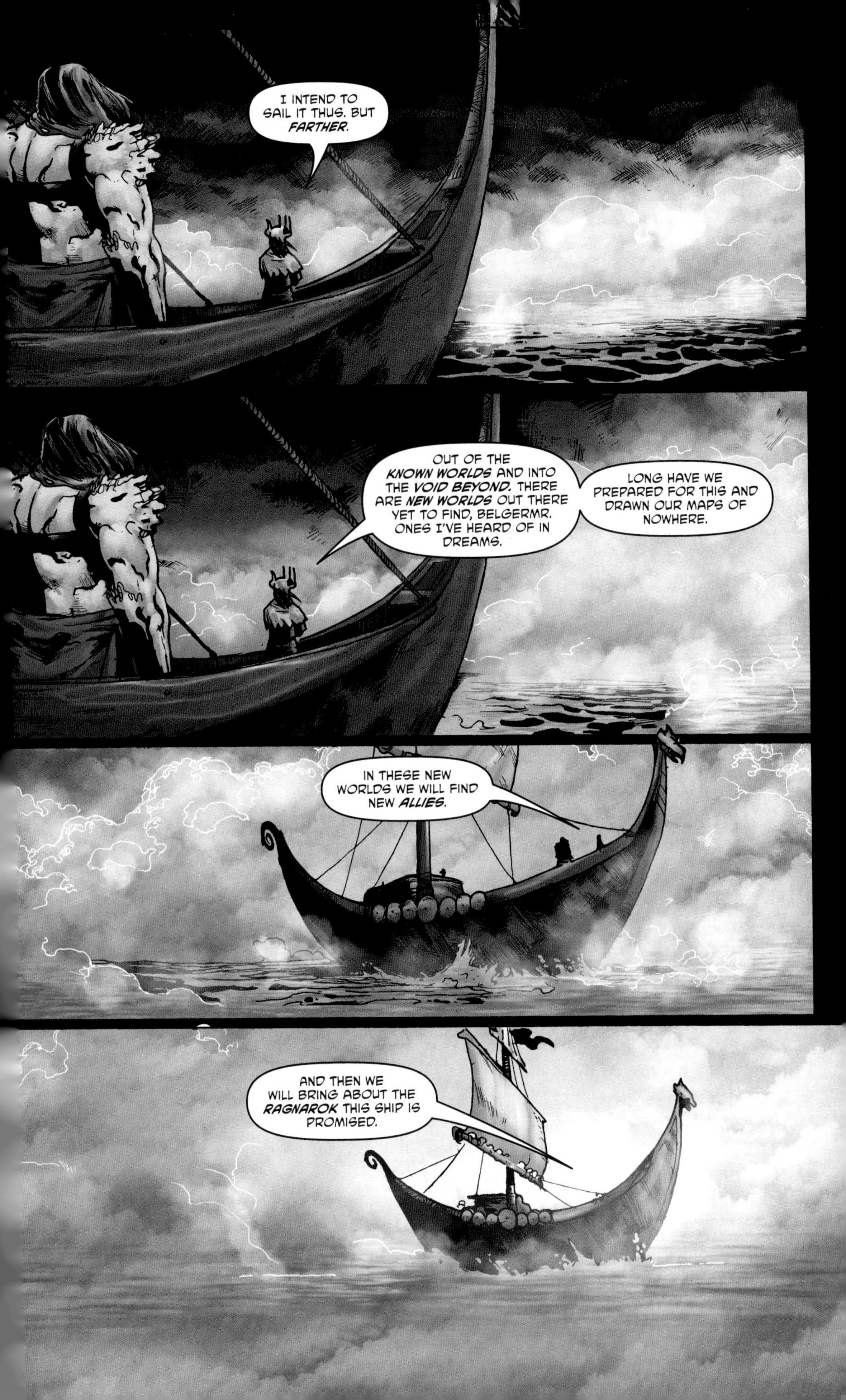
I INTEND TO SAIL IT THUS. BUT *FARTHER*.
OUT OF THE *KNOWN WORLDS* AND INTO THE *VOID BEYOND.* THERE ARE *NEW WORLDS* OUT THERE YET TO FIND, BELGERMR. ONES I'VE HEARD OF IN DREAMS.
LONG HAVE WE PREPARED FOR THIS AND DRAWN OUR MAPS OF NOWHERE.
IN THESE NEW WORLDS WE WILL FIND NEW *ALLIES*.
AND THEN WE WILL BRING ABOUT THE *RAGNAROK* THIS SHIP IS PROMISED.

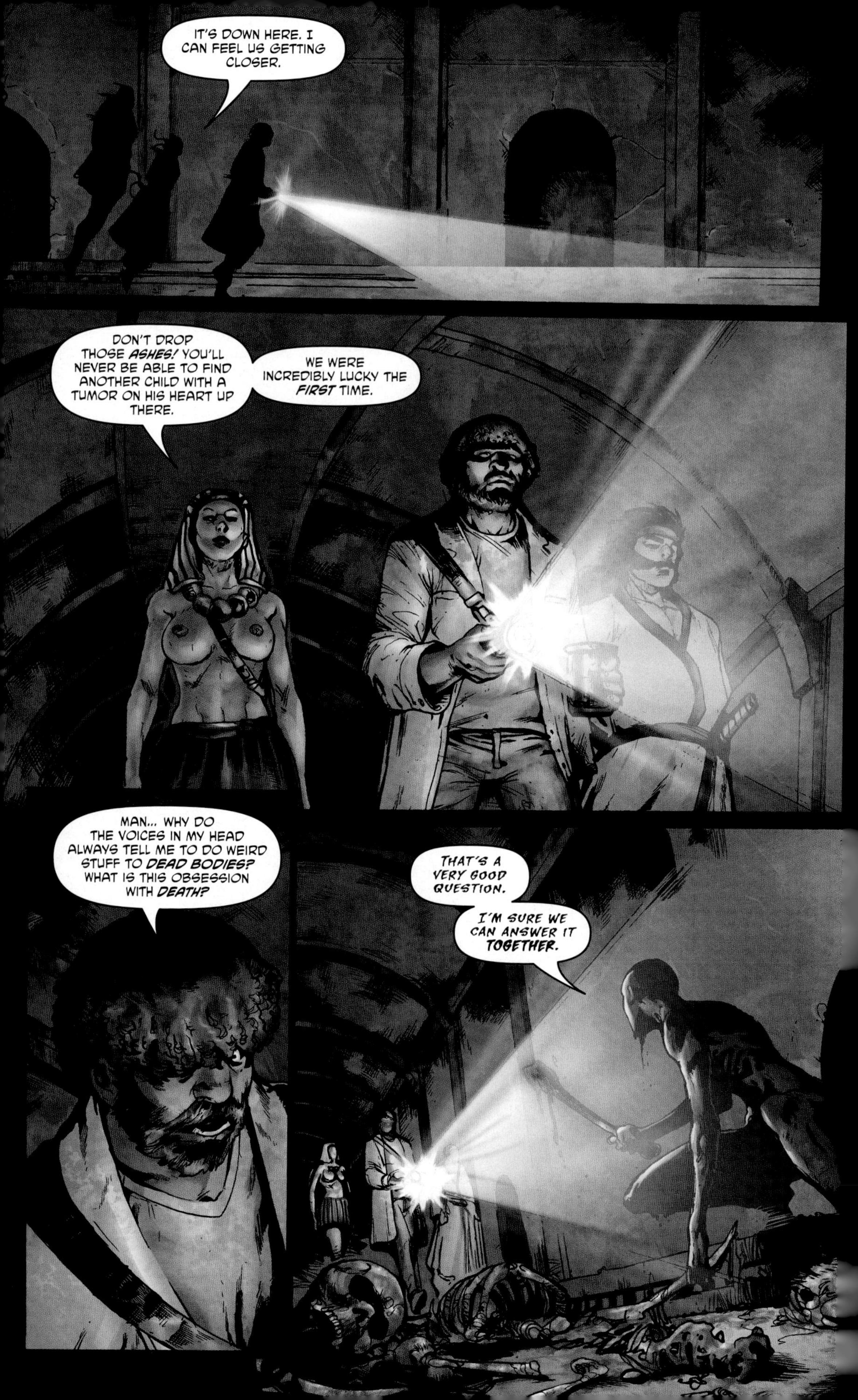
IT'S DOWN HERE. I CAN FEEL US GETTING CLOSER.
DON'T DROP THOSE *ASHES!* YOU'LL NEVER BE ABLE TO FIND ANOTHER CHILD WITH A TUMOR ON HIS HEART UP THERE.
WE WERE INCREDIBLY LUCKY THE *FIRST* TIME.
MAN... WHY DO THE VOICES IN MY HEAD ALWAYS TELL ME TO DO WEIRD STUFF TO *DEAD BODIES?* WHAT IS THIS OBSESSION WITH *DEATH?*
THAT'S A VERY GOOD QUESTION.
I'M SURE WE CAN ANSWER IT **TOGETHER.**

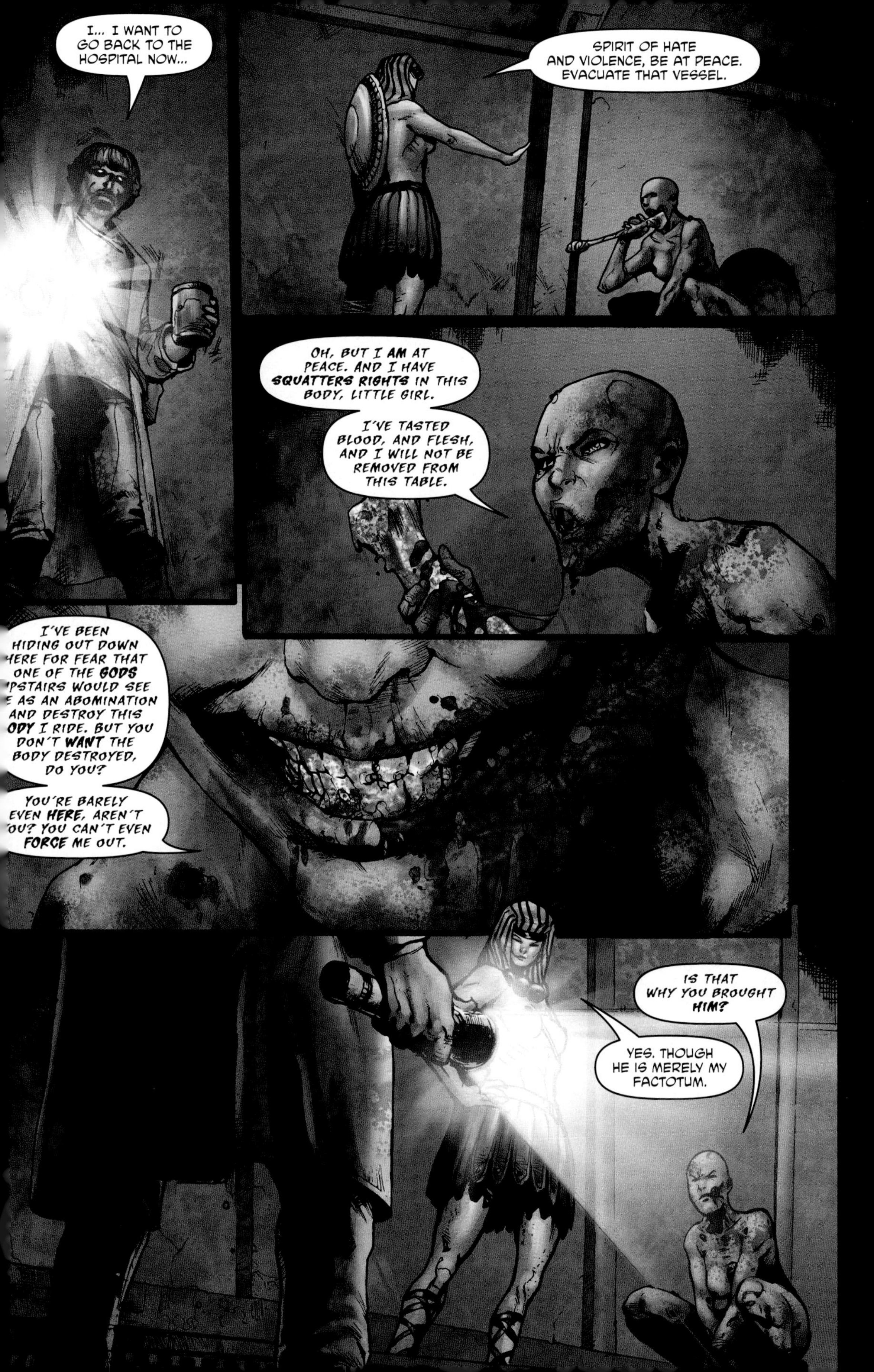

I... I WANT TO GO BACK TO THE HOSPITAL NOW...
SPIRIT OF HATE AND VIOLENCE, BE AT PEACE. EVACUATE THAT VESSEL.
OH, BUT I AM AT PEACE. AND I HAVE SQUATTERS RIGHTS IN THIS BODY, LITTLE GIRL.
I'VE TASTED BLOOD, AND FLESH, AND I WILL NOT BE REMOVED FROM THIS TABLE.
I'VE BEEN HIDING OUT DOWN HERE FOR FEAR THAT ONE OF THE GODS UPSTAIRS WOULD SEE ME AS AN ABOMINATION AND DESTROY THIS BODY I RIDE. BUT YOU DON'T WANT THE BODY DESTROYED, DO YOU?
YOU'RE BARELY EVEN HERE, AREN'T YOU? YOU CAN'T EVEN FORCE ME OUT.
IS THAT WHY YOU BROUGHT HIM?
YES. THOUGH HE IS MERELY MY FACTOTUM.

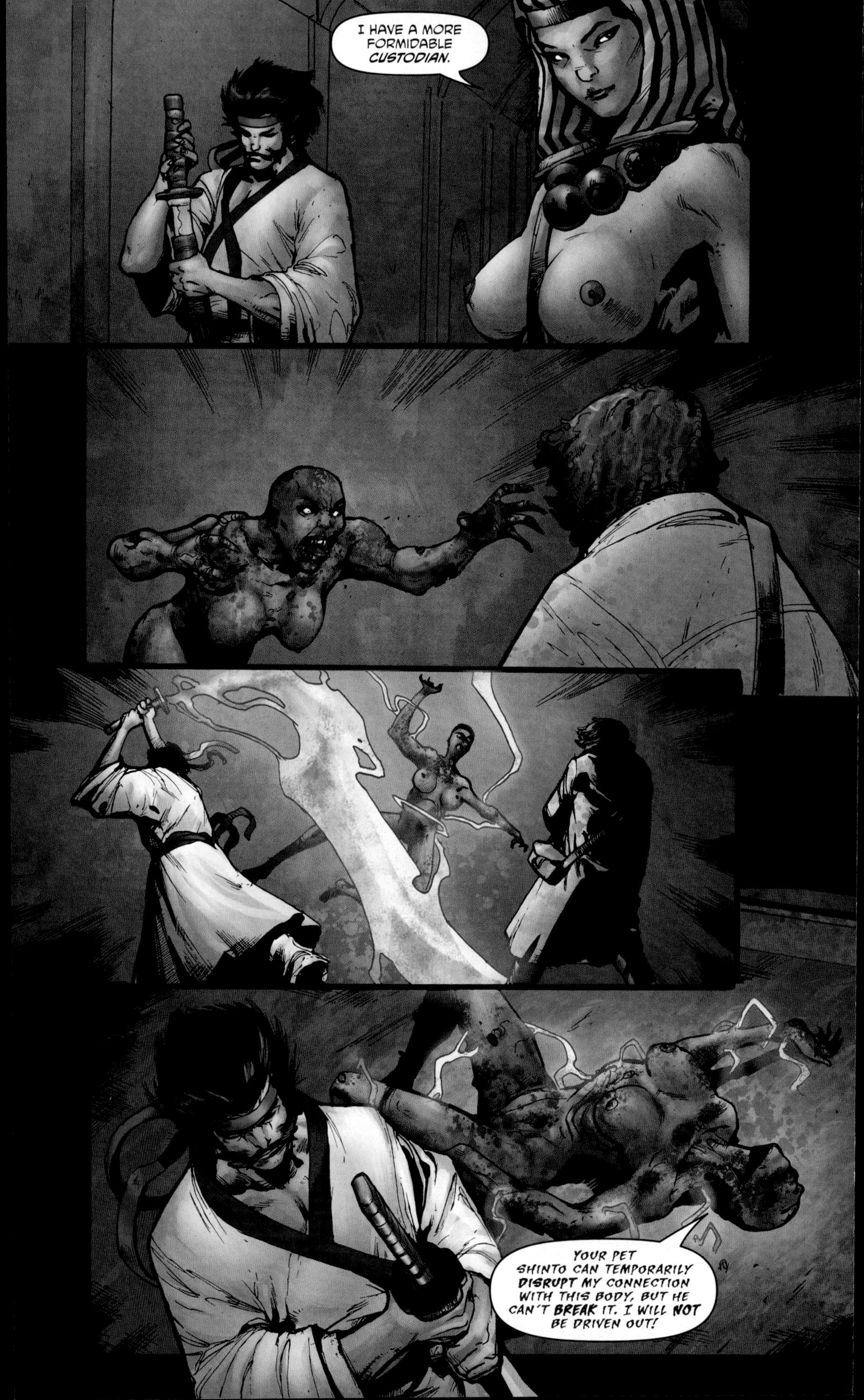
I HAVE A MORE FORMIDABLE CUSTODIAN.
YOUR PET SHINTO CAN TEMPORARILY DISRUPT MY CONNECTION WITH THIS BODY, BUT HE CAN'T BREAK IT. I WILL NOT BE DRIVEN OUT!

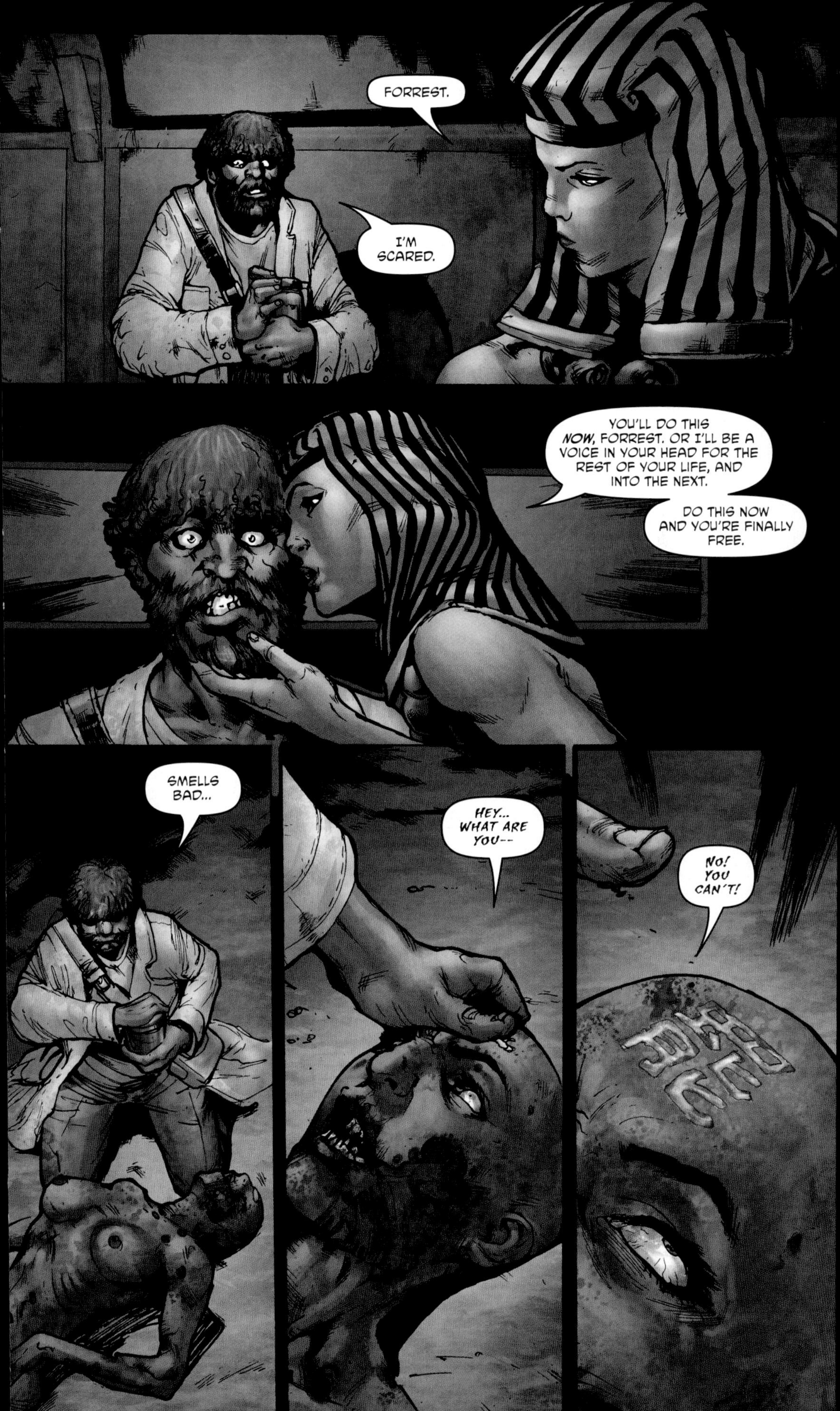
FORREST.
I'M SCARED.
YOU'LL DO THIS *NOW*, FORREST. OR I'LL BE A VOICE IN YOUR HEAD FOR THE REST OF YOUR LIFE, AND INTO THE NEXT.
DO THIS NOW AND YOU'RE FINALLY FREE.
SMELLS BAD...
HEY... WHAT ARE YOU--
NO! YOU CAN'T!

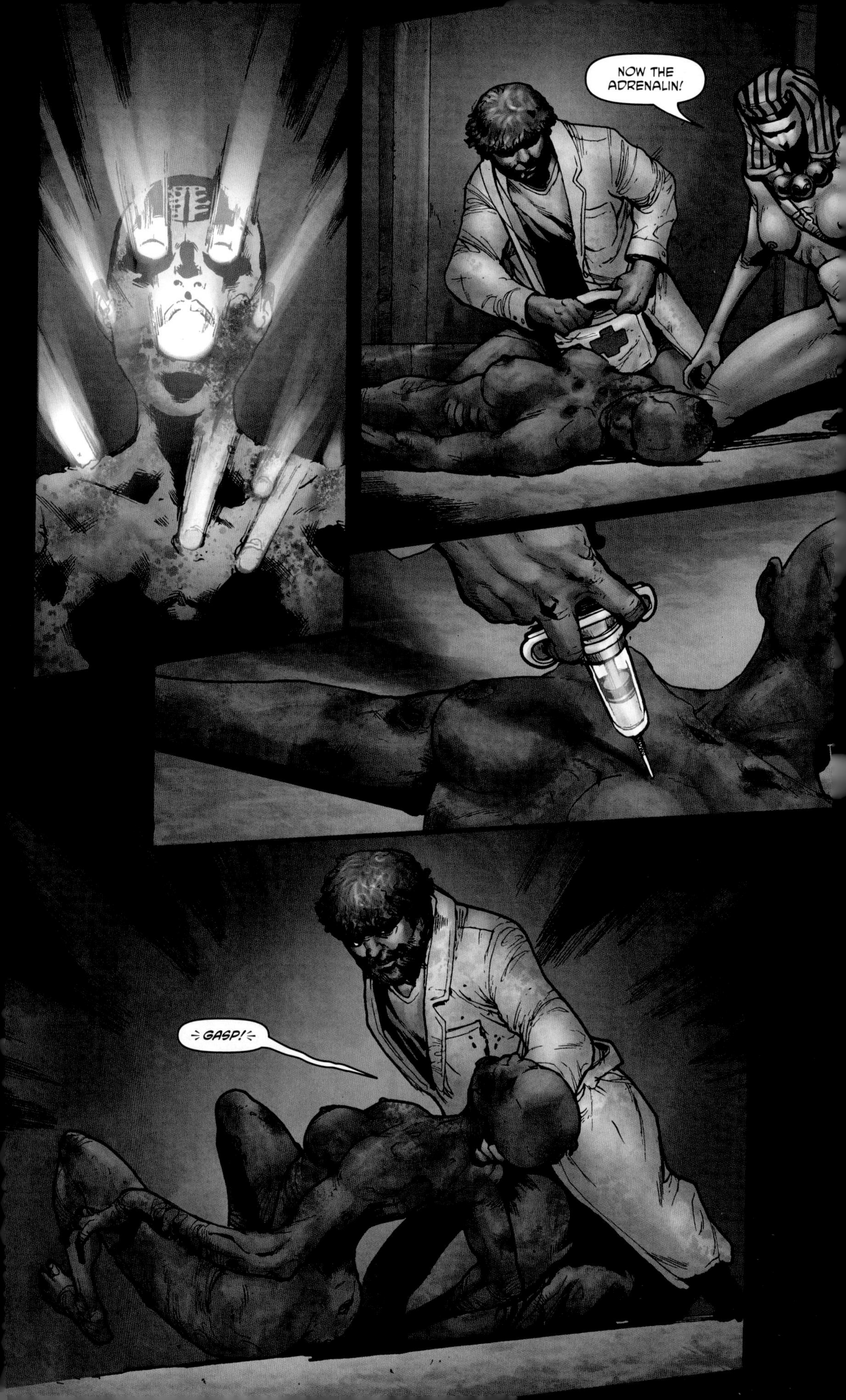
NOW THE ADRENALIN!
GASP!

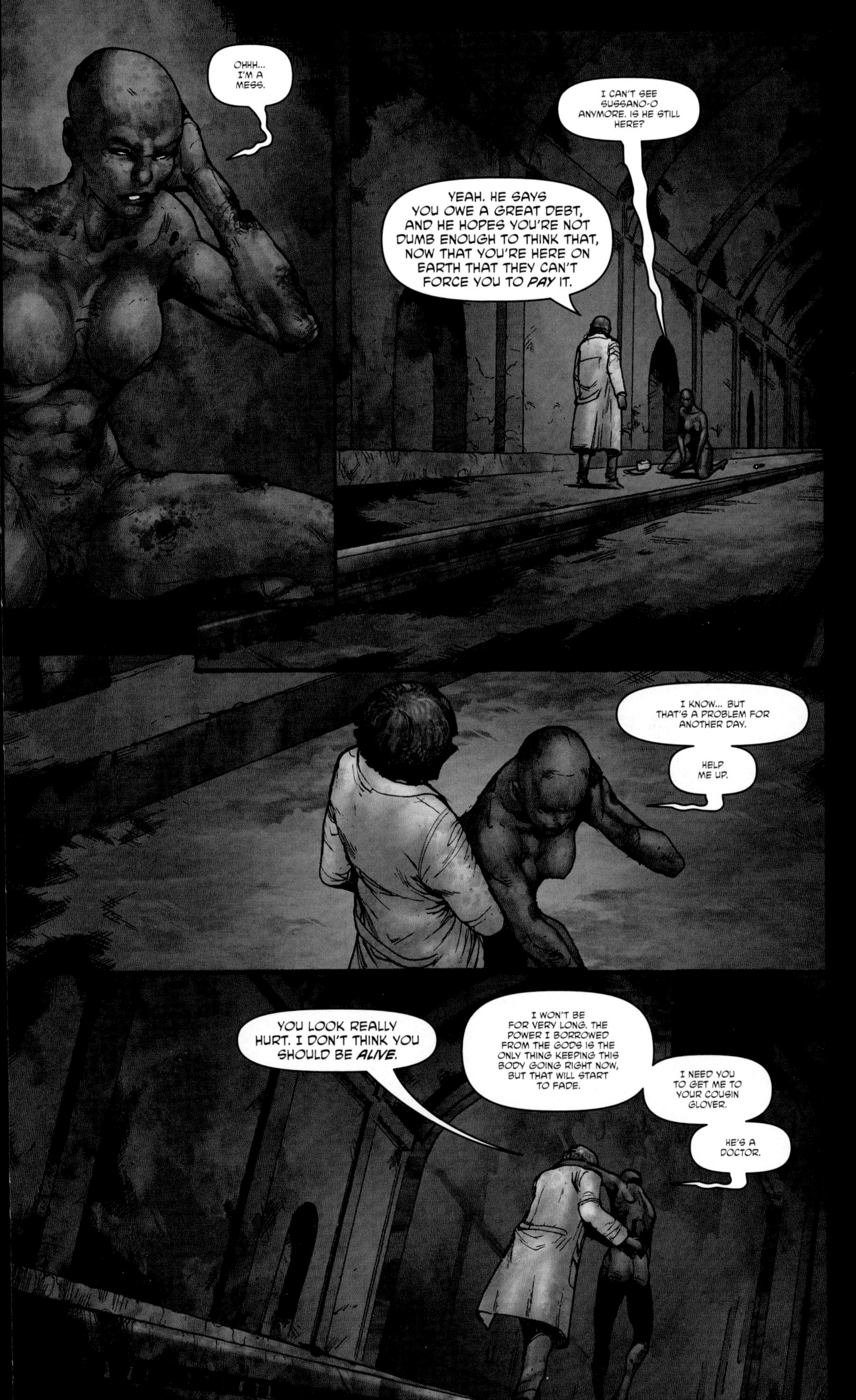
OHHH... I'M A MESS.
I CAN'T SEE SUSSANO-O ANYMORE. IS HE STILL HERE?
YEAH. HE SAYS YOU OWE A GREAT DEBT, AND HE HOPES YOU'RE NOT DUMB ENOUGH TO THINK THAT, NOW THAT YOU'RE HERE ON EARTH THAT THEY CAN'T FORCE YOU TO PAY IT.
I KNOW... BUT THAT'S A PROBLEM FOR ANOTHER DAY.
HELP ME UP.
YOU LOOK REALLY HURT. I DON'T THINK YOU SHOULD BE ALIVE.
I WON'T BE FOR VERY LONG. THE POWER I BORROWED FROM THE GODS IS THE ONLY THING KEEPING THIS BODY GOING RIGHT NOW, BUT THAT WILL START TO FADE.
I NEED YOU TO GET ME TO YOUR COUSIN GLOVER.
HE'S A DOCTOR.

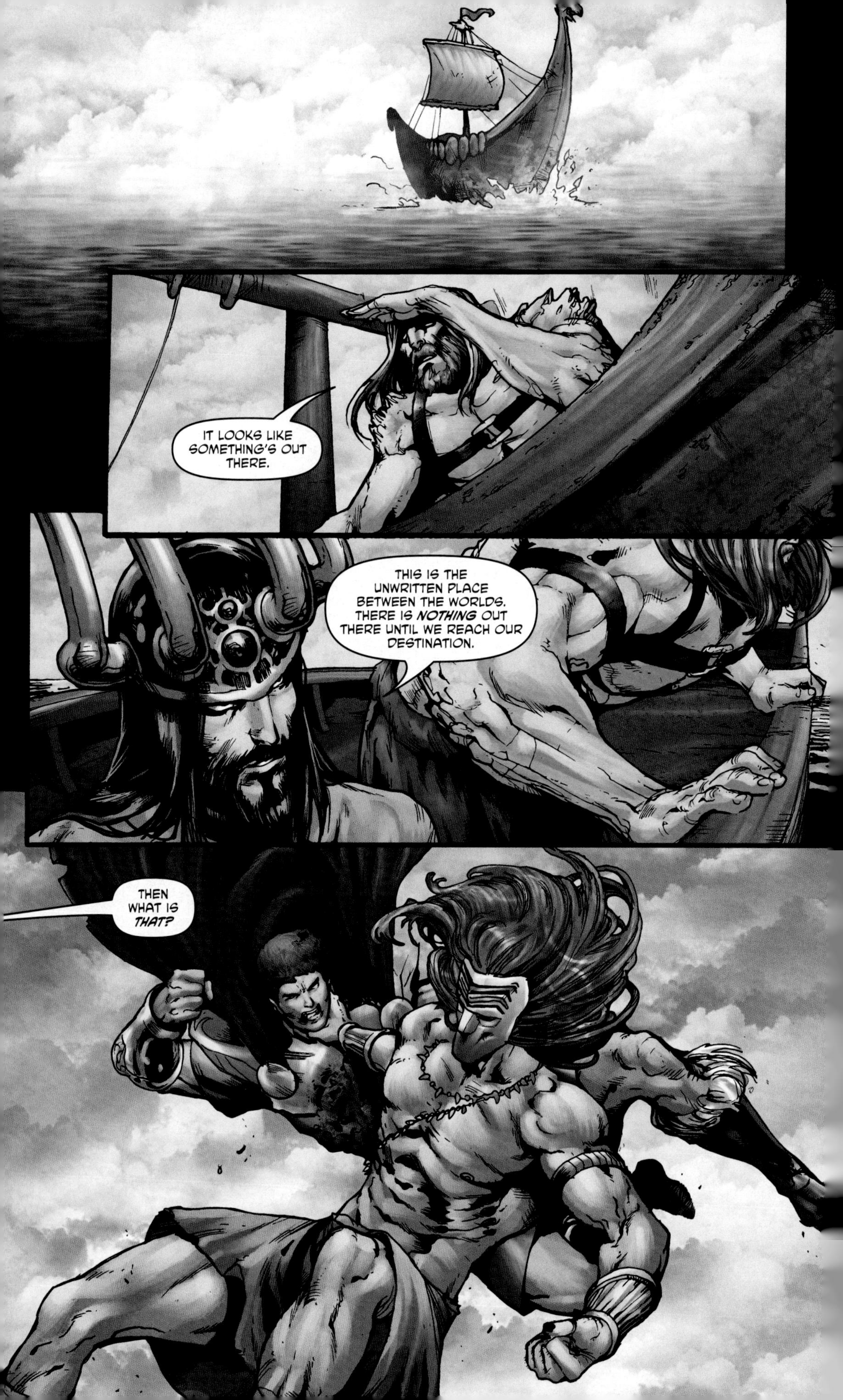
IT LOOKS LIKE SOMETHING'S OUT THERE.
THIS IS THE UNWRITTEN PLACE BETWEEN THE WORLDS. THERE IS *NOTHING* OUT THERE UNTIL WE REACH OUR DESTINATION.
THEN WHAT IS *THAT?*

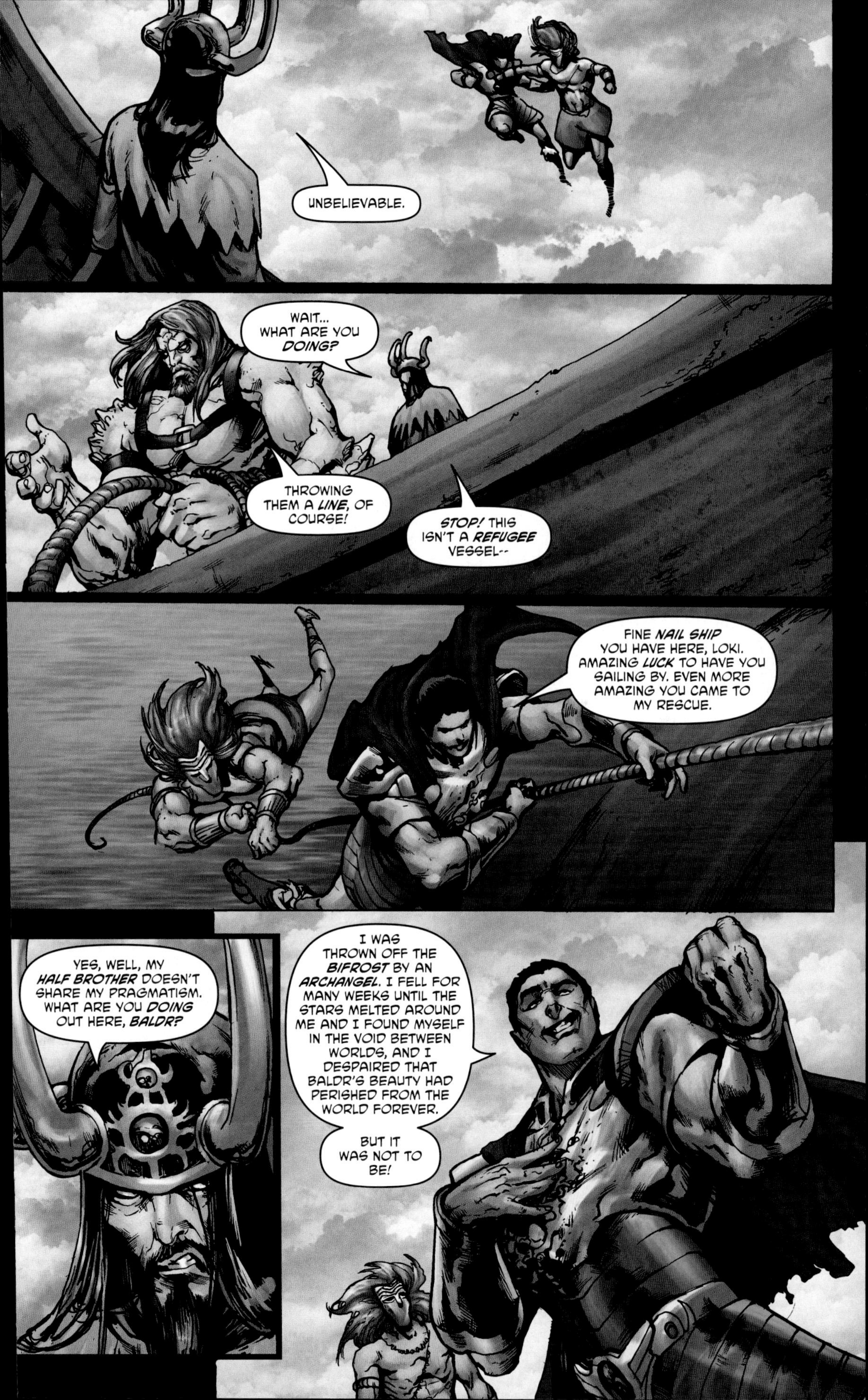
UNBELIEVABLE.
WAIT... WHAT ARE YOU DOING?
THROWING THEM A LINE, OF COURSE!
STOP! THIS ISN'T A REFUGEE VESSEL--
FINE NAIL SHIP YOU HAVE HERE, LOKI. AMAZING LUCK TO HAVE YOU SAILING BY. EVEN MORE AMAZING YOU CAME TO MY RESCUE.
YES, WELL, MY HALF BROTHER DOESN'T SHARE MY PRAGMATISM. WHAT ARE YOU DOING OUT HERE, BALDR?
I WAS THROWN OFF THE BIFROST BY AN ARCHANGEL. I FELL FOR MANY WEEKS UNTIL THE STARS MELTED AROUND ME AND I FOUND MYSELF IN THE VOID BETWEEN WORLDS, AND I DESPAIRED THAT BALDR'S BEAUTY HAD PERISHED FROM THE WORLD FOREVER.
BUT IT WAS NOT TO BE!

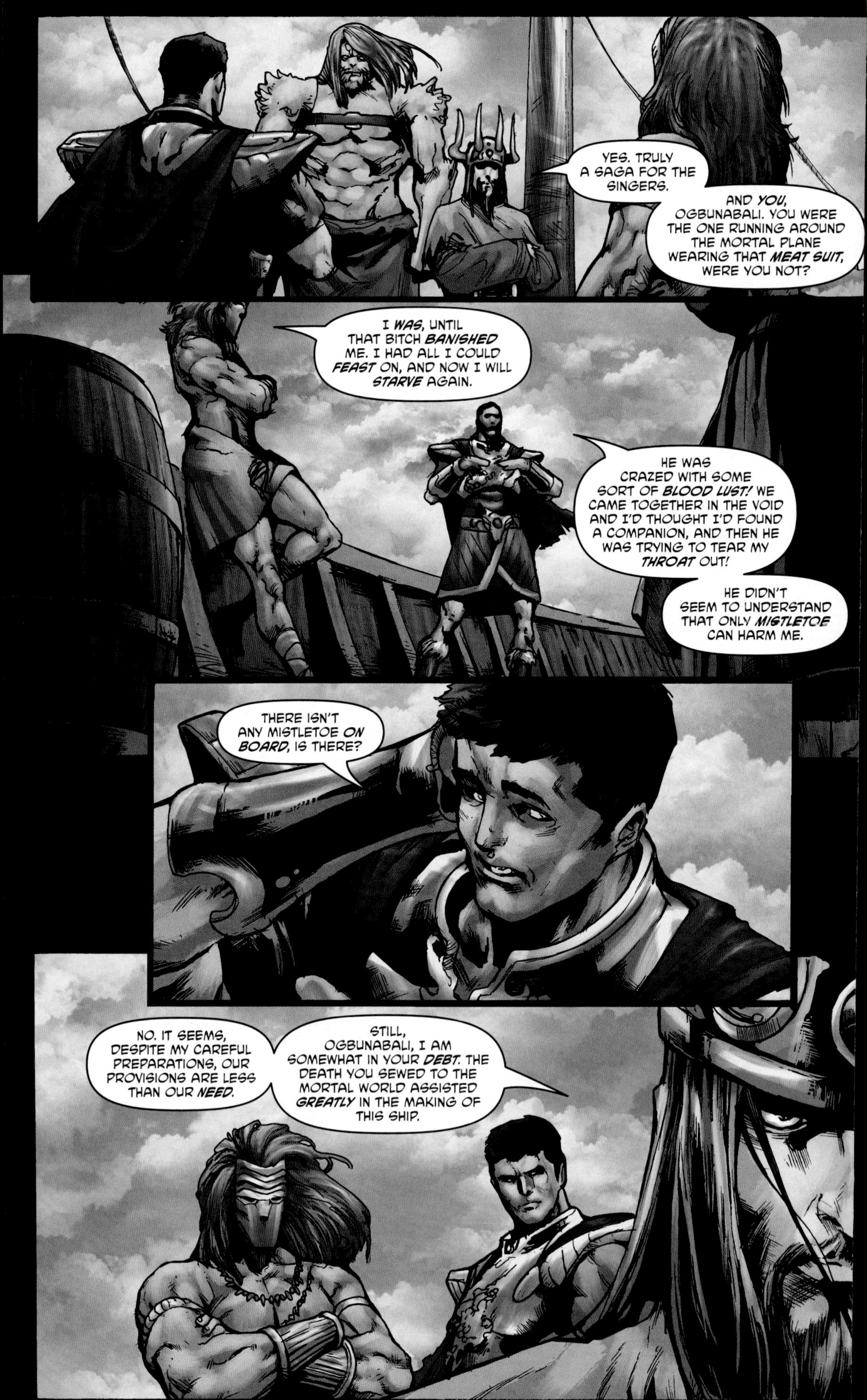
YES. TRULY A SAGA FOR THE SINGERS.
AND *YOU*, OGBUNABALI. YOU WERE THE ONE RUNNING AROUND THE MORTAL PLANE WEARING THAT *MEAT SUIT*, WERE YOU NOT?
I *WAS*, UNTIL THAT BITCH *BANISHED* ME. I HAD ALL I COULD *FEAST* ON, AND NOW I WILL *STARVE* AGAIN.
HE WAS CRAZED WITH SOME SORT OF *BLOOD LUST!* WE CAME TOGETHER IN THE VOID AND I'D THOUGHT I'D FOUND A COMPANION, AND THEN HE WAS TRYING TO TEAR MY *THROAT* OUT!
HE DIDN'T SEEM TO UNDERSTAND THAT ONLY *MISTLETOE* CAN HARM ME.
THERE ISN'T ANY MISTLETOE *ON BOARD*, IS THERE?
NO. IT SEEMS, DESPITE MY CAREFUL PREPARATIONS, OUR PROVISIONS ARE LESS THAN OUR *NEED*.
STILL, OGBUNABALI, I AM SOMEWHAT IN YOUR *DEBT*. THE DEATH YOU SEWED TO THE MORTAL WORLD ASSISTED *GREATLY* IN THE MAKING OF THIS SHIP.

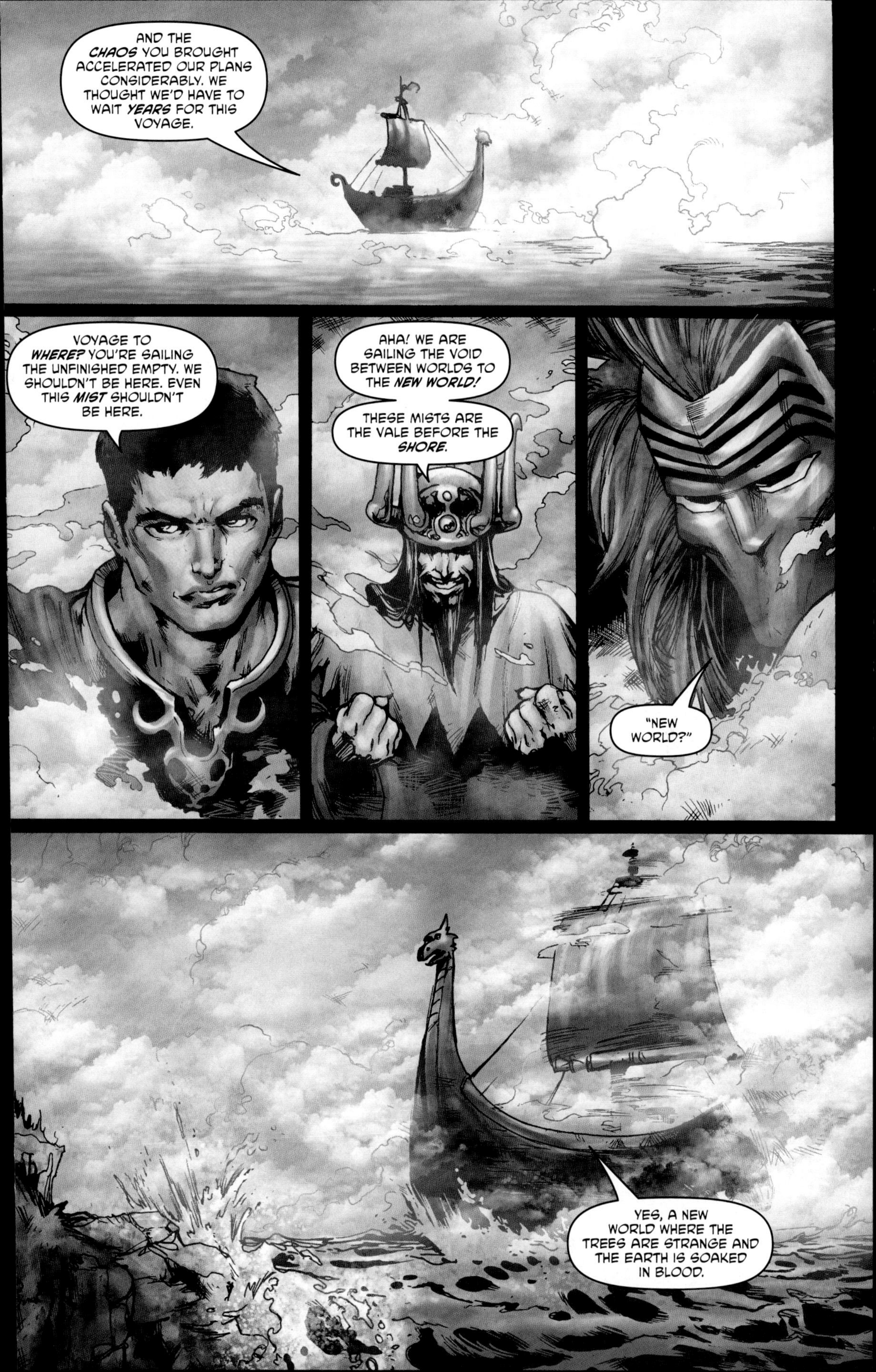
AND THE CHAOS YOU BROUGHT ACCELERATED OUR PLANS CONSIDERABLY. WE THOUGHT WE'D HAVE TO WAIT YEARS FOR THIS VOYAGE.
VOYAGE TO WHERE? YOU'RE SAILING THE UNFINISHED EMPTY. WE SHOULDN'T BE HERE. EVEN THIS MIST SHOULDN'T BE HERE.
AHA! WE ARE SAILING THE VOID BETWEEN WORLDS TO THE NEW WORLD!
THESE MISTS ARE THE VALE BEFORE THE SHORE.
"NEW WORLD?"
YES, A NEW WORLD WHERE THE TREES ARE STRANGE AND THE EARTH IS SOAKED IN BLOOD.

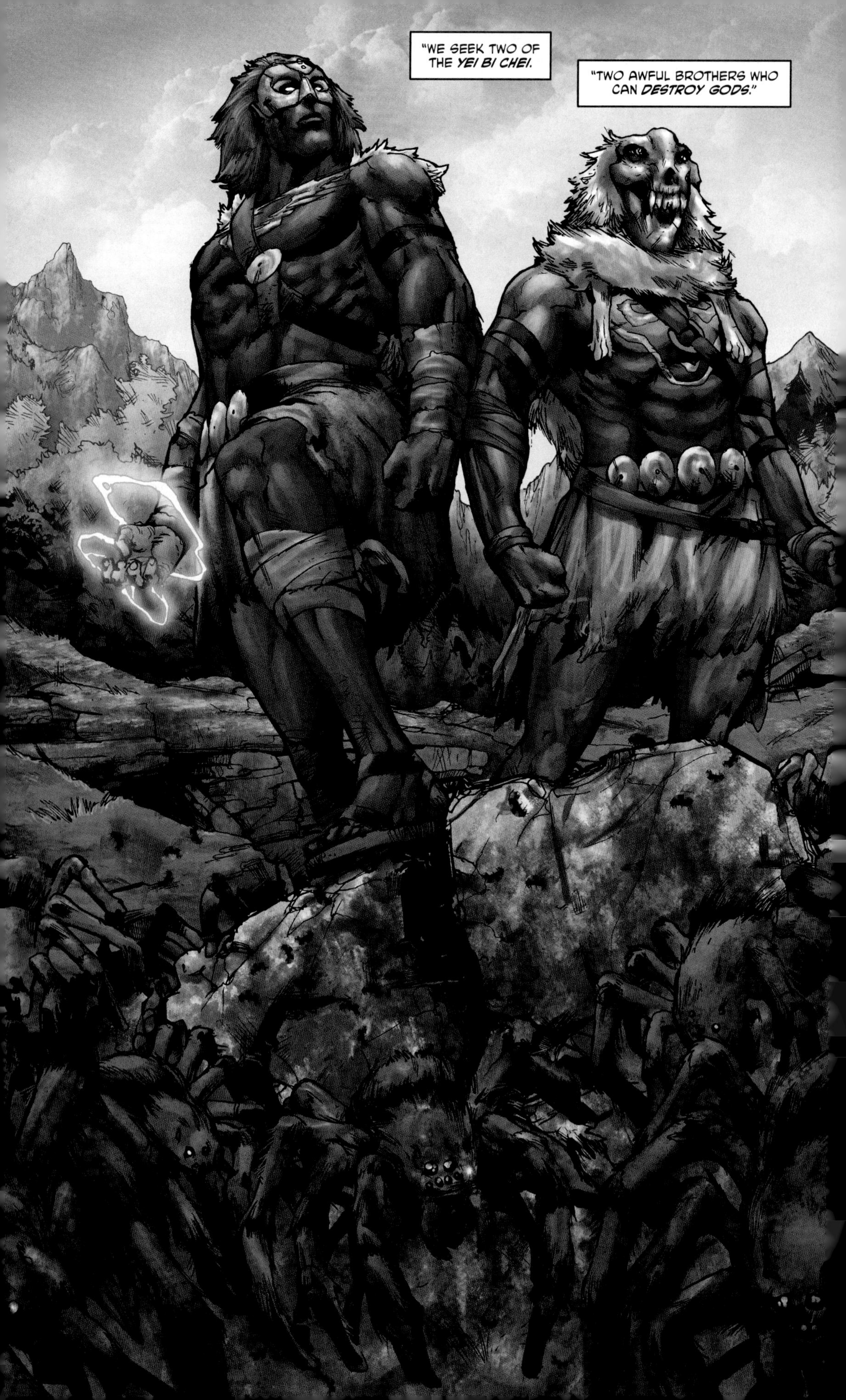
"WE SEEK TWO OF THE YEI BI CHEI.
"TWO AWFUL BROTHERS WHO CAN DESTROY GODS."

FOUR

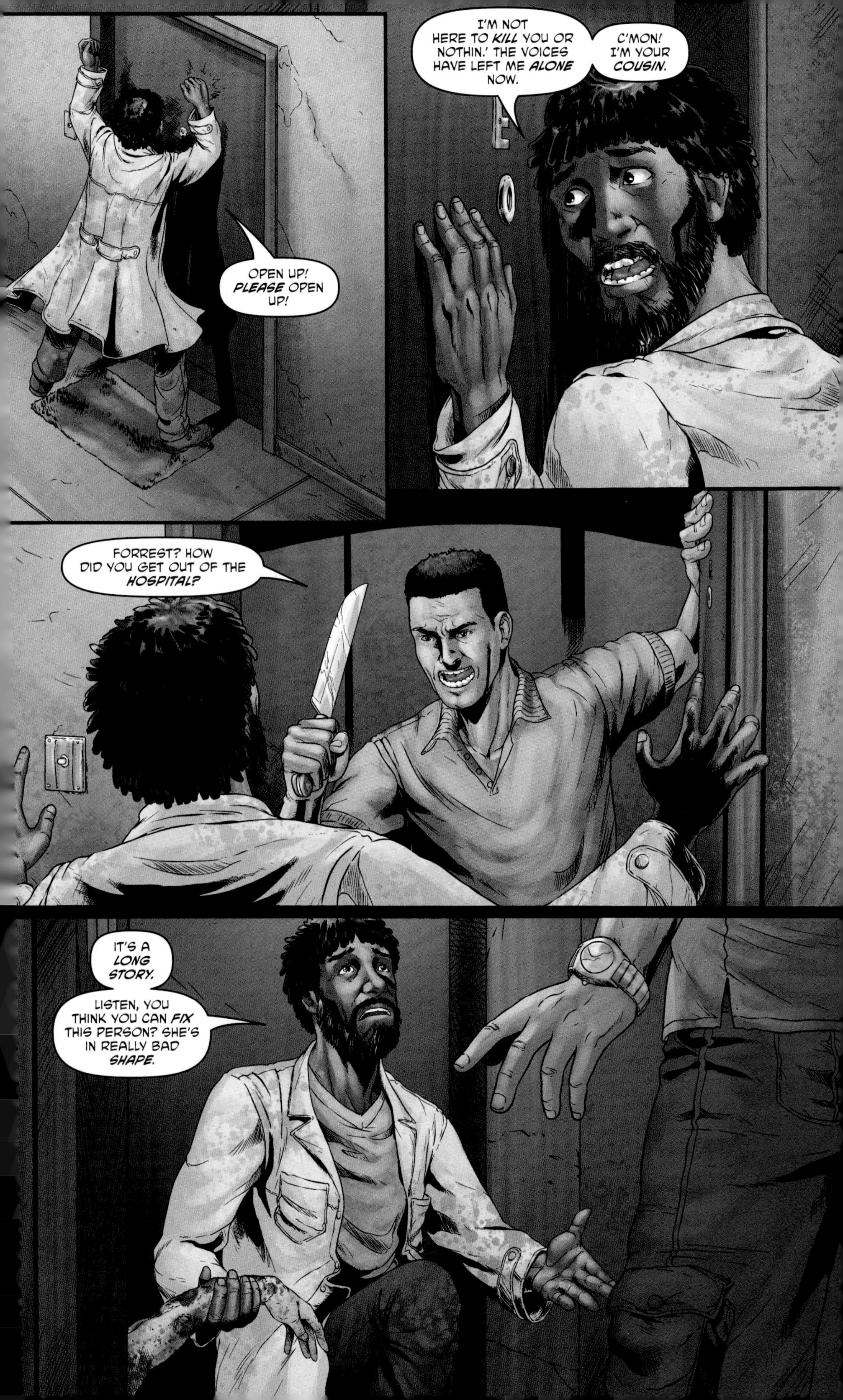
OPEN UP! PLEASE OPEN UP!
I'M NOT HERE TO KILL YOU OR NOTHIN.' THE VOICES HAVE LEFT ME ALONE NOW.
C'MON! I'M YOUR COUSIN.
FORREST? HOW DID YOU GET OUT OF THE HOSPITAL?
IT'S A LONG STORY.
LISTEN, YOU THINK YOU CAN FIX THIS PERSON? SHE'S IN REALLY BAD SHAPE.

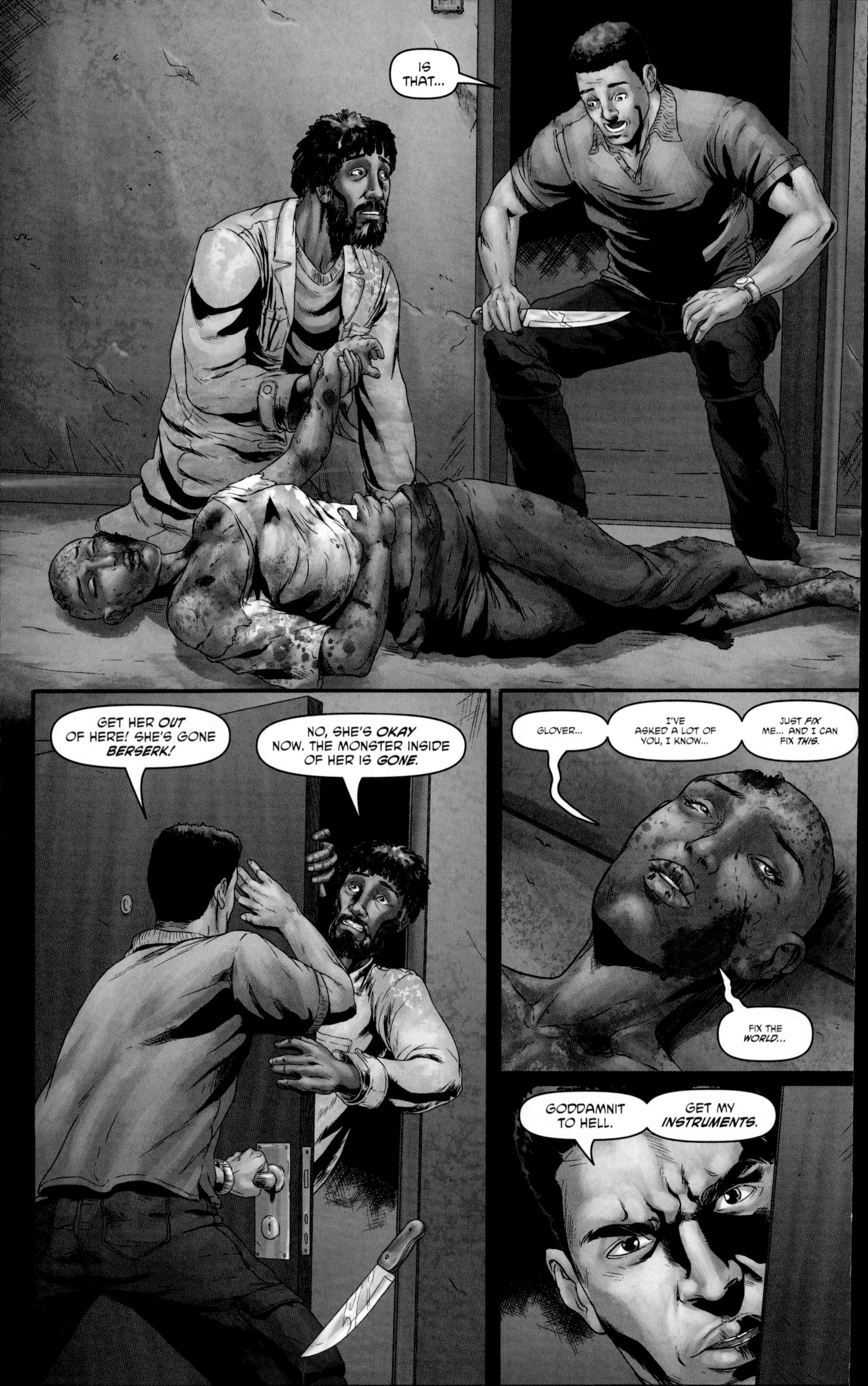
IS THAT...
GET HER OUT OF HERE! SHE'S GONE BERSERK!
NO, SHE'S OKAY NOW. THE MONSTER INSIDE OF HER IS GONE.
GLOVER...
I'VE ASKED A LOT OF YOU, I KNOW...
JUST FIX ME... AND I CAN FIX THIS.
FIX THE WORLD...
GODDAMNIT TO HELL.
GET MY INSTRUMENTS.

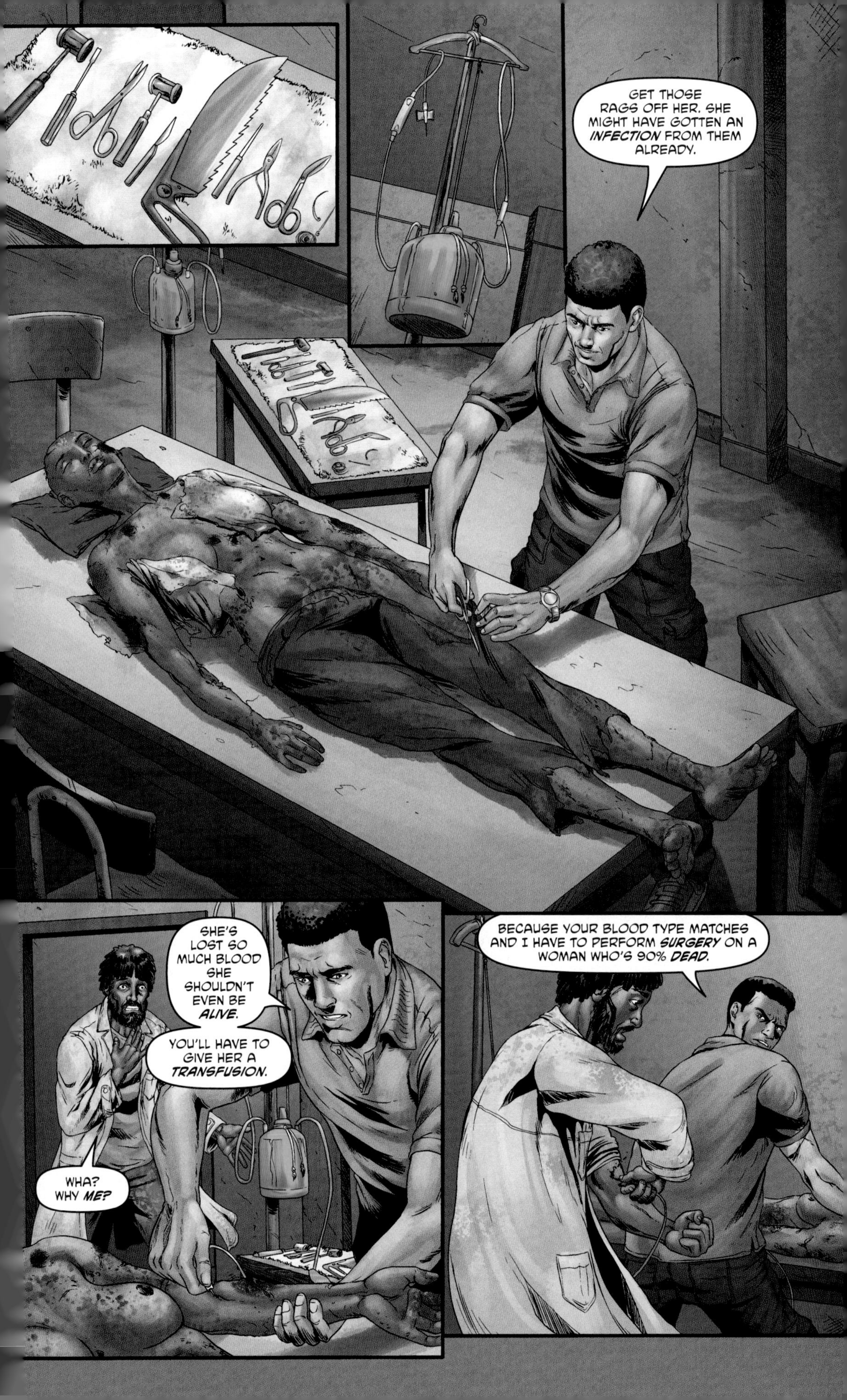

GET THOSE RAGS OFF HER. SHE MIGHT HAVE GOTTEN AN *INFECTION* FROM THEM ALREADY.
SHE'S LOST SO MUCH BLOOD SHE SHOULDN'T EVEN BE *ALIVE*.
YOU'LL HAVE TO GIVE HER A *TRANSFUSION*.
WHA? WHY *ME?*
BECAUSE YOUR BLOOD TYPE MATCHES AND I HAVE TO PERFORM *SURGERY* ON A WOMAN WHO'S 90% *DEAD*.

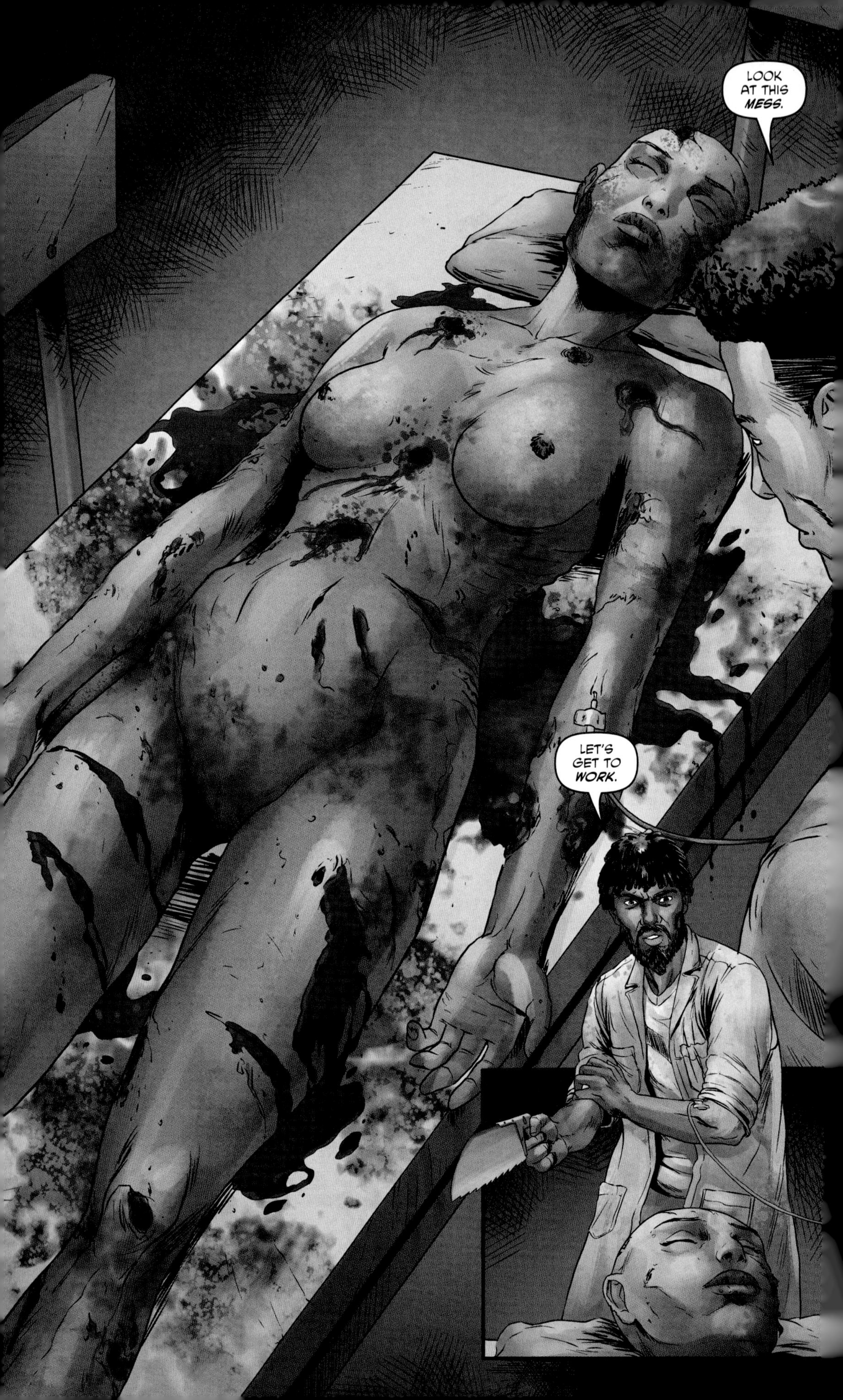
LOOK AT THIS MESS.
LET'S GET TO WORK.

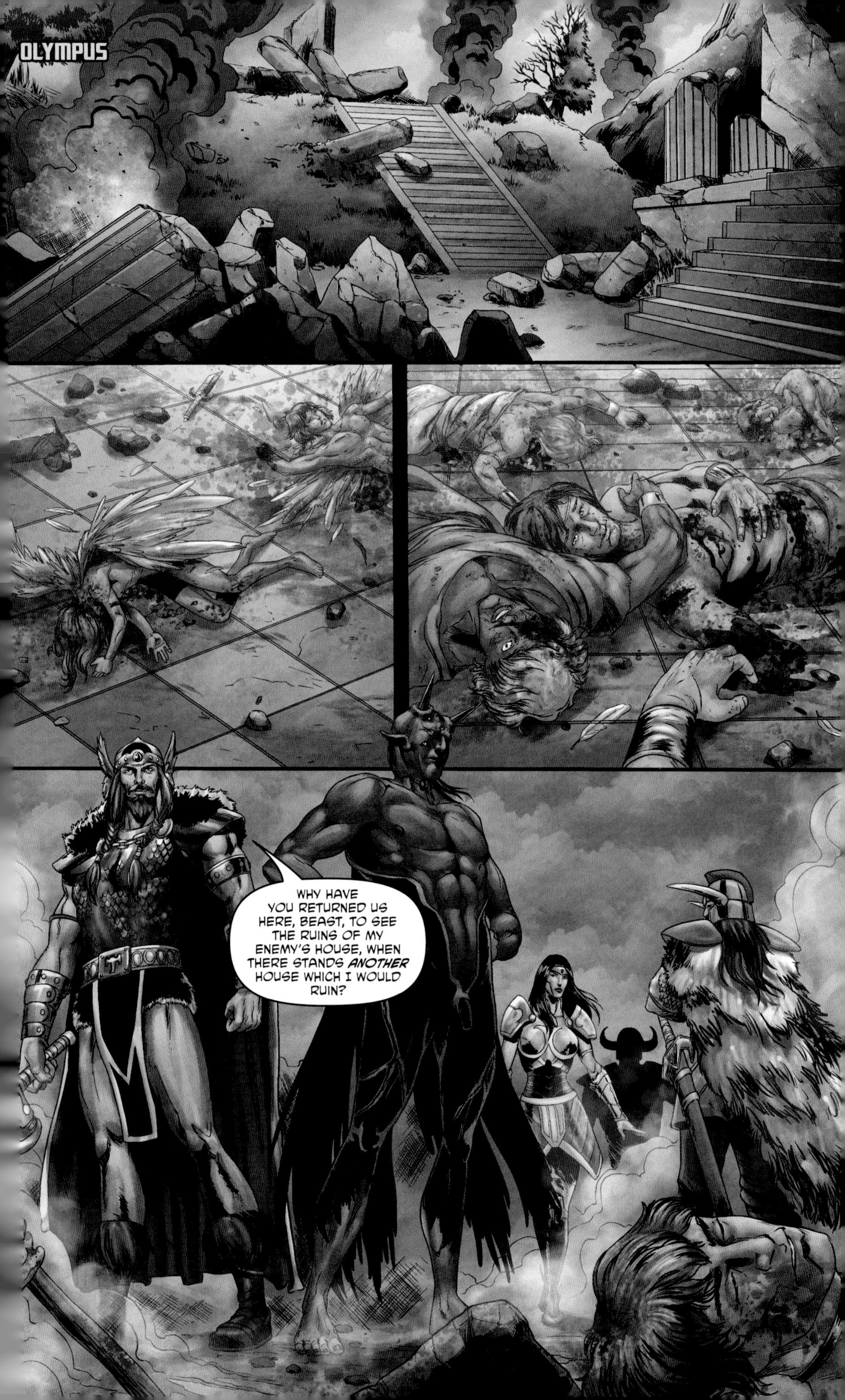
OLYMPUS
WHY HAVE YOU RETURNED US HERE, BEAST, TO SEE THE RUINS OF MY ENEMY'S HOUSE, WHEN THERE STANDS *ANOTHER* HOUSE WHICH I WOULD RUIN?

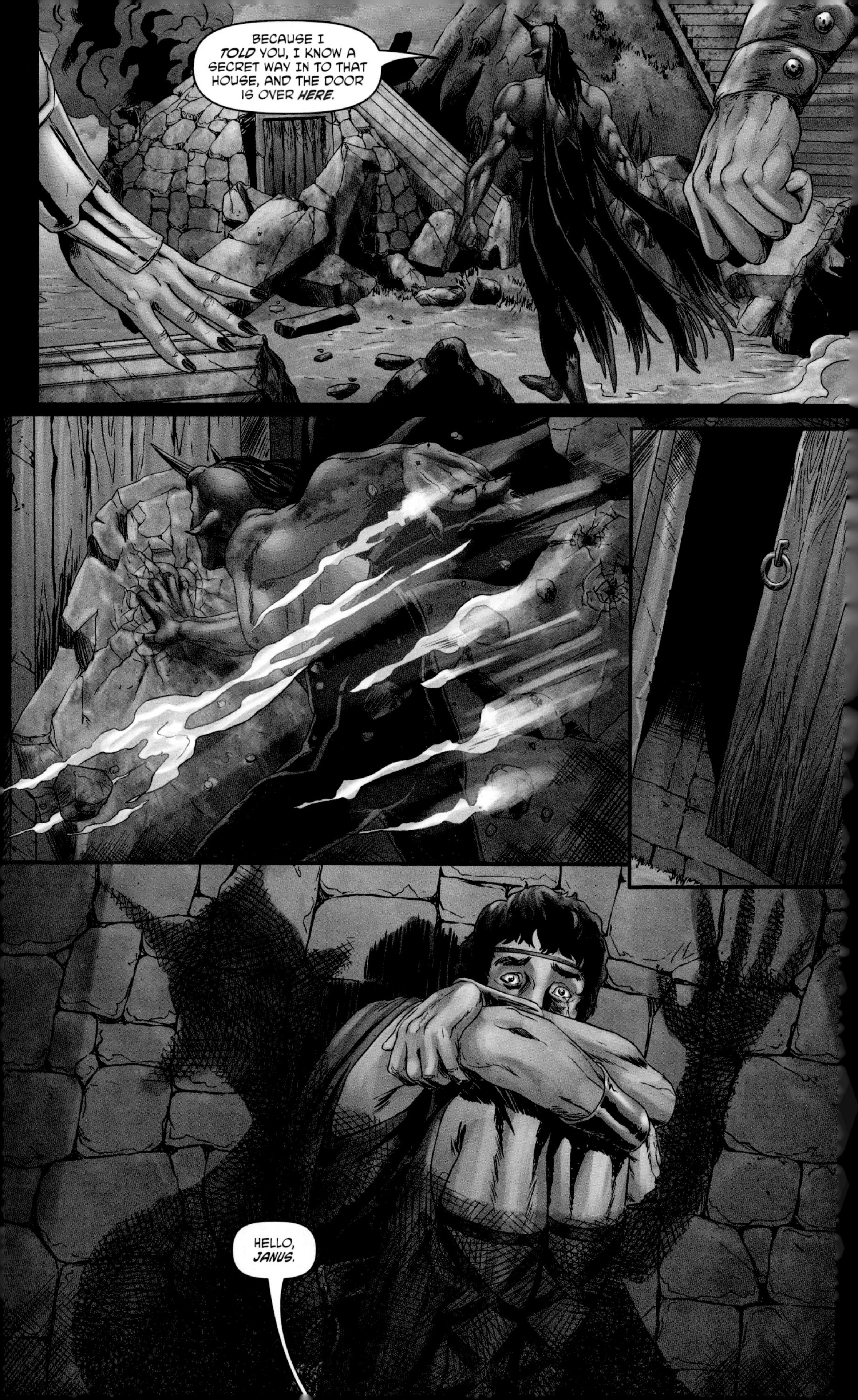
BECAUSE I TOLD YOU, I KNOW A SECRET WAY IN TO THAT HOUSE, AND THE DOOR IS OVER HERE.
HELLO, JANUS.

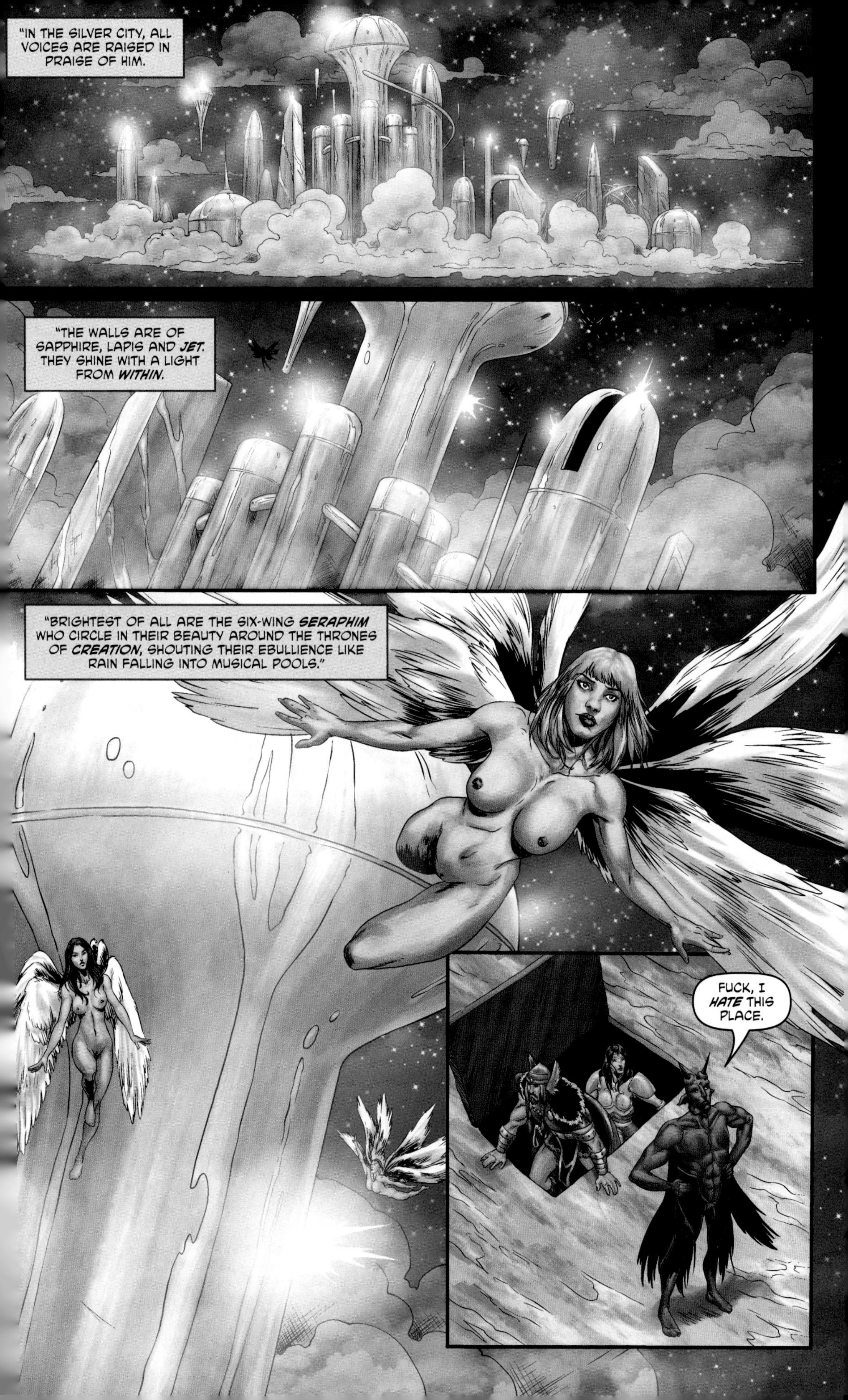
"IN THE SILVER CITY, ALL VOICES ARE RAISED IN PRAISE OF HIM.
"THE WALLS ARE OF SAPPHIRE, LAPIS AND JET. THEY SHINE WITH A LIGHT FROM WITHIN.
"BRIGHTEST OF ALL ARE THE SIX-WING SERAPHIM WHO CIRCLE IN THEIR BEAUTY AROUND THE THRONES OF CREATION, SHOUTING THEIR EBULLIENCE LIKE RAIN FALLING INTO MUSICAL POOLS."
FUCK, I HATE THIS PLACE.

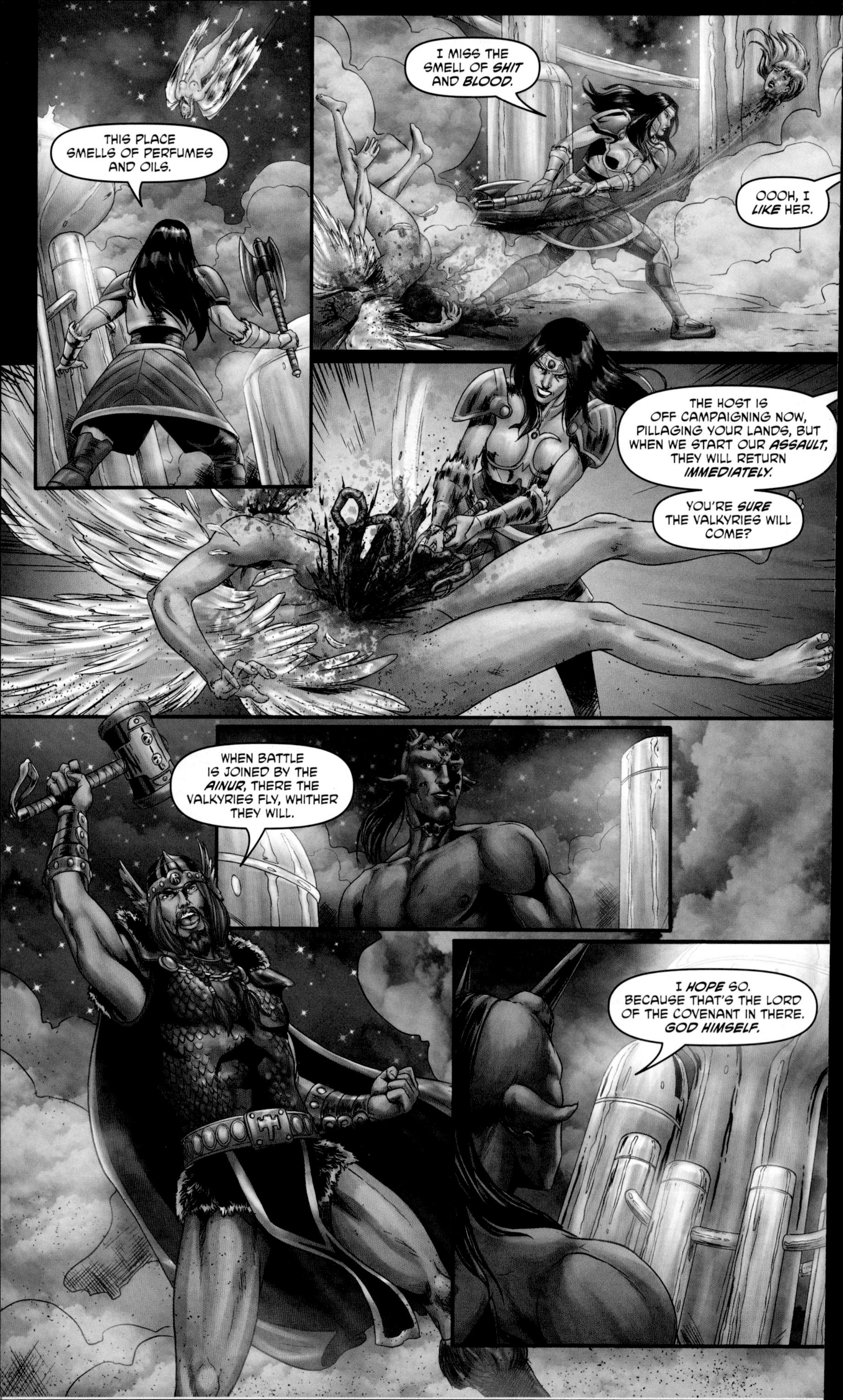
THIS PLACE SMELLS OF PERFUMES AND OILS.
I MISS THE SMELL OF SHIT AND BLOOD.
OOOH, I LIKE HER.
THE HOST IS OFF CAMPAIGNING NOW, PILLAGING YOUR LANDS, BUT WHEN WE START OUR ASSAULT, THEY WILL RETURN IMMEDIATELY.
YOU'RE SURE THE VALKYRIES WILL COME?
WHEN BATTLE IS JOINED BY THE AINUR, THERE THE VALKYRIES FLY, WHITHER THEY WILL.
I HOPE SO. BECAUSE THAT'S THE LORD OF THE COVENANT IN THERE. GOD HIMSELF.

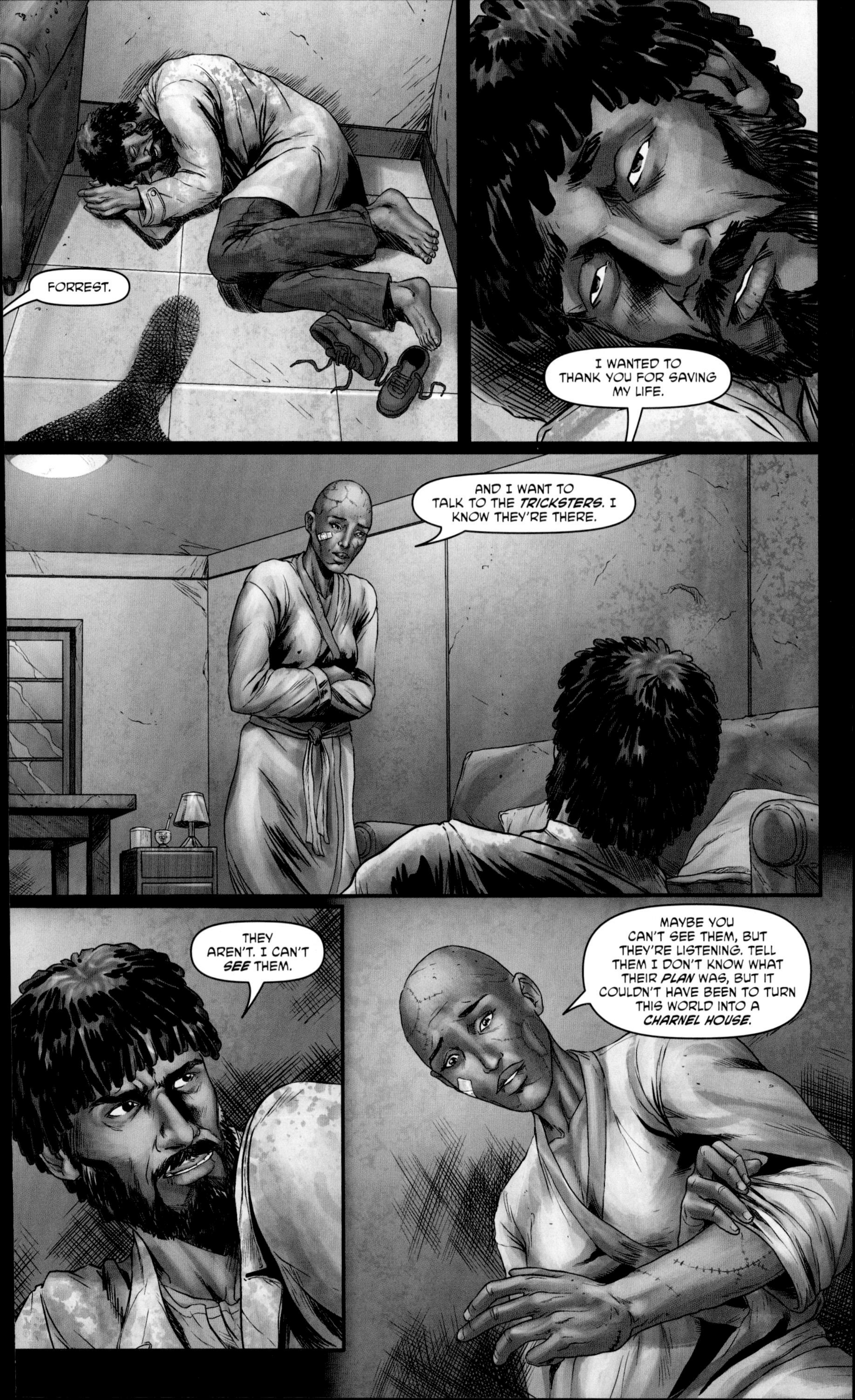

FORREST.
I WANTED TO THANK YOU FOR SAVING MY LIFE.
AND I WANT TO TALK TO THE *TRICKSTERS*. I KNOW THEY'RE THERE.
THEY AREN'T. I CAN'T *SEE* THEM.
MAYBE YOU CAN'T SEE THEM, BUT THEY'RE LISTENING. TELL THEM I DON'T KNOW WHAT THEIR *PLAN* WAS, BUT IT COULDN'T HAVE BEEN TO TURN THIS WORLD INTO A *CHARNEL HOUSE*.

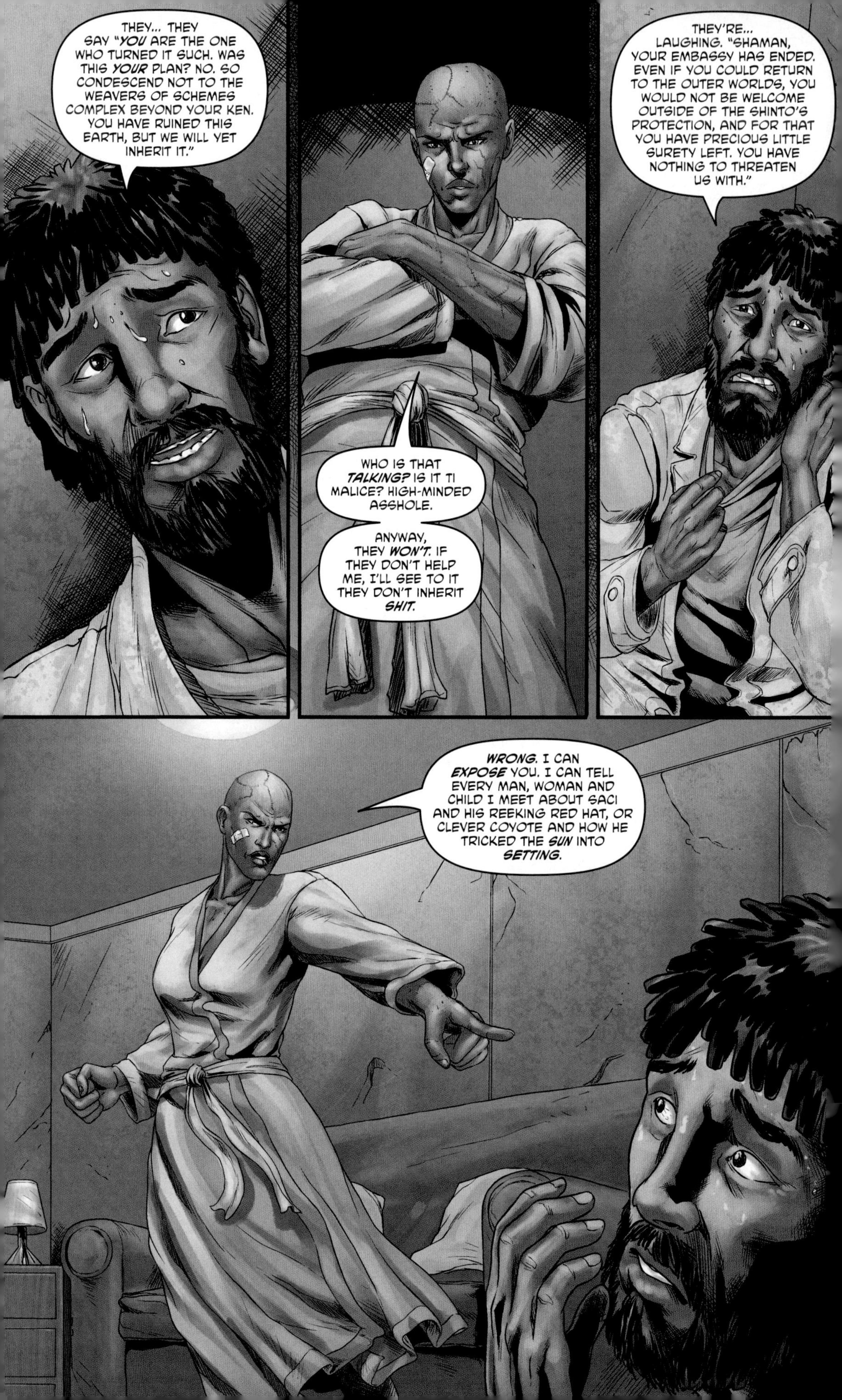
THEY... THEY SAY "YOU ARE THE ONE WHO TURNED IT SUCH. WAS THIS YOUR PLAN? NO. SO CONDESCEND NOT TO THE WEAVERS OF SCHEMES COMPLEX BEYOND YOUR KEN. YOU HAVE RUINED THIS EARTH, BUT WE WILL YET INHERIT IT."
WHO IS THAT TALKING? IS IT TI MALICE? HIGH-MINDED ASSHOLE.
ANYWAY, THEY WON'T. IF THEY DON'T HELP ME, I'LL SEE TO IT THEY DON'T INHERIT SHIT.
THEY'RE... LAUGHING. "SHAMAN, YOUR EMBASSY HAS ENDED. EVEN IF YOU COULD RETURN TO THE OUTER WORLDS, YOU WOULD NOT BE WELCOME OUTSIDE OF THE SHINTO'S PROTECTION, AND FOR THAT YOU HAVE PRECIOUS LITTLE SURETY LEFT. YOU HAVE NOTHING TO THREATEN US WITH."
WRONG. I CAN EXPOSE YOU. I CAN TELL EVERY MAN, WOMAN AND CHILD I MEET ABOUT SACI AND HIS REEKING RED HAT, OR CLEVER COYOTE AND HOW HE TRICKED THE SUN INTO SETTING.

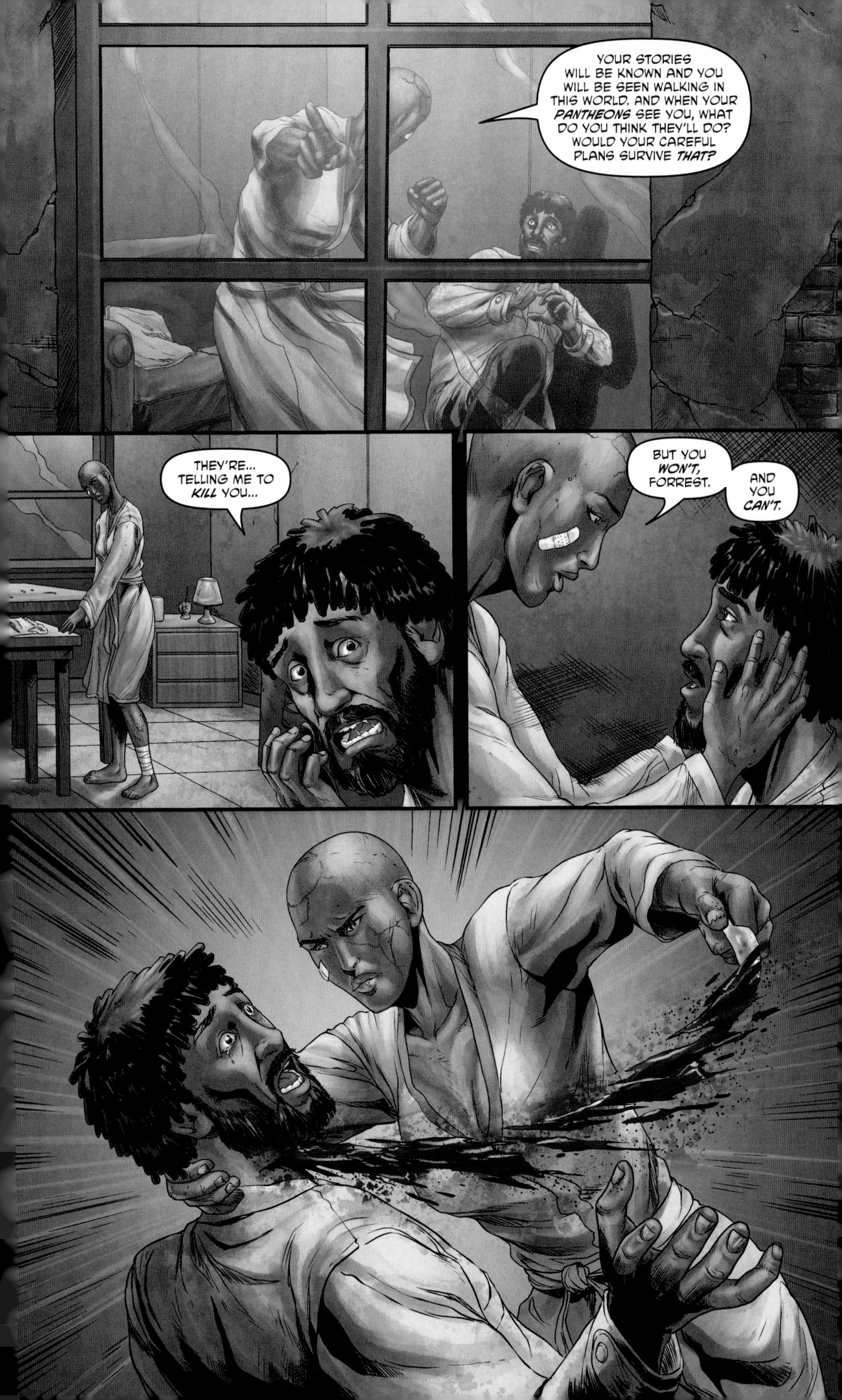
YOUR STORIES WILL BE KNOWN AND YOU WILL BE SEEN WALKING IN THIS WORLD. AND WHEN YOUR *PANTHEONS* SEE YOU, WHAT DO YOU THINK THEY'LL DO? WOULD YOUR CAREFUL PLANS SURVIVE *THAT?*
THEY'RE... TELLING ME TO *KILL* YOU...
BUT YOU *WON'T,* FORREST.
AND YOU *CAN'T.*

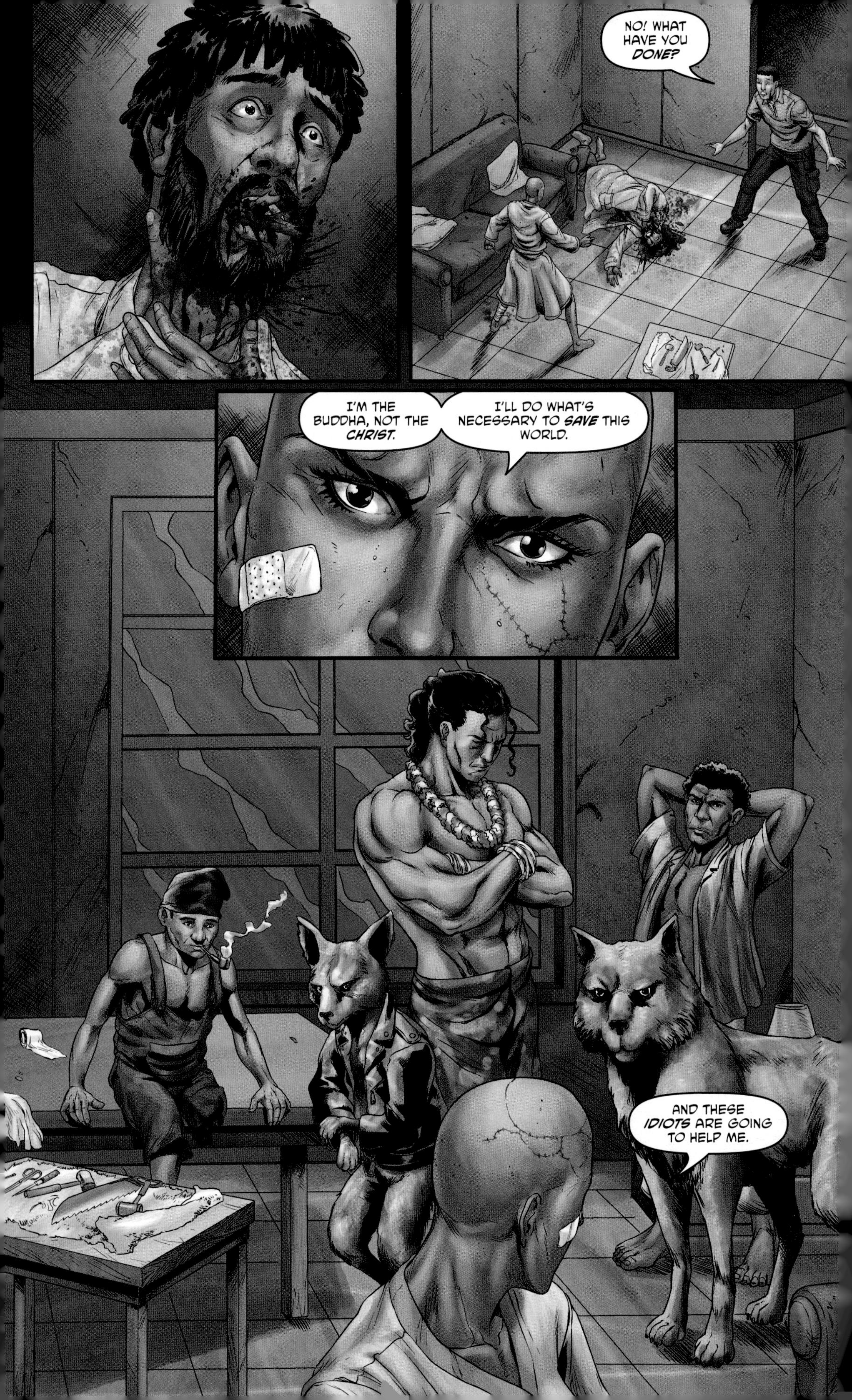
NO! WHAT HAVE YOU DONE?
I'M THE BUDDHA, NOT THE CHRIST.
I'LL DO WHAT'S NECESSARY TO SAVE THIS WORLD.
AND THESE IDIOTS ARE GOING TO HELP ME.

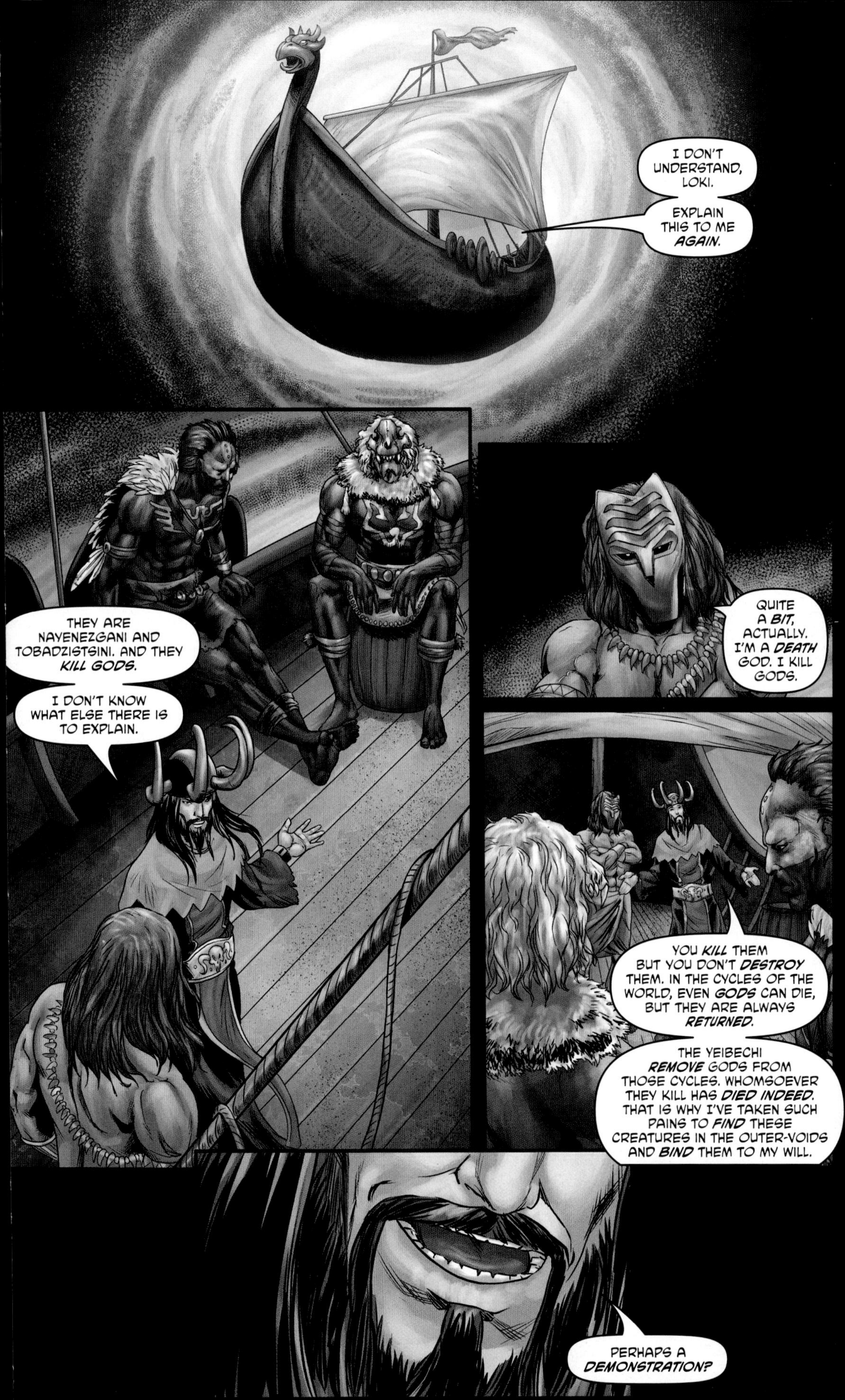
I DON'T UNDERSTAND, LOKI.
EXPLAIN THIS TO ME AGAIN.
THEY ARE NAYENEZGANI AND TOBADZISTSINI. AND THEY KILL GODS.
I DON'T KNOW WHAT ELSE THERE IS TO EXPLAIN.
QUITE A BIT, ACTUALLY. I'M A DEATH GOD. I KILL GODS.
YOU KILL THEM BUT YOU DON'T DESTROY THEM. IN THE CYCLES OF THE WORLD, EVEN GODS CAN DIE, BUT THEY ARE ALWAYS RETURNED.
THE YEIBECHI REMOVE GODS FROM THOSE CYCLES. WHOMSOEVER THEY KILL HAS DIED INDEED. THAT IS WHY I'VE TAKEN SUCH PAINS TO FIND THESE CREATURES IN THE OUTER-VOIDS AND BIND THEM TO MY WILL.
PERHAPS A DEMONSTRATION?

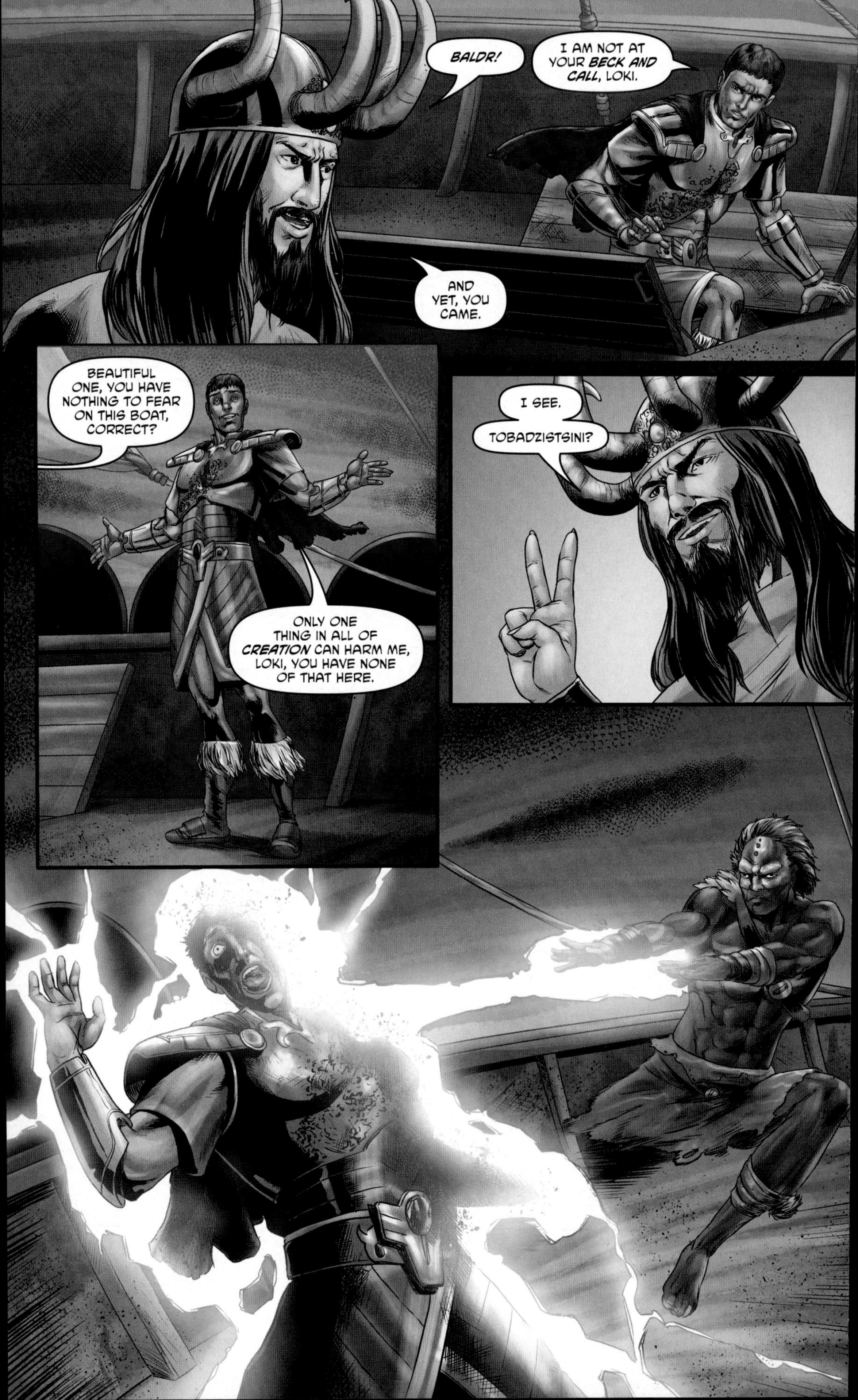
BALDR!
I AM NOT AT YOUR BECK AND CALL, LOKI.
AND YET, YOU CAME.
BEAUTIFUL ONE, YOU HAVE NOTHING TO FEAR ON THIS BOAT, CORRECT?
ONLY ONE THING IN ALL OF CREATION CAN HARM ME, LOKI, YOU HAVE NONE OF THAT HERE.
I SEE.
TOBADZISTSINI?

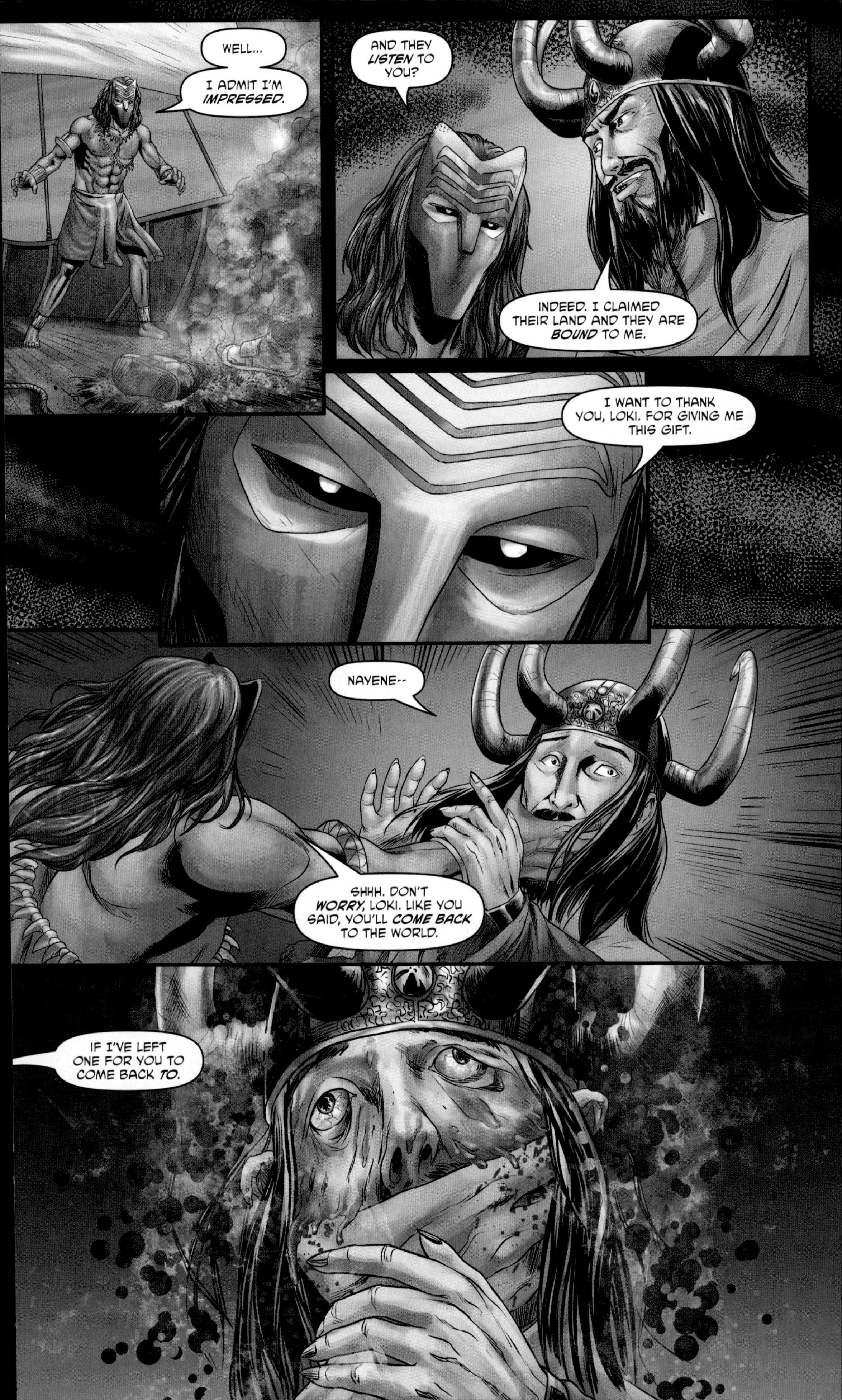
WELL...
I ADMIT I'M *IMPRESSED.*
AND THEY *LISTEN* TO YOU?
INDEED. I CLAIMED THEIR LAND AND THEY ARE *BOUND* TO ME.
I WANT TO THANK YOU, LOKI. FOR GIVING ME THIS GIFT.
NAYENE--
SHHH. DON'T *WORRY,* LOKI. LIKE YOU SAID, YOU'LL *COME BACK* TO THE WORLD.
IF I'VE LEFT ONE FOR YOU TO COME BACK *TO.*

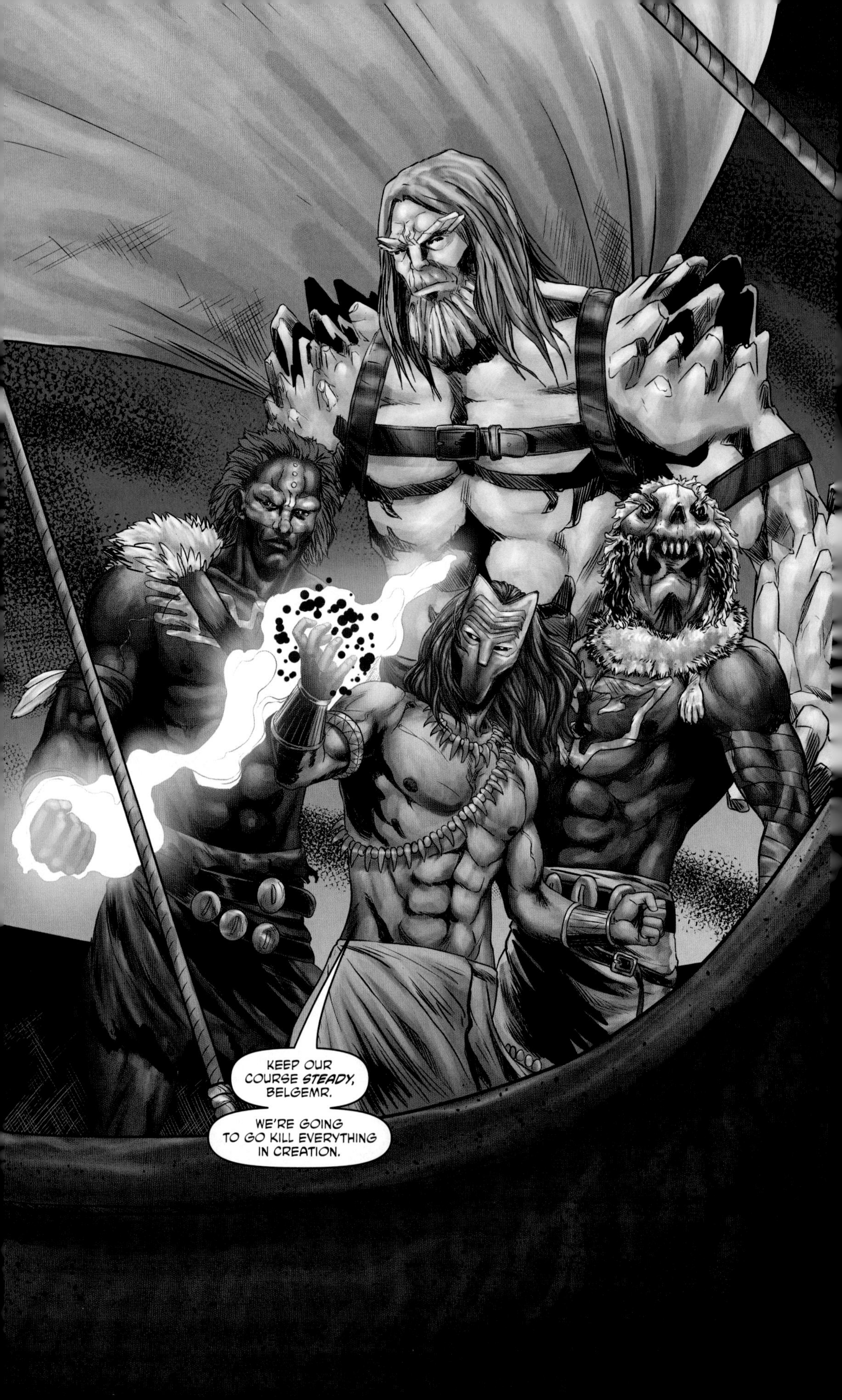
KEEP OUR COURSE STEADY, BELGEMR.
WE'RE GOING TO GO KILL EVERYTHING IN CREATION.

FIVE

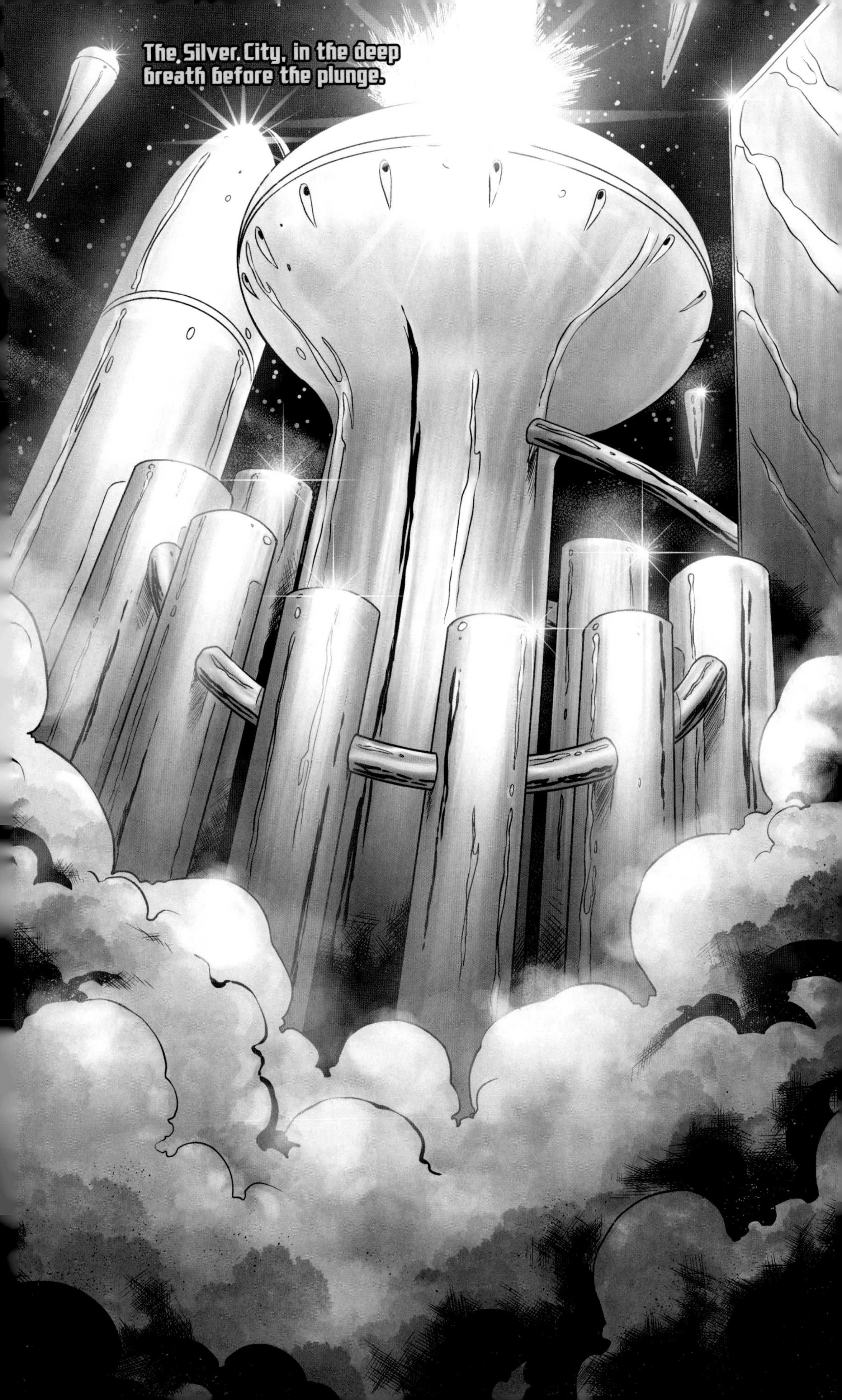
The Silver City, in the deep breath before the plunge.

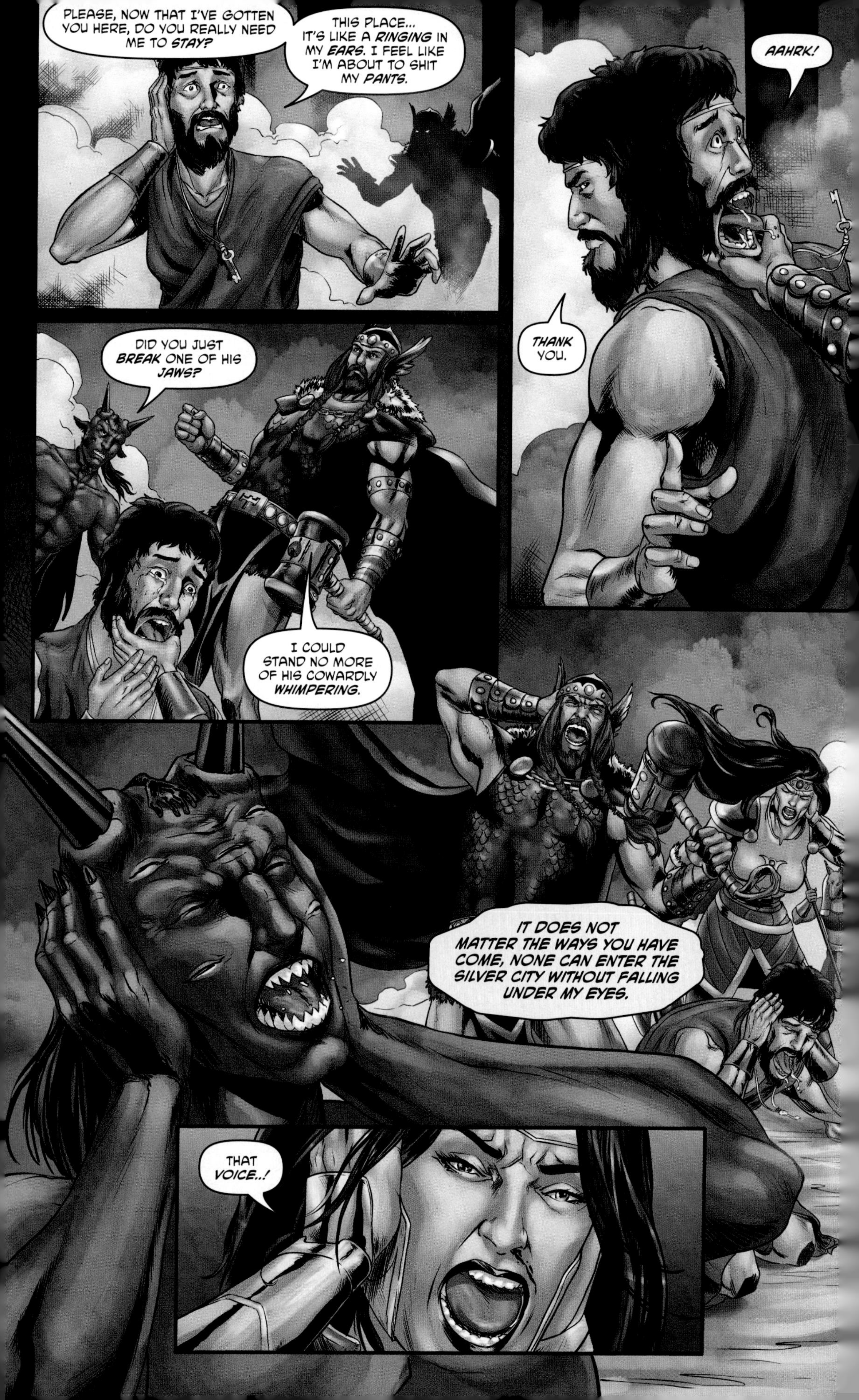
PLEASE, NOW THAT I'VE GOTTEN YOU HERE, DO YOU REALLY NEED ME TO STAY?
THIS PLACE... IT'S LIKE A RINGING IN MY EARS. I FEEL LIKE I'M ABOUT TO SHIT MY PANTS.
AAHRK!
THANK YOU.
DID YOU JUST BREAK ONE OF HIS JAWS?
I COULD STAND NO MORE OF HIS COWARDLY WHIMPERING.
IT DOES NOT MATTER THE WAYS YOU HAVE COME, NONE CAN ENTER THE SILVER CITY WITHOUT FALLING UNDER MY EYES.
THAT VOICE..!

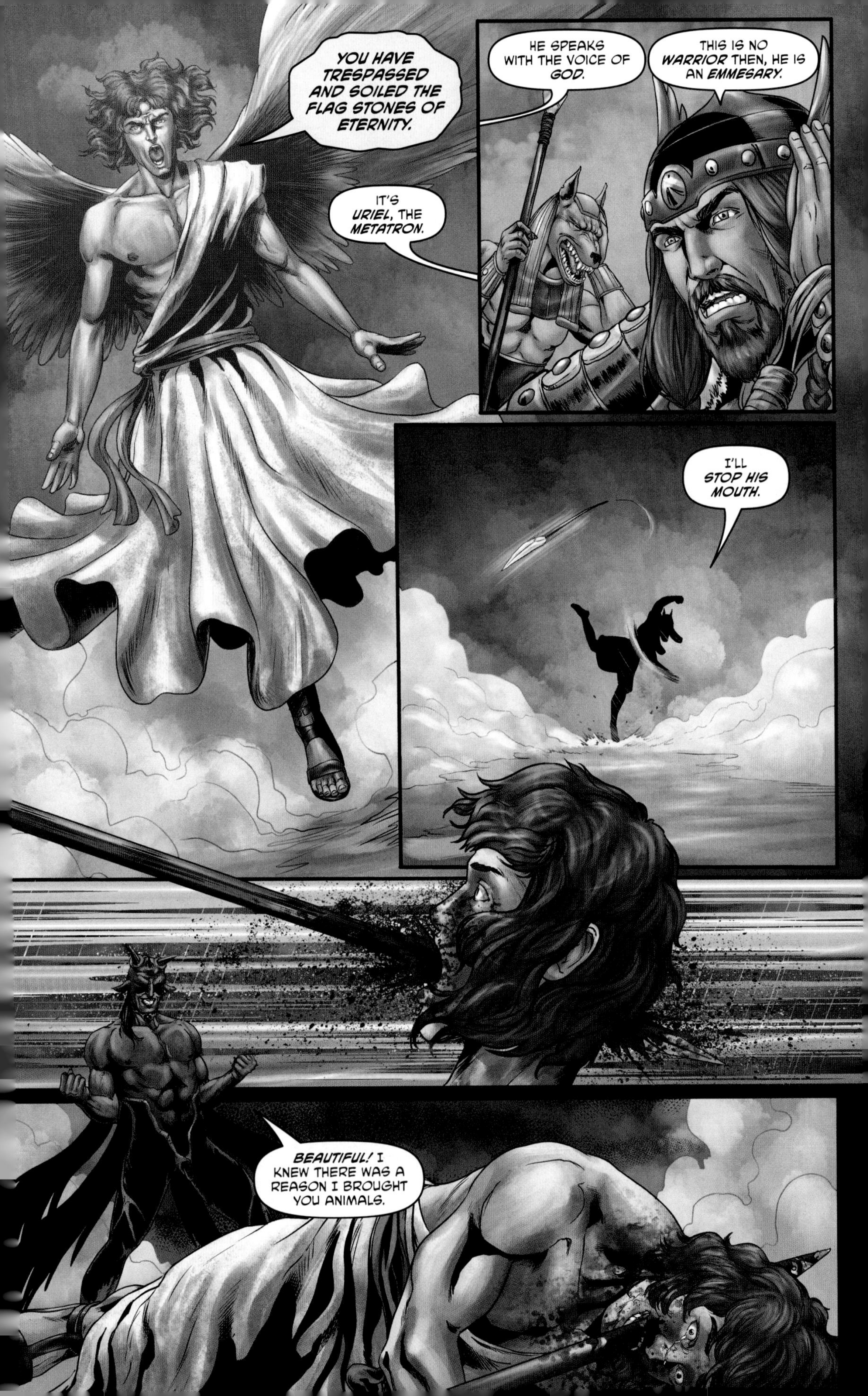
YOU HAVE TRESPASSED AND SOILED THE FLAG STONES OF ETERNITY.
IT'S URIEL, THE METATRON.
HE SPEAKS WITH THE VOICE OF GOD.
THIS IS NO WARRIOR THEN, HE IS AN EMMESARY.
I'LL STOP HIS MOUTH.
BEAUTIFUL! I KNEW THERE WAS A REASON I BROUGHT YOU ANIMALS.

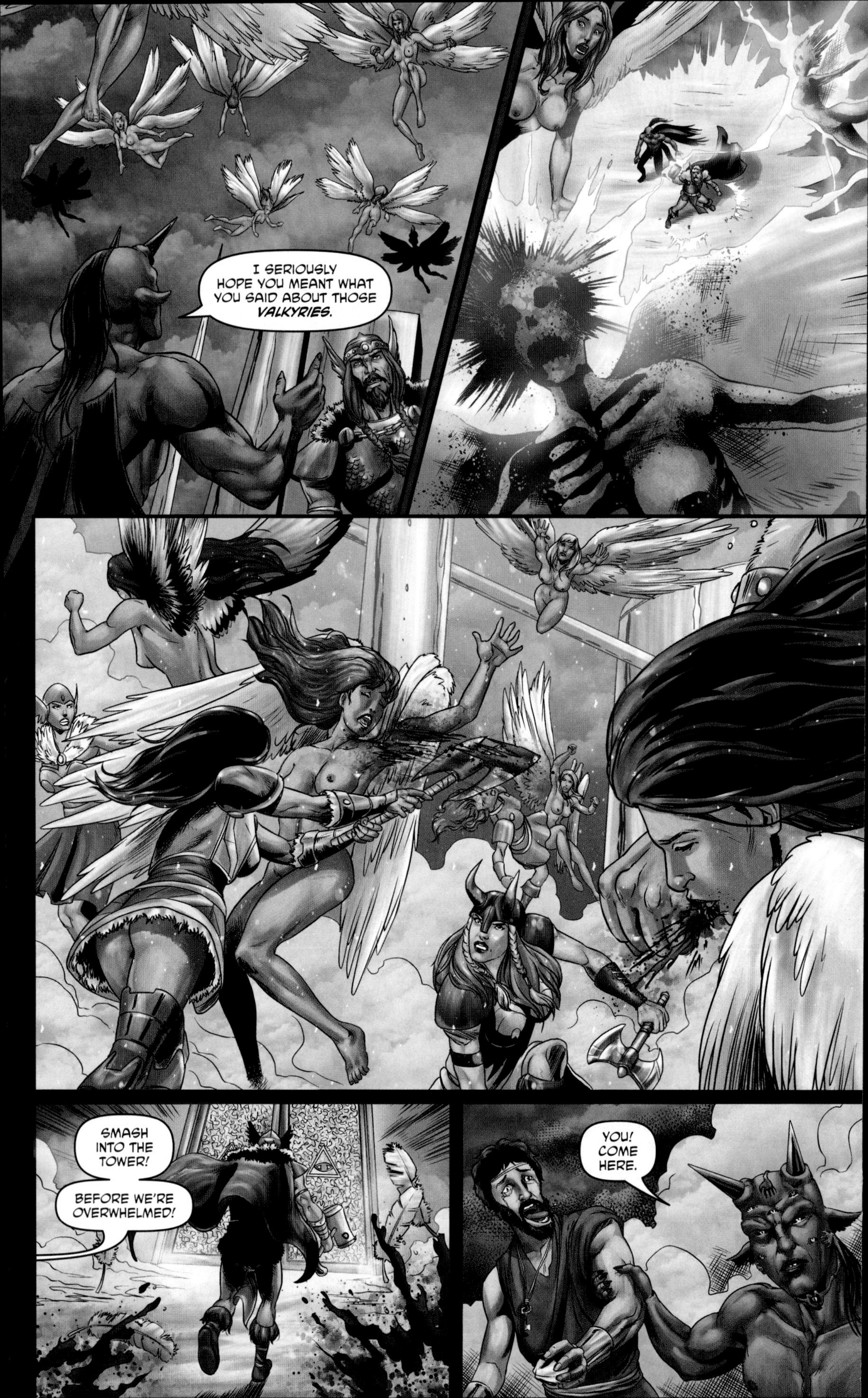

I SERIOUSLY HOPE YOU MEANT WHAT YOU SAID ABOUT THOSE VALKYRIES.
SMASH INTO THE TOWER!
BEFORE WE'RE OVERWHELMED!
YOU! COME HERE.

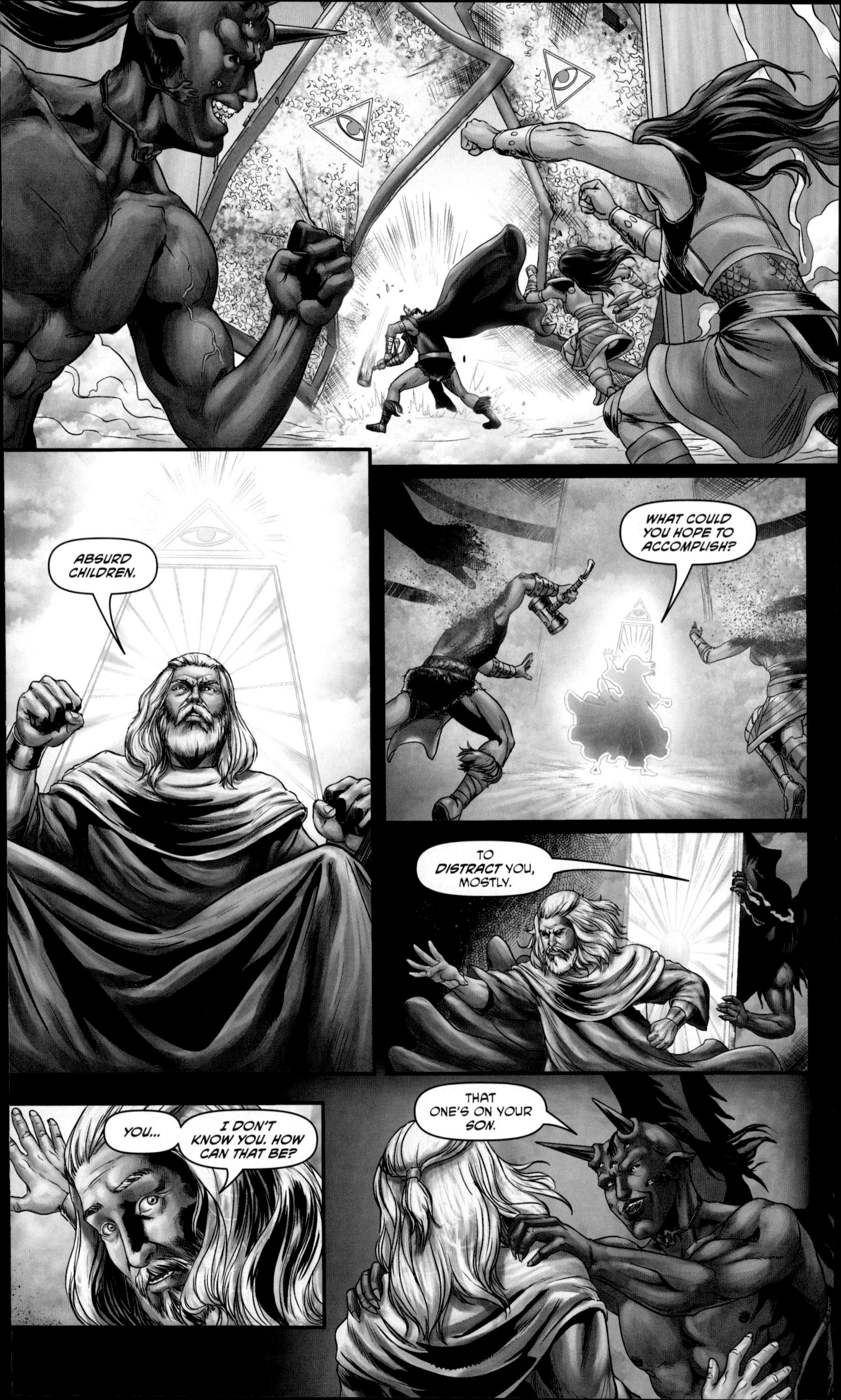
ABSURD CHILDREN.
WHAT COULD YOU HOPE TO ACCOMPLISH?
TO *DISTRACT* YOU, MOSTLY.
YOU...
I DON'T KNOW YOU. HOW CAN THAT BE?
THAT ONE'S ON YOUR *SON*.

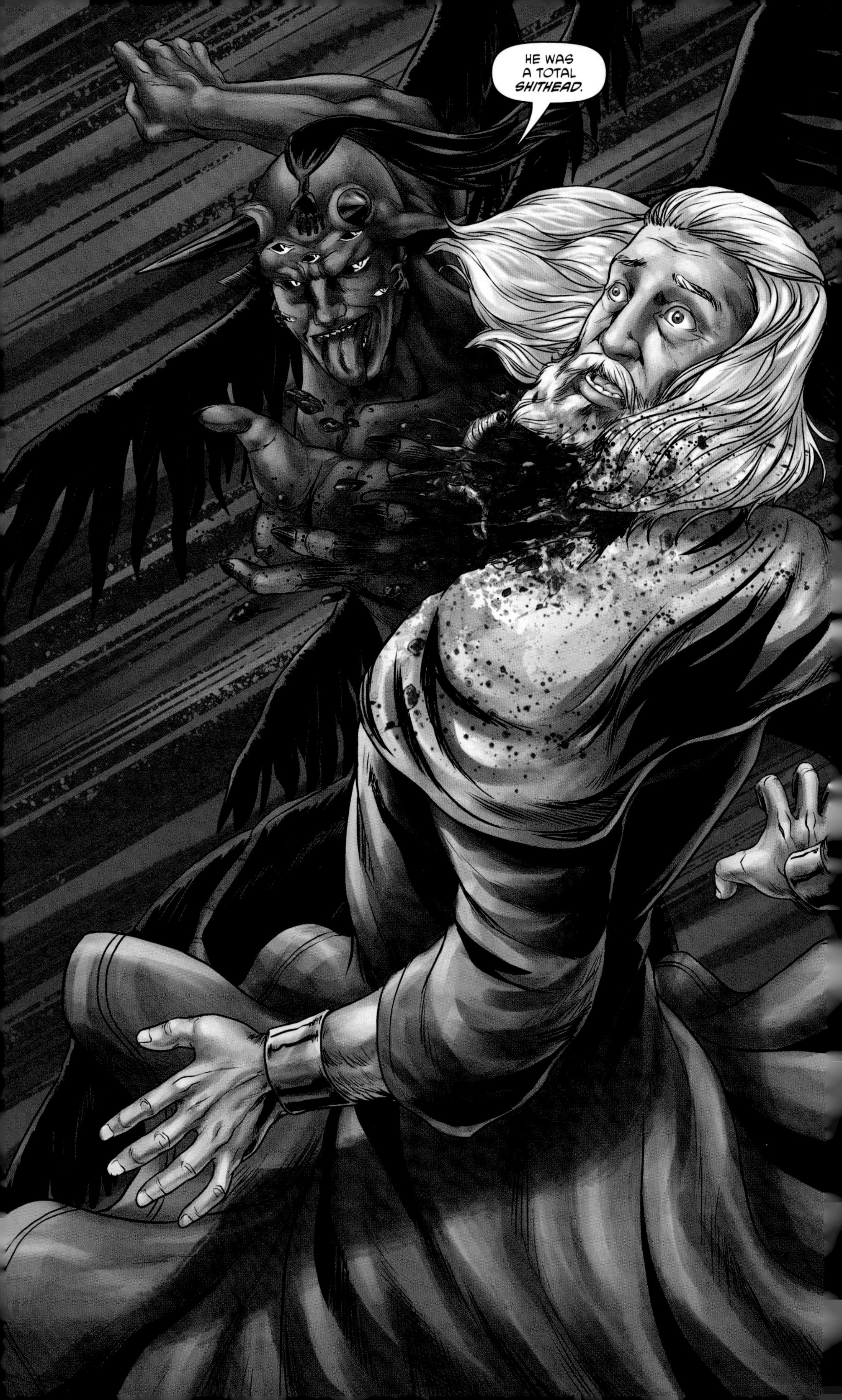
HE WAS A TOTAL *SHITHEAD.*

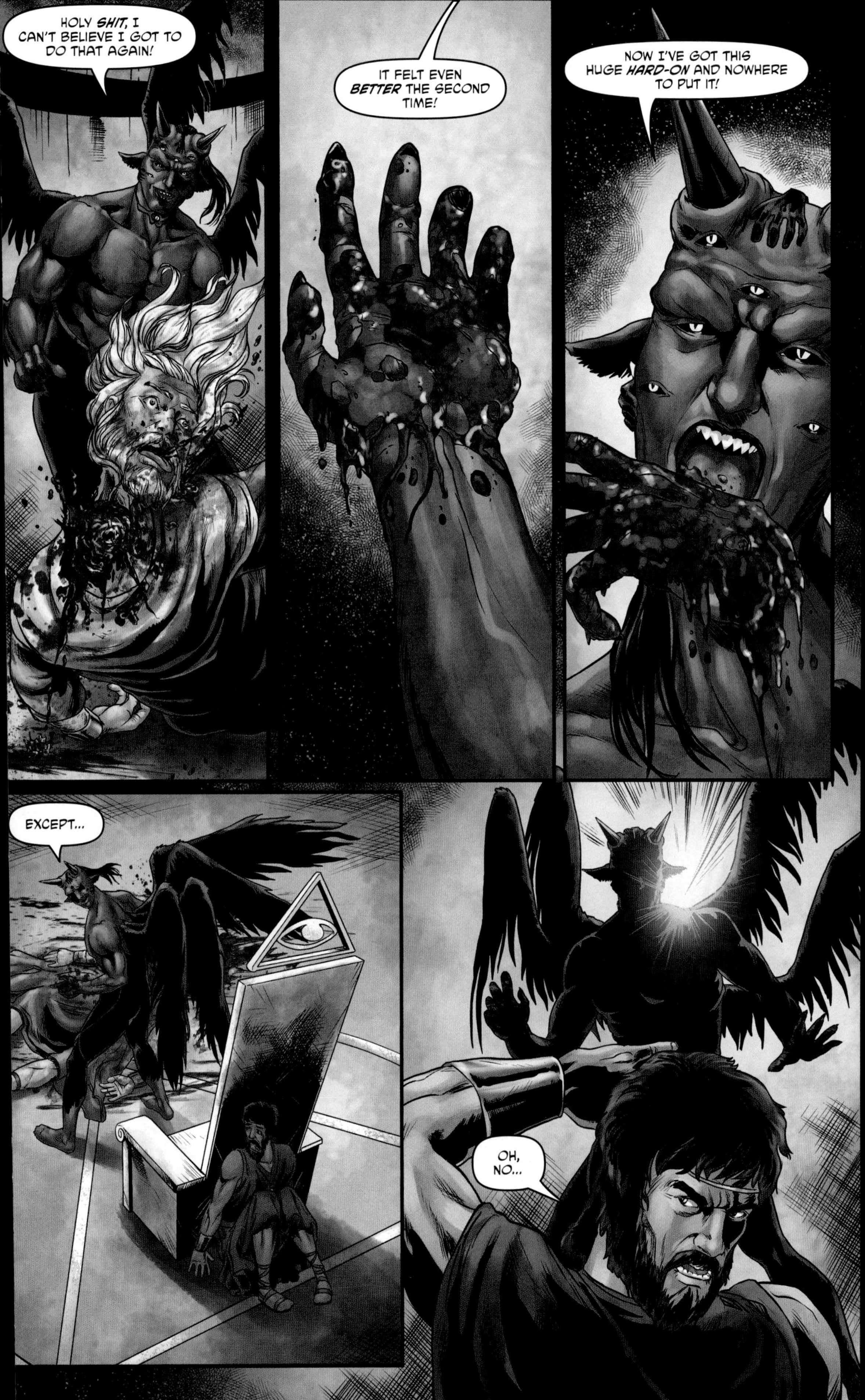
HOLY SHIT, I CAN'T BELIEVE I GOT TO DO THAT AGAIN!
IT FELT EVEN BETTER THE SECOND TIME!
NOW I'VE GOT THIS HUGE HARD-ON AND NOWHERE TO PUT IT!
EXCEPT...
OH, NO...

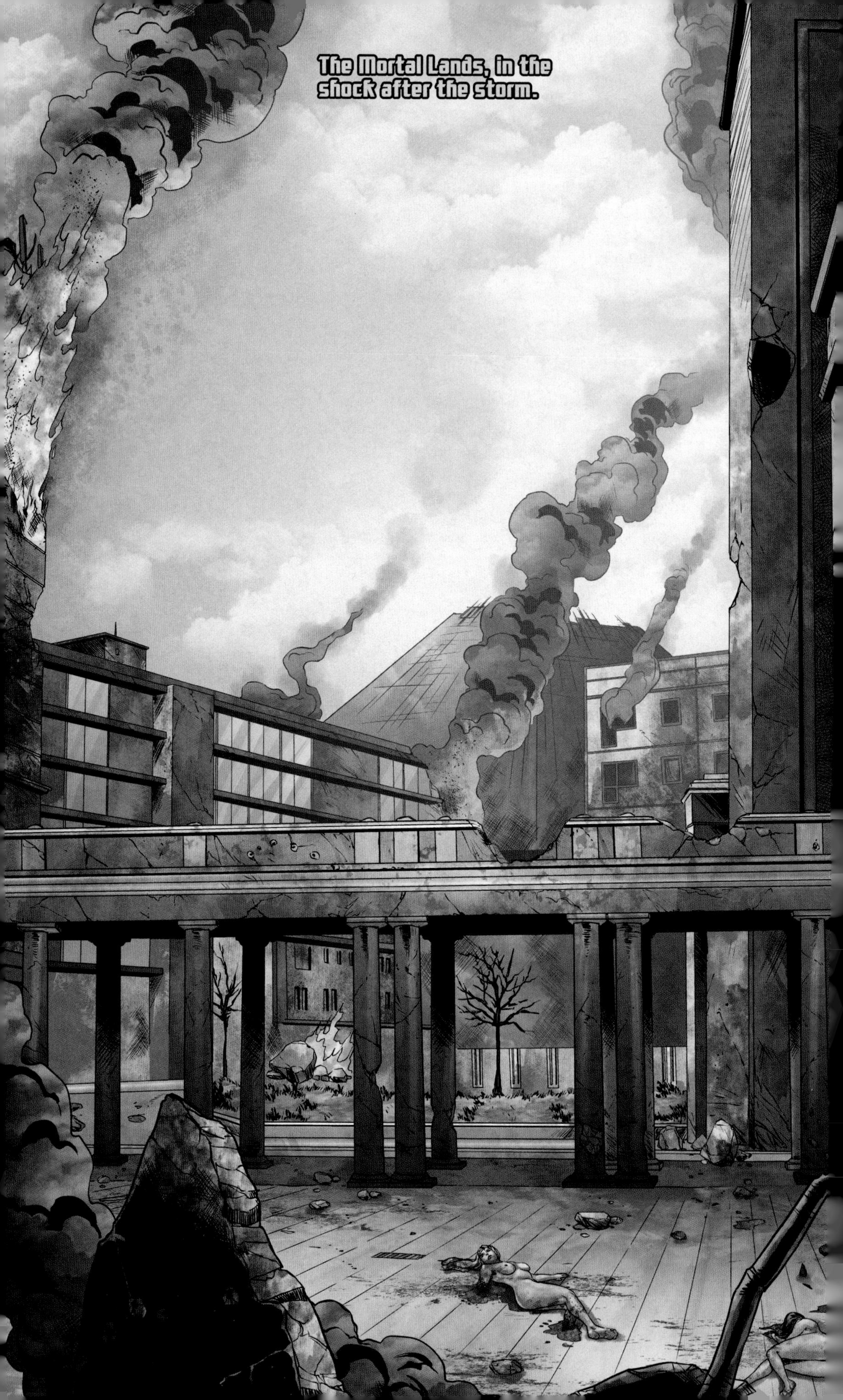
The Mortal Lands, in the shock after the storm.

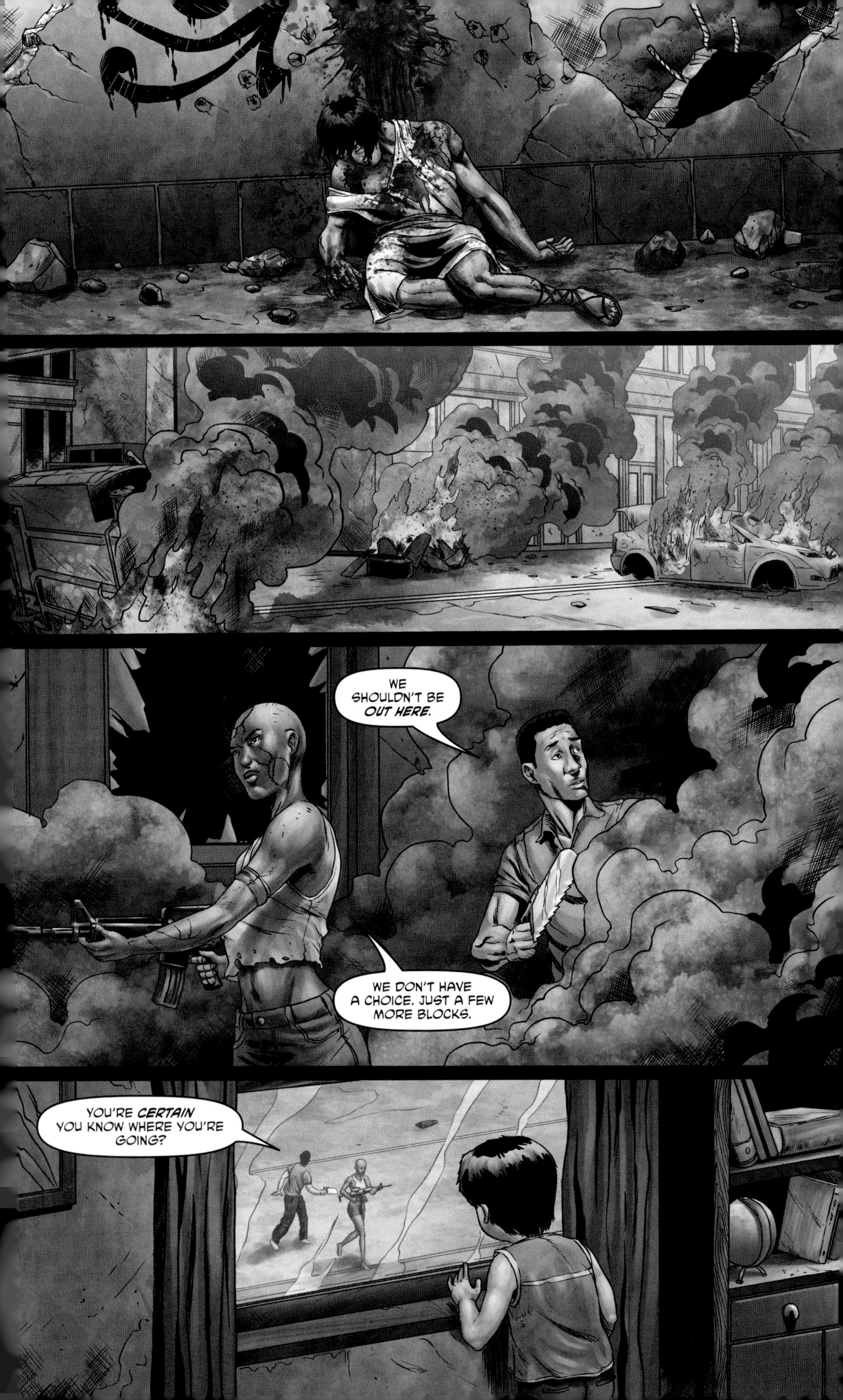
WE SHOULDN'T BE OUT HERE.
WE DON'T HAVE A CHOICE. JUST A FEW MORE BLOCKS.
YOU'RE CERTAIN YOU KNOW WHERE YOU'RE GOING?

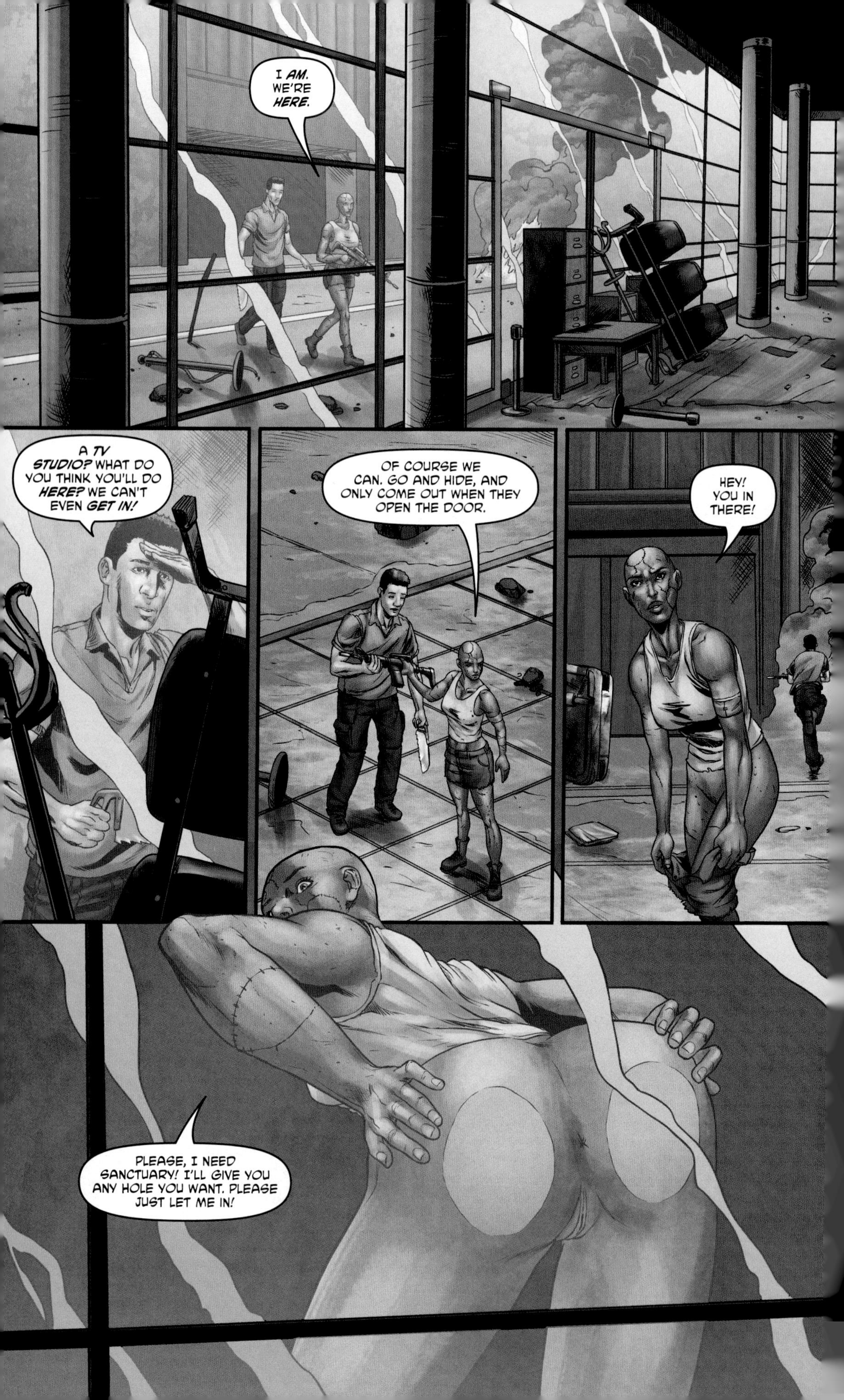
I AM. WE'RE HERE.
A TV STUDIO? WHAT DO YOU THINK YOU'LL DO HERE? WE CAN'T EVEN GET IN!
OF COURSE WE CAN. GO AND HIDE, AND ONLY COME OUT WHEN THEY OPEN THE DOOR.
HEY! YOU IN THERE!
PLEASE, I NEED SANCTUARY! I'LL GIVE YOU ANY HOLE YOU WANT. PLEASE JUST LET ME IN!

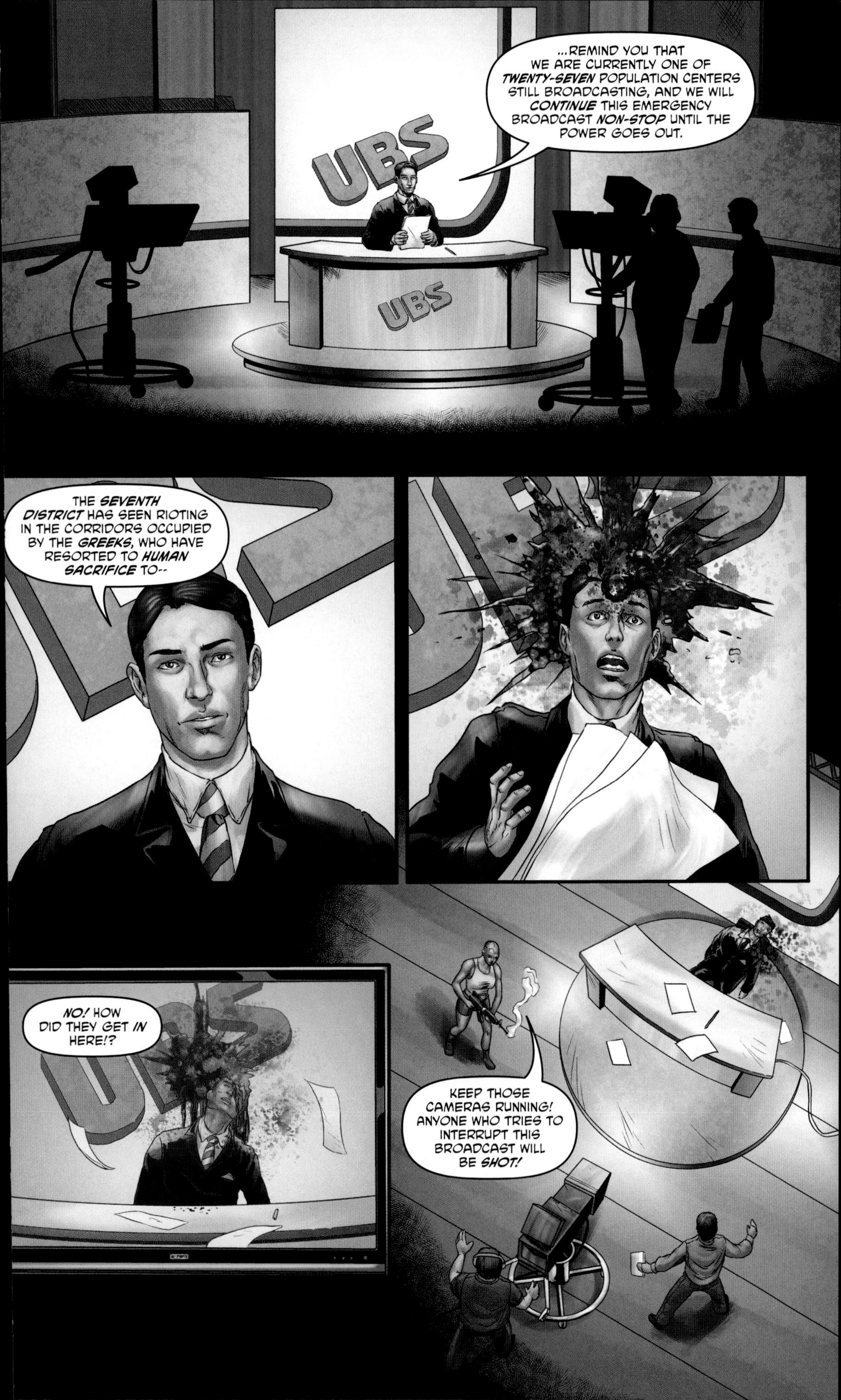
...REMIND YOU THAT WE ARE CURRENTLY ONE OF TWENTY-SEVEN POPULATION CENTERS STILL BROADCASTING, AND WE WILL CONTINUE THIS EMERGENCY BROADCAST NON-STOP UNTIL THE POWER GOES OUT.
THE SEVENTH DISTRICT HAS SEEN RIOTING IN THE CORRIDORS OCCUPIED BY THE GREEKS, WHO HAVE RESORTED TO HUMAN SACRIFICE TO--
NO! HOW DID THEY GET IN HERE!?
KEEP THOSE CAMERAS RUNNING! ANYONE WHO TRIES TO INTERRUPT THIS BROADCAST WILL BE SHOT!

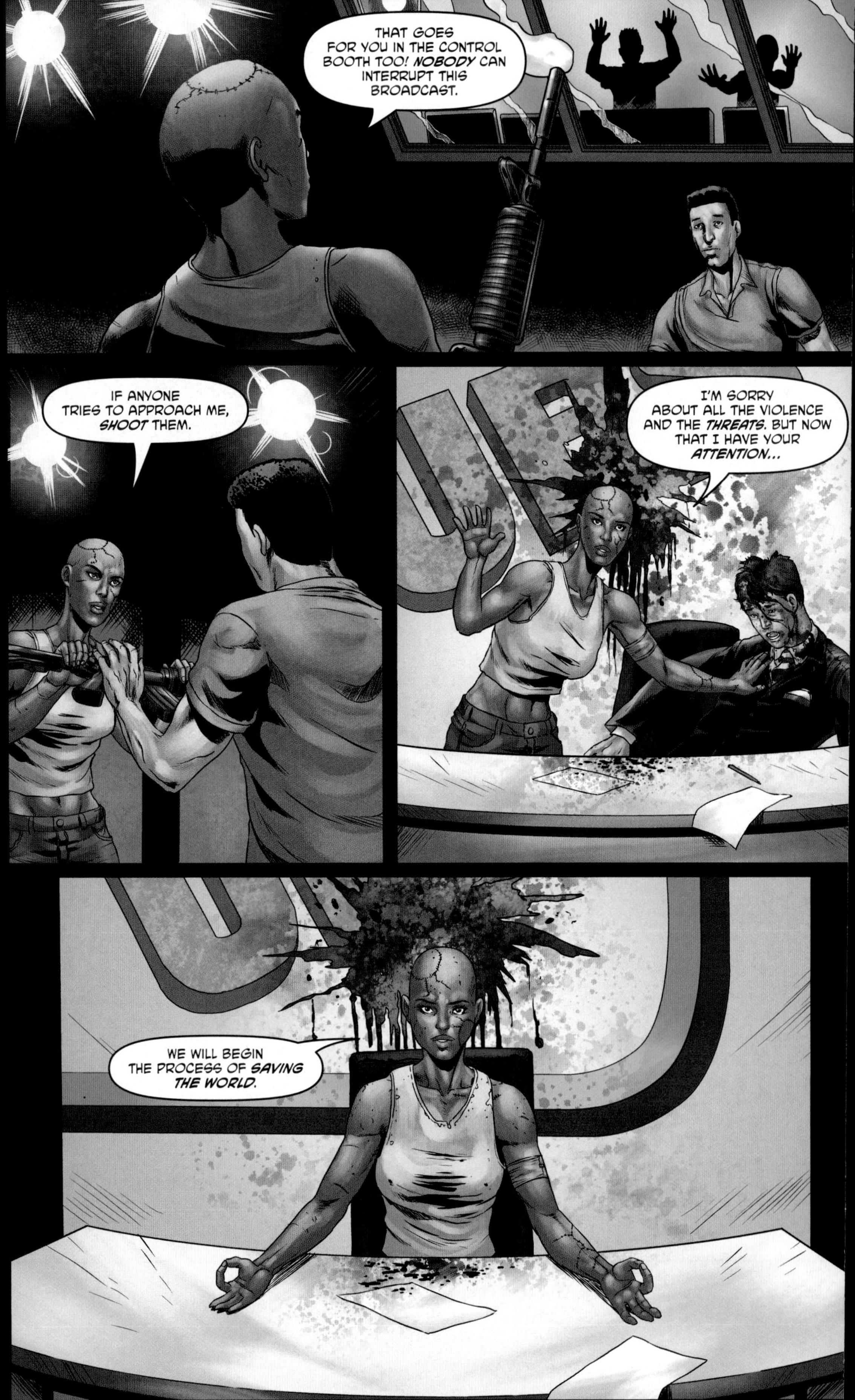
THAT GOES FOR YOU IN THE CONTROL BOOTH TOO! *NOBODY* CAN INTERRUPT THIS BROADCAST.
IF ANYONE TRIES TO APPROACH ME, *SHOOT* THEM.
I'M SORRY ABOUT ALL THE VIOLENCE AND THE *THREATS*. BUT NOW THAT I HAVE YOUR *ATTENTION*...
WE WILL BEGIN THE PROCESS OF *SAVING THE WORLD*.

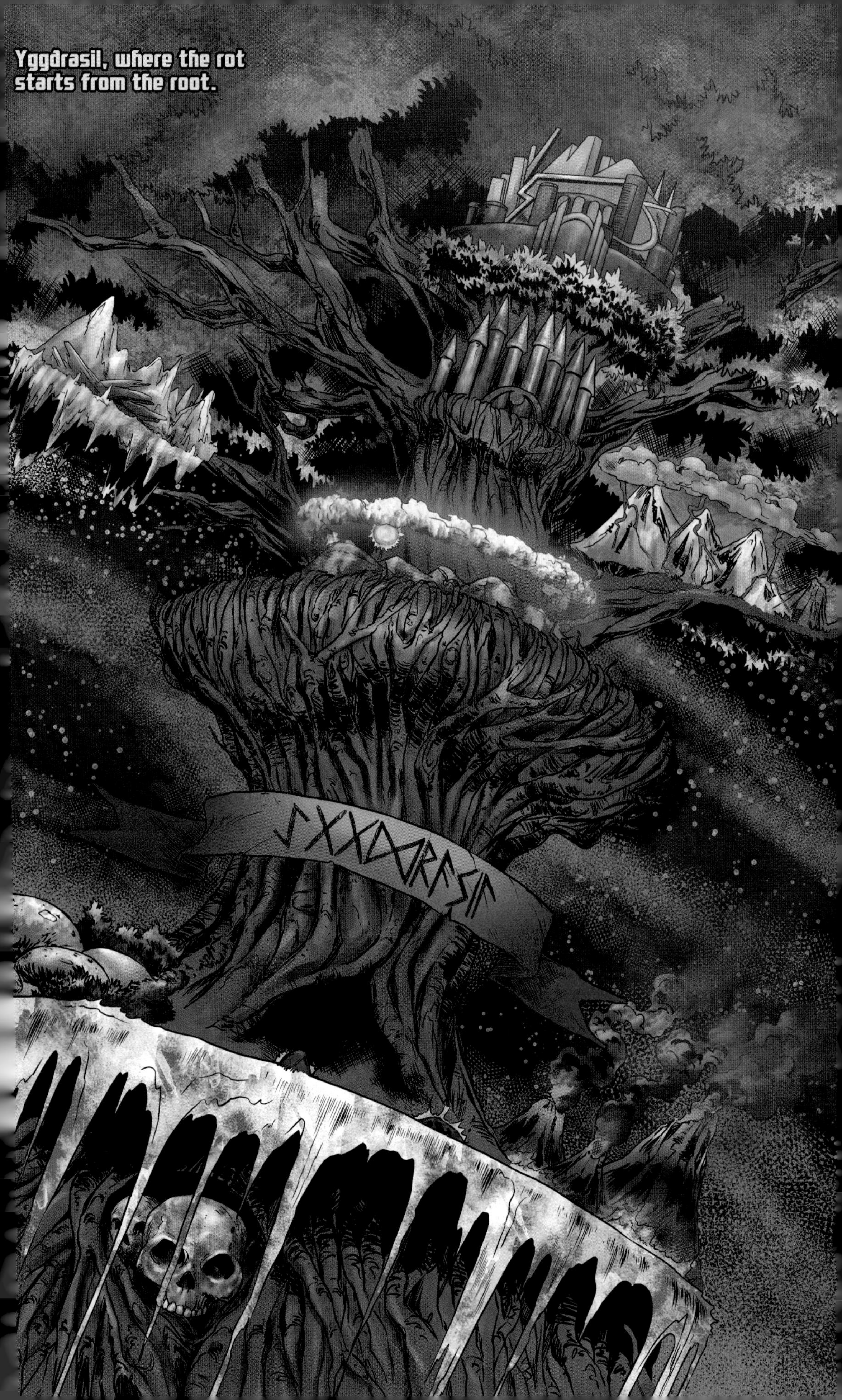
Yggdrasil, where the rot starts from the root.

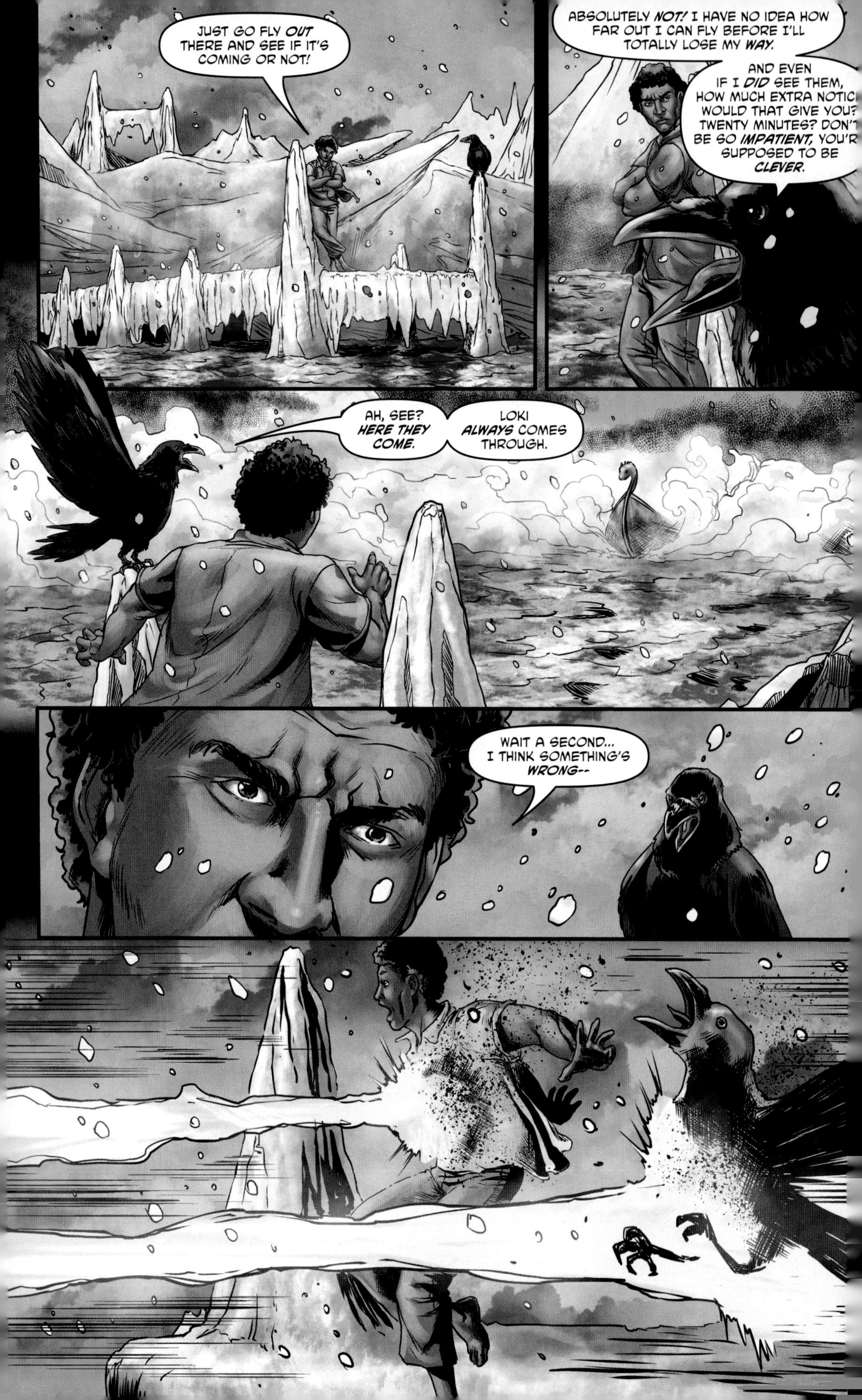
JUST GO FLY OUT THERE AND SEE IF IT'S COMING OR NOT!
ABSOLUTELY NOT! I HAVE NO IDEA HOW FAR OUT I CAN FLY BEFORE I'LL TOTALLY LOSE MY WAY.
AND EVEN IF I DID SEE THEM, HOW MUCH EXTRA NOTIC WOULD THAT GIVE YOU? TWENTY MINUTES? DON'T BE SO IMPATIENT, YOU'R SUPPOSED TO BE CLEVER.
AH, SEE? HERE THEY COME.
LOKI ALWAYS COMES THROUGH.
WAIT A SECOND... I THINK SOMETHING'S WRONG--

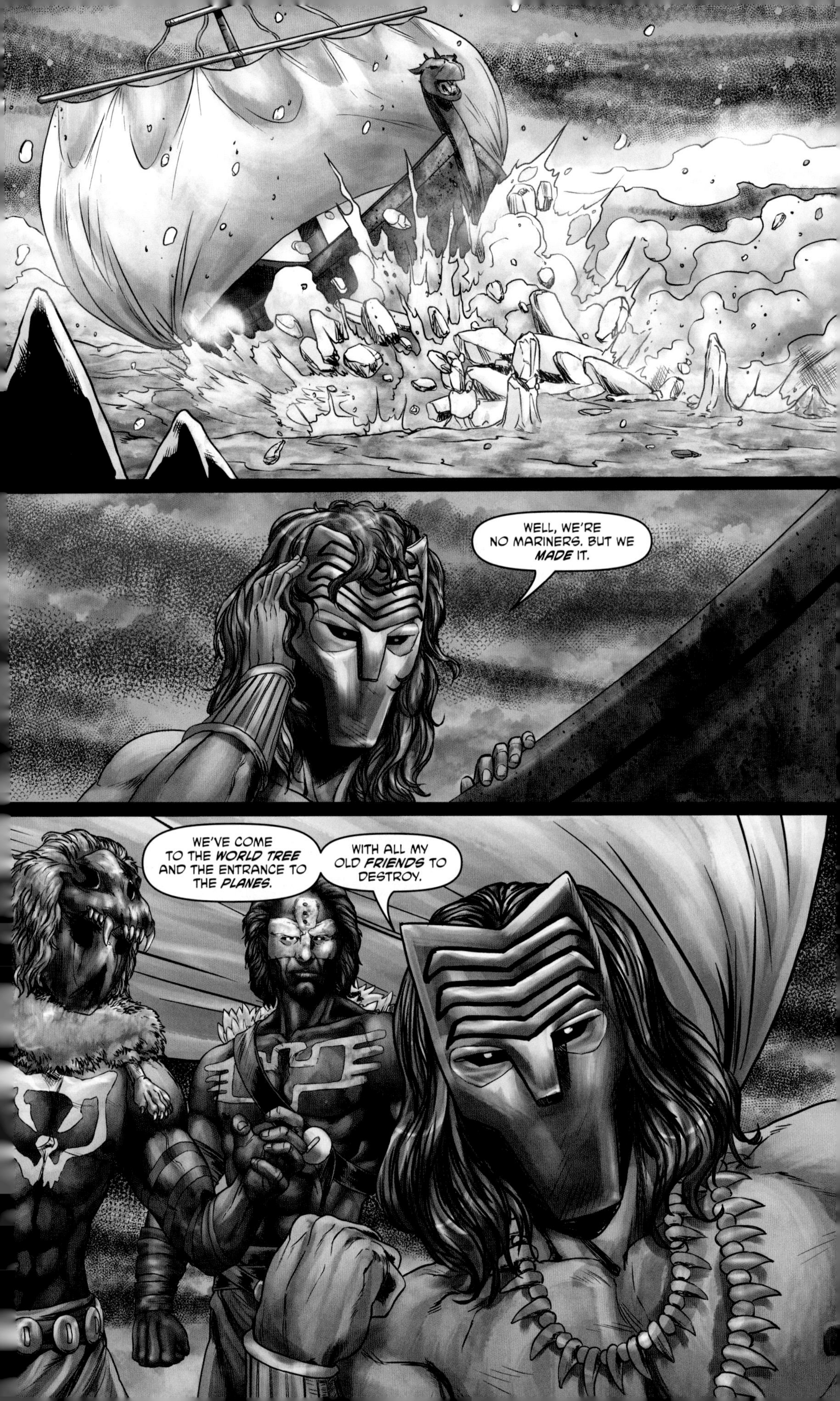
WELL, WE'RE NO MARINERS. BUT WE *MADE* IT.
WE'VE COME TO THE *WORLD TREE* AND THE ENTRANCE TO THE *PLANES*.
WITH ALL MY OLD *FRIENDS* TO DESTROY.

SIX

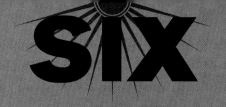

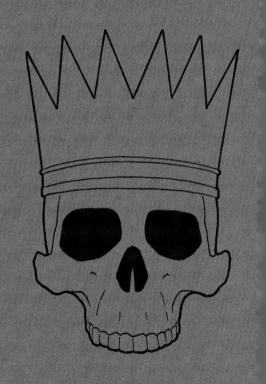

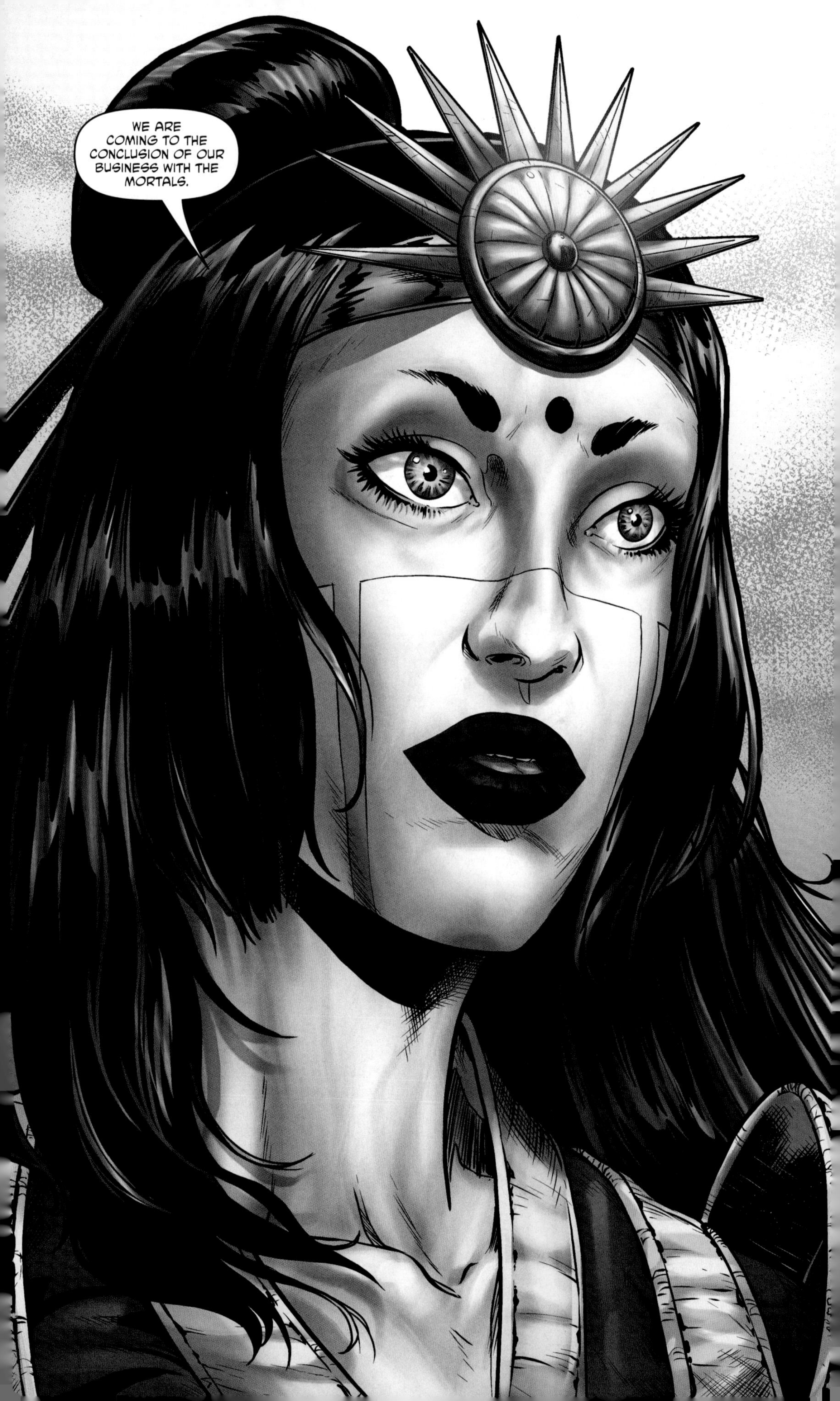
WE ARE COMING TO THE CONCLUSION OF OUR BUSINESS WITH THE MORTALS.

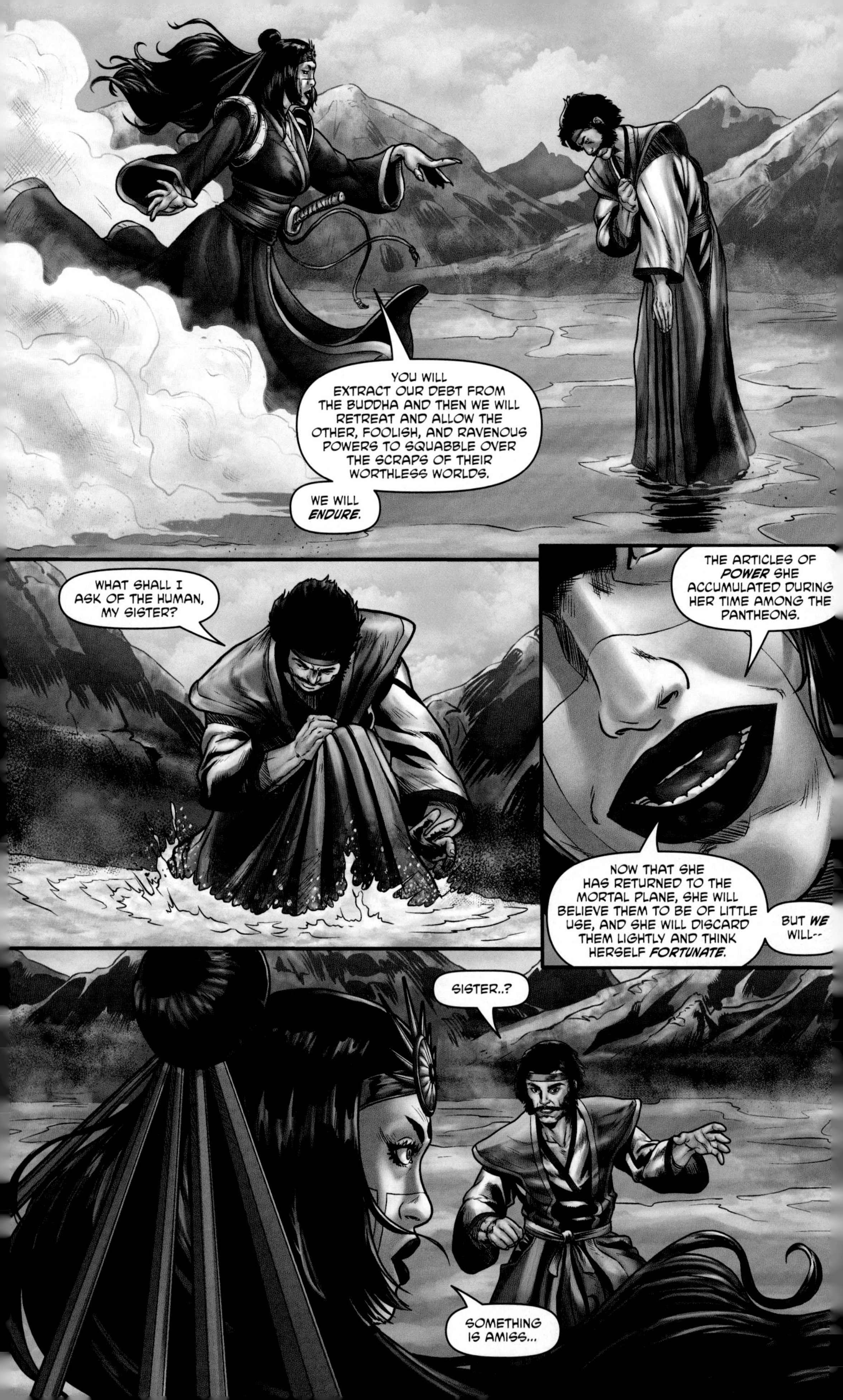
YOU WILL EXTRACT OUR DEBT FROM THE BUDDHA AND THEN WE WILL RETREAT AND ALLOW THE OTHER, FOOLISH, AND RAVENOUS POWERS TO SQUABBLE OVER THE SCRAPS OF THEIR WORTHLESS WORLDS.
WE WILL *ENDURE*.
WHAT SHALL I ASK OF THE HUMAN, MY SISTER?
THE ARTICLES OF *POWER* SHE ACCUMULATED DURING HER TIME AMONG THE PANTHEONS.
NOW THAT SHE HAS RETURNED TO THE MORTAL PLANE, SHE WILL BELIEVE THEM TO BE OF LITTLE USE, AND SHE WILL DISCARD THEM LIGHTLY AND THINK HERSELF *FORTUNATE*.
BUT *WE* WILL--
SISTER..?
SOMETHING IS AMISS...

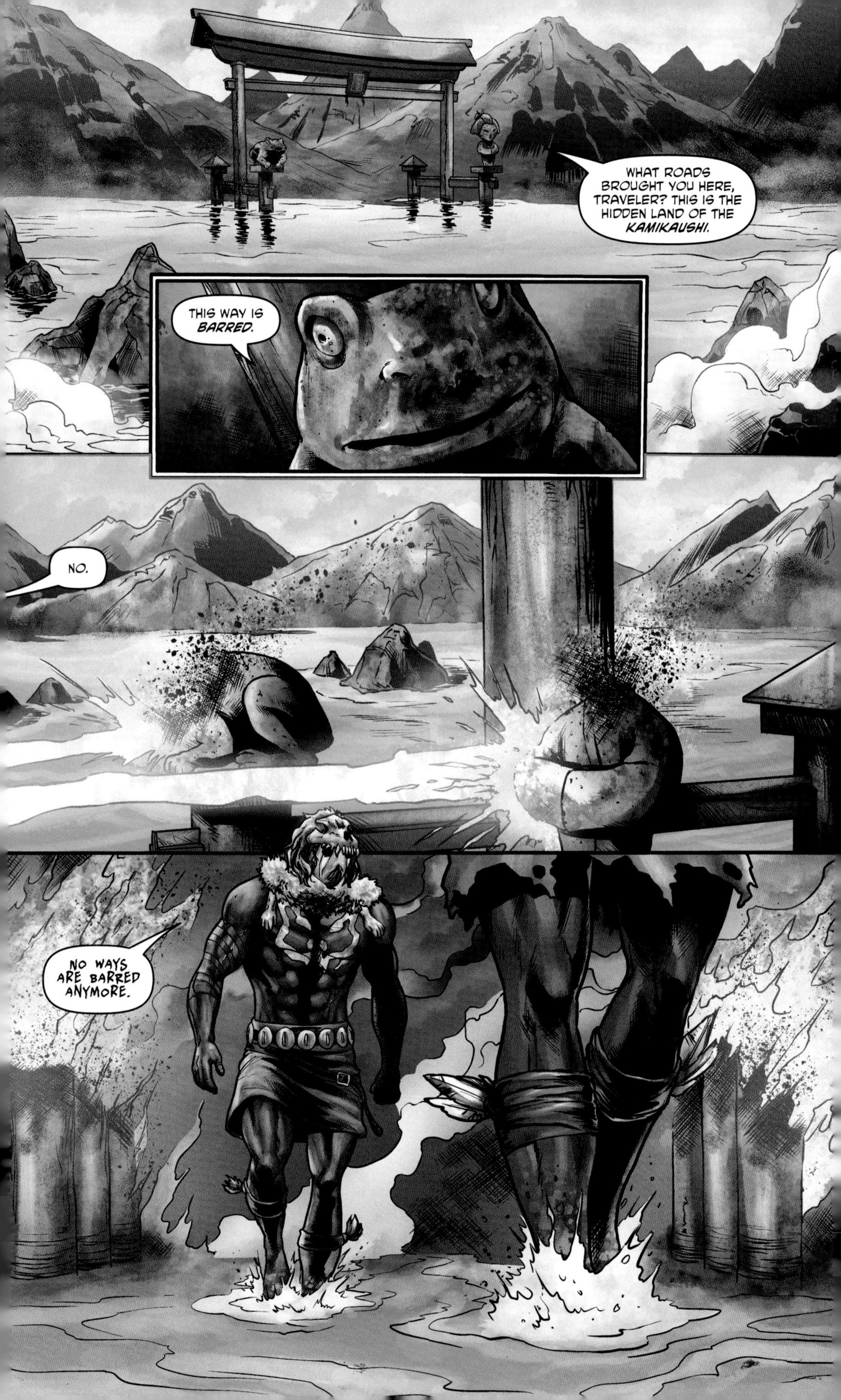
WHAT ROADS BROUGHT YOU HERE, TRAVELER? THIS IS THE HIDDEN LAND OF THE *KAMIKAUSHI*.
THIS WAY IS *BARRED*.
NO.
NO WAYS ARE BARRED ANYMORE.

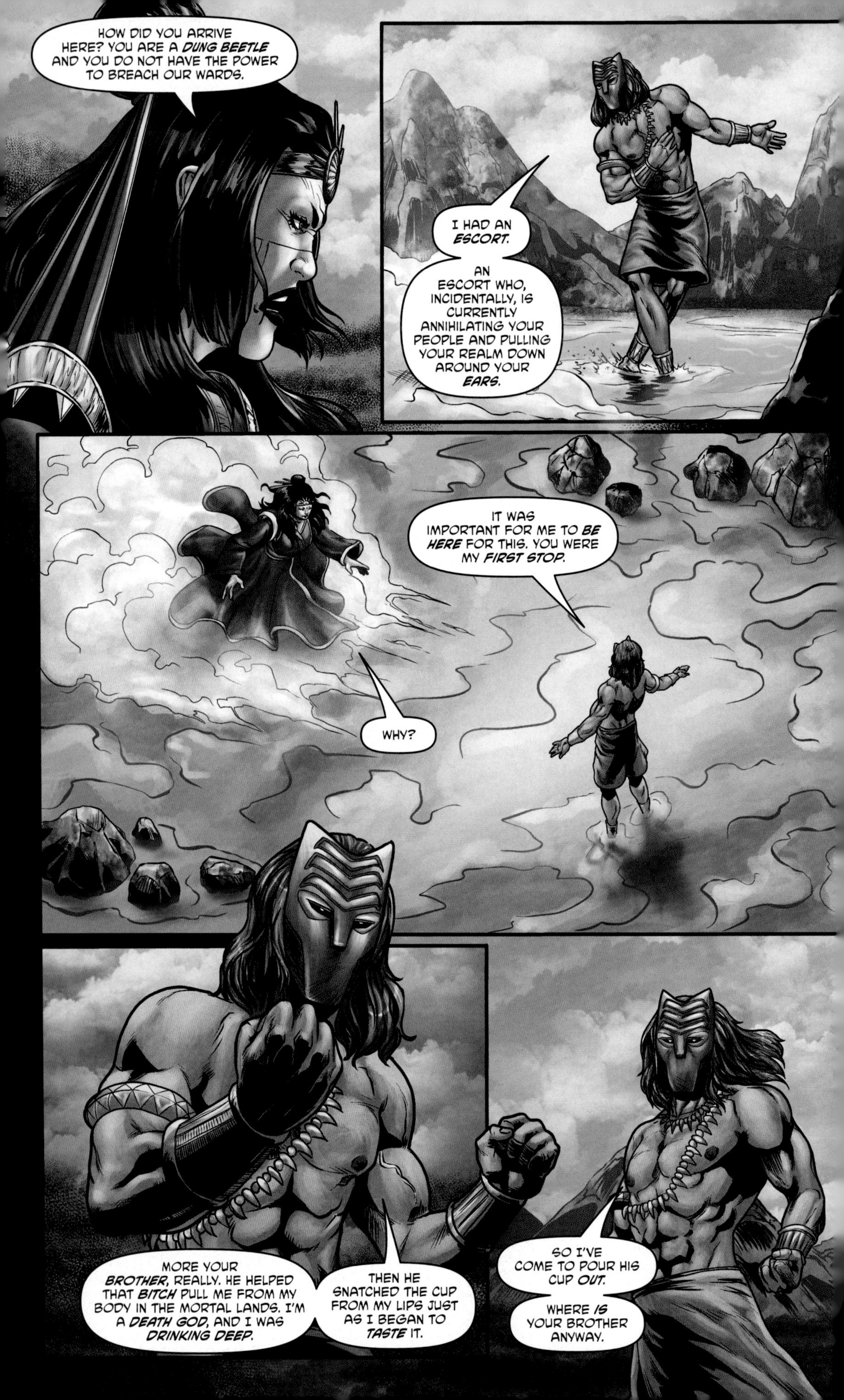
HOW DID YOU ARRIVE HERE? YOU ARE A DUNG BEETLE AND YOU DO NOT HAVE THE POWER TO BREACH OUR WARDS.
I HAD AN ESCORT.
AN ESCORT WHO, INCIDENTALLY, IS CURRENTLY ANNIHILATING YOUR PEOPLE AND PULLING YOUR REALM DOWN AROUND YOUR EARS.
IT WAS IMPORTANT FOR ME TO BE HERE FOR THIS. YOU WERE MY FIRST STOP.
WHY?
MORE YOUR BROTHER, REALLY. HE HELPED THAT BITCH PULL ME FROM MY BODY IN THE MORTAL LANDS. I'M A DEATH GOD, AND I WAS DRINKING DEEP.
THEN HE SNATCHED THE CUP FROM MY LIPS JUST AS I BEGAN TO TASTE IT.
SO I'VE COME TO POUR HIS CUP OUT.
WHERE IS YOUR BROTHER ANYWAY.

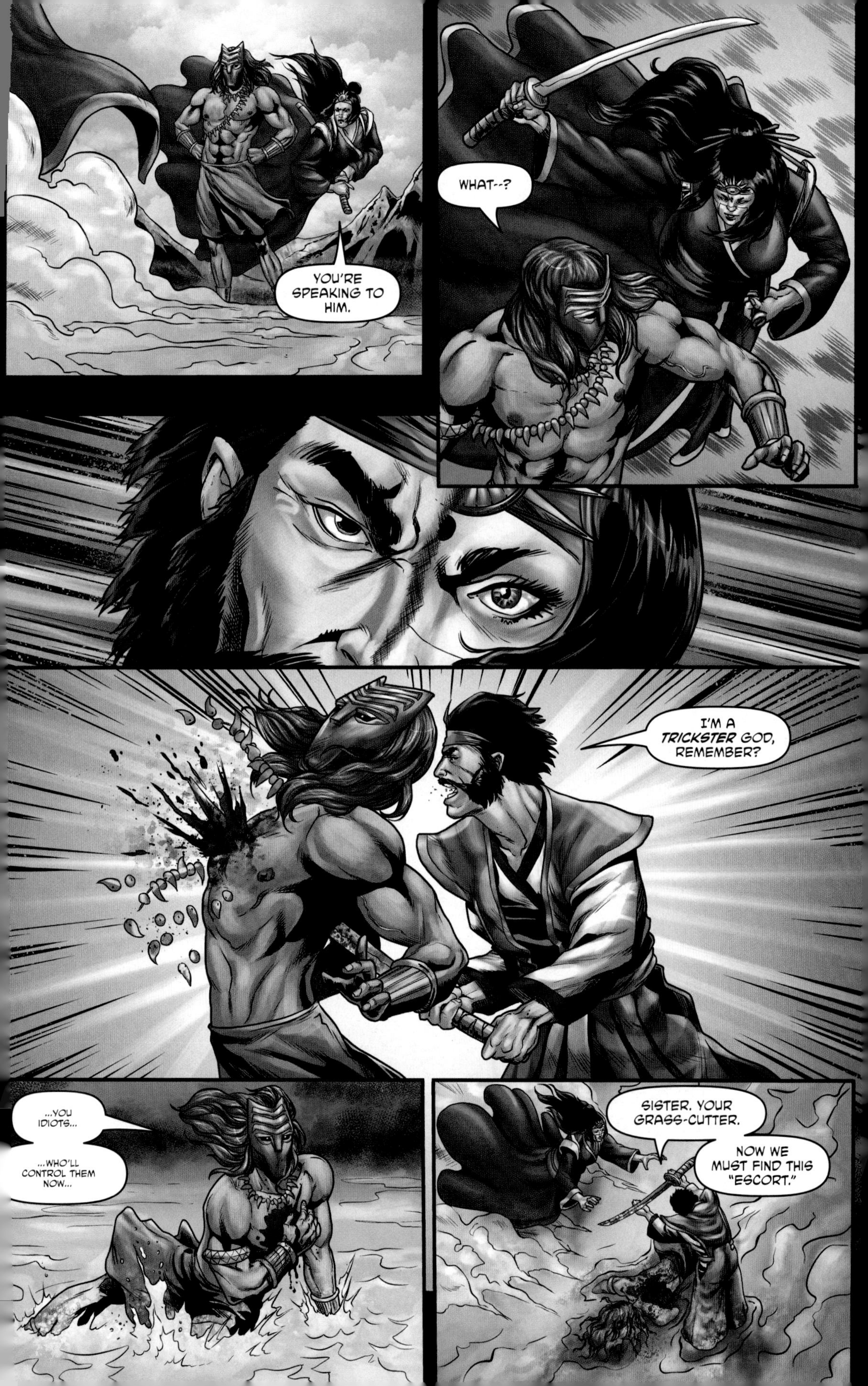
YOU'RE SPEAKING TO HIM.
WHAT--?
I'M A *TRICKSTER* GOD, REMEMBER?
...YOU IDIOTS...
...WHO'LL CONTROL THEM NOW...
SISTER. YOUR GRASS-CUTTER.
NOW WE MUST FIND THIS "ESCORT."

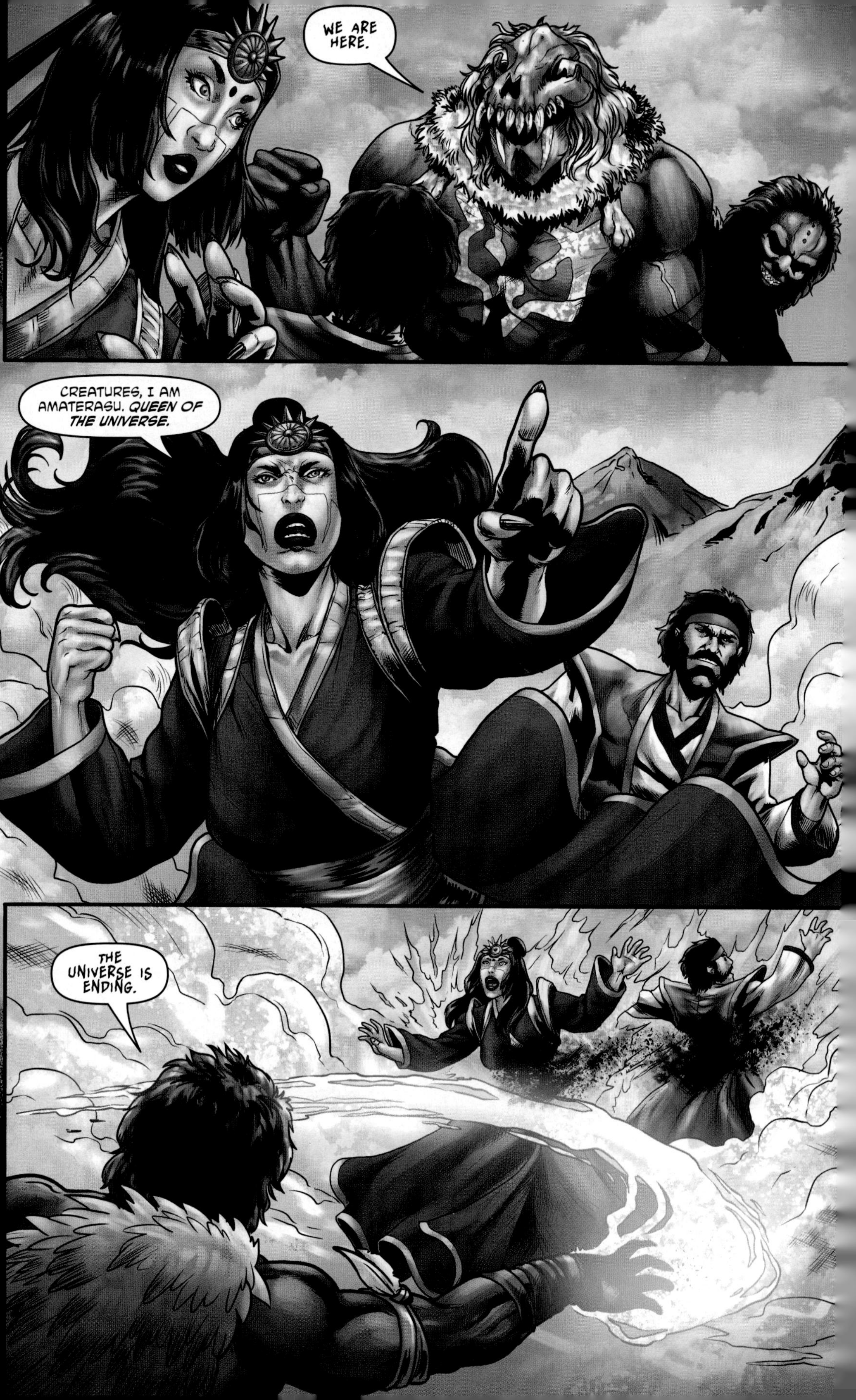
WE ARE HERE.
CREATURES, I AM AMATERASU. *QUEEN OF THE UNIVERSE.*
THE UNIVERSE IS ENDING.

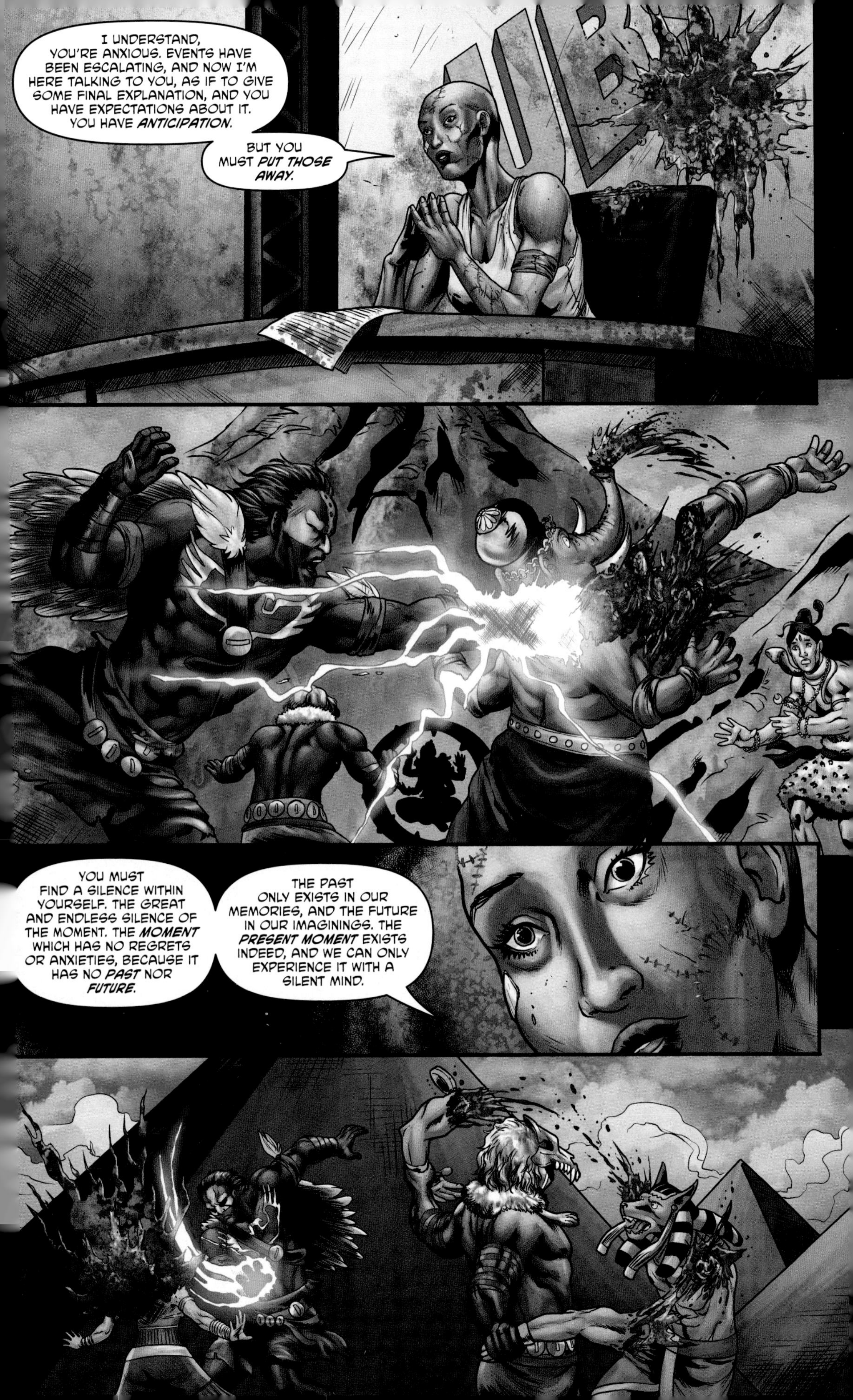
I UNDERSTAND, YOU'RE ANXIOUS. EVENTS HAVE BEEN ESCALATING, AND NOW I'M HERE TALKING TO YOU, AS IF TO GIVE SOME FINAL EXPLANATION, AND YOU HAVE EXPECTATIONS ABOUT IT. YOU HAVE ***ANTICIPATION***.
BUT YOU MUST ***PUT THOSE AWAY***.
YOU MUST FIND A SILENCE WITHIN YOURSELF. THE GREAT AND ENDLESS SILENCE OF THE MOMENT. THE ***MOMENT*** WHICH HAS NO REGRETS OR ANXIETIES, BECAUSE IT HAS NO ***PAST*** NOR ***FUTURE***.
THE PAST ONLY EXISTS IN OUR MEMORIES, AND THE FUTURE IN OUR IMAGININGS. THE ***PRESENT MOMENT*** EXISTS INDEED, AND WE CAN ONLY EXPERIENCE IT WITH A SILENT MIND.

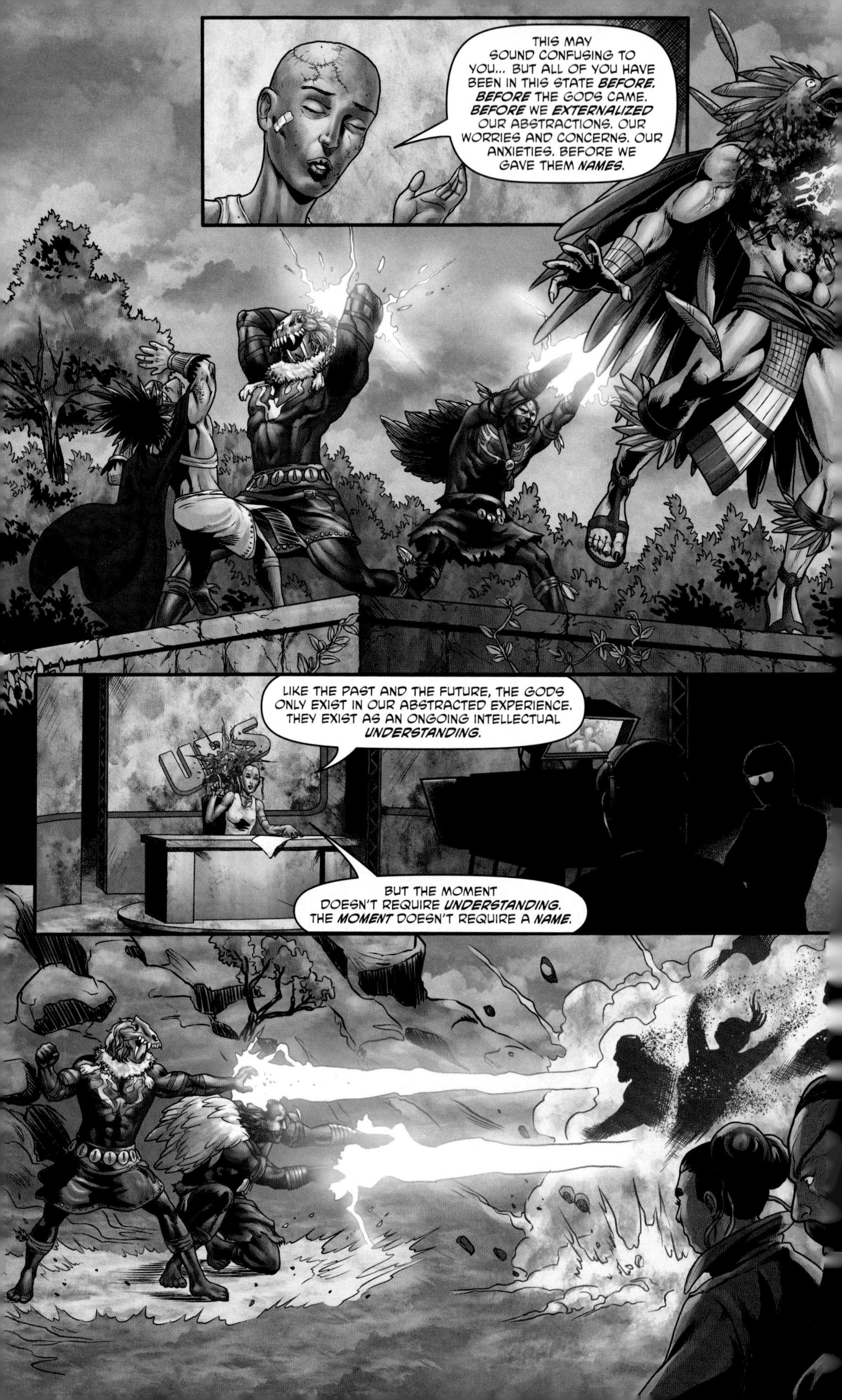
THIS MAY SOUND CONFUSING TO YOU... BUT ALL OF YOU HAVE BEEN IN THIS STATE ***BEFORE. BEFORE*** THE GODS CAME. ***BEFORE*** WE ***EXTERNALIZED*** OUR ABSTRACTIONS. OUR WORRIES AND CONCERNS. OUR ANXIETIES. BEFORE WE GAVE THEM ***NAMES***.
LIKE THE PAST AND THE FUTURE, THE GODS ONLY EXIST IN OUR ABSTRACTED EXPERIENCE. THEY EXIST AS AN ONGOING INTELLECTUAL ***UNDERSTANDING***.
BUT THE MOMENT DOESN'T REQUIRE ***UNDERSTANDING***. THE ***MOMENT*** DOESN'T REQUIRE A ***NAME***.

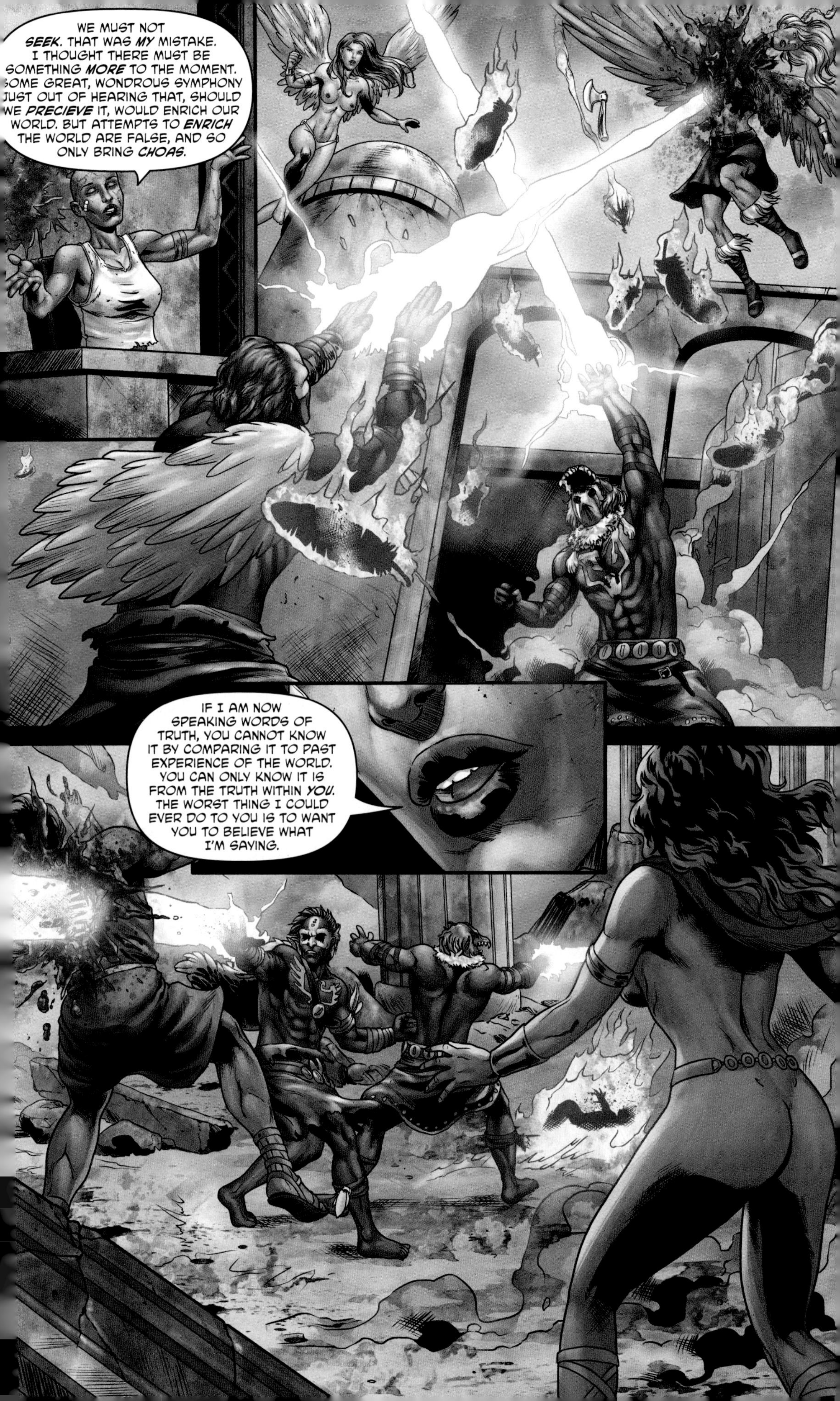
WE MUST NOT SEEK. THAT WAS MY MISTAKE. I THOUGHT THERE MUST BE SOMETHING MORE TO THE MOMENT. SOME GREAT, WONDROUS SYMPHONY JUST OUT OF HEARING THAT, SHOULD WE PRECIEVE IT, WOULD ENRICH OUR WORLD. BUT ATTEMPTS TO ENRICH THE WORLD ARE FALSE, AND SO ONLY BRING CHOAS.
IF I AM NOW SPEAKING WORDS OF TRUTH, YOU CANNOT KNOW IT BY COMPARING IT TO PAST EXPERIENCE OF THE WORLD. YOU CAN ONLY KNOW IT IS FROM THE TRUTH WITHIN YOU. THE WORST THING I COULD EVER DO TO YOU IS TO WANT YOU TO BELIEVE WHAT I'M SAYING.

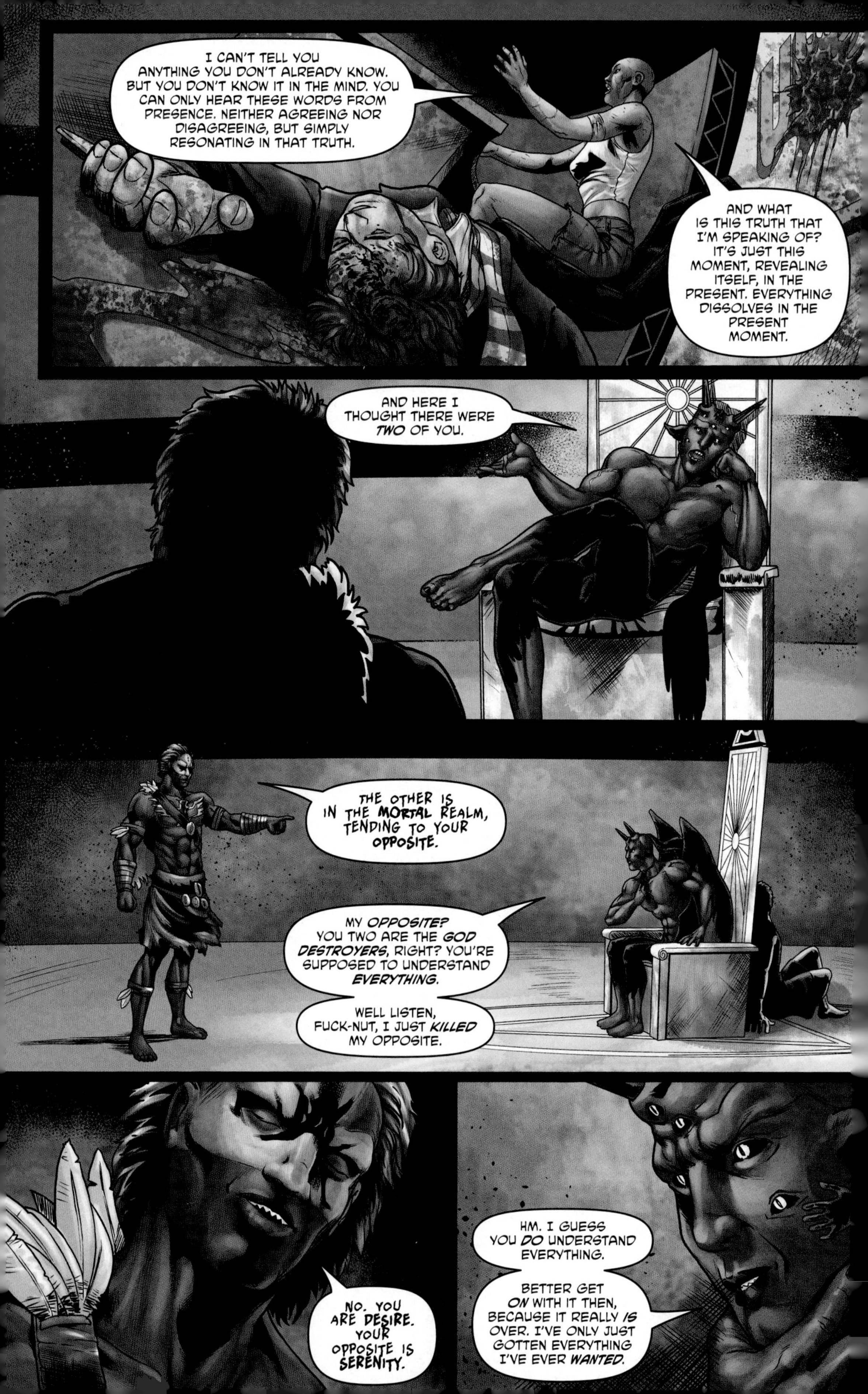
I CAN'T TELL YOU ANYTHING YOU DON'T ALREADY KNOW. BUT YOU DON'T KNOW IT IN THE MIND. YOU CAN ONLY HEAR THESE WORDS FROM PRESENCE. NEITHER AGREEING NOR DISAGREEING, BUT SIMPLY RESONATING IN THAT TRUTH.
AND WHAT IS THIS TRUTH THAT I'M SPEAKING OF? IT'S JUST THIS MOMENT, REVEALING ITSELF, IN THE PRESENT. EVERYTHING DISSOLVES IN THE PRESENT MOMENT.
AND HERE I THOUGHT THERE WERE *TWO* OF YOU.
THE OTHER IS IN THE **MORTAL** REALM, TENDING TO YOUR **OPPOSITE.**
MY *OPPOSITE?* YOU TWO ARE THE *GOD DESTROYERS*, RIGHT? YOU'RE SUPPOSED TO UNDERSTAND *EVERYTHING*.
WELL LISTEN, FUCK-NUT, I JUST *KILLED* MY OPPOSITE.
NO. YOU ARE **DESIRE.** YOUR OPPOSITE IS **SERENITY.**
HM. I GUESS YOU *DO* UNDERSTAND EVERYTHING.
BETTER GET *ON* WITH IT THEN, BECAUSE IT REALLY *IS* OVER. I'VE ONLY JUST GOTTEN EVERYTHING I'VE EVER *WANTED*.

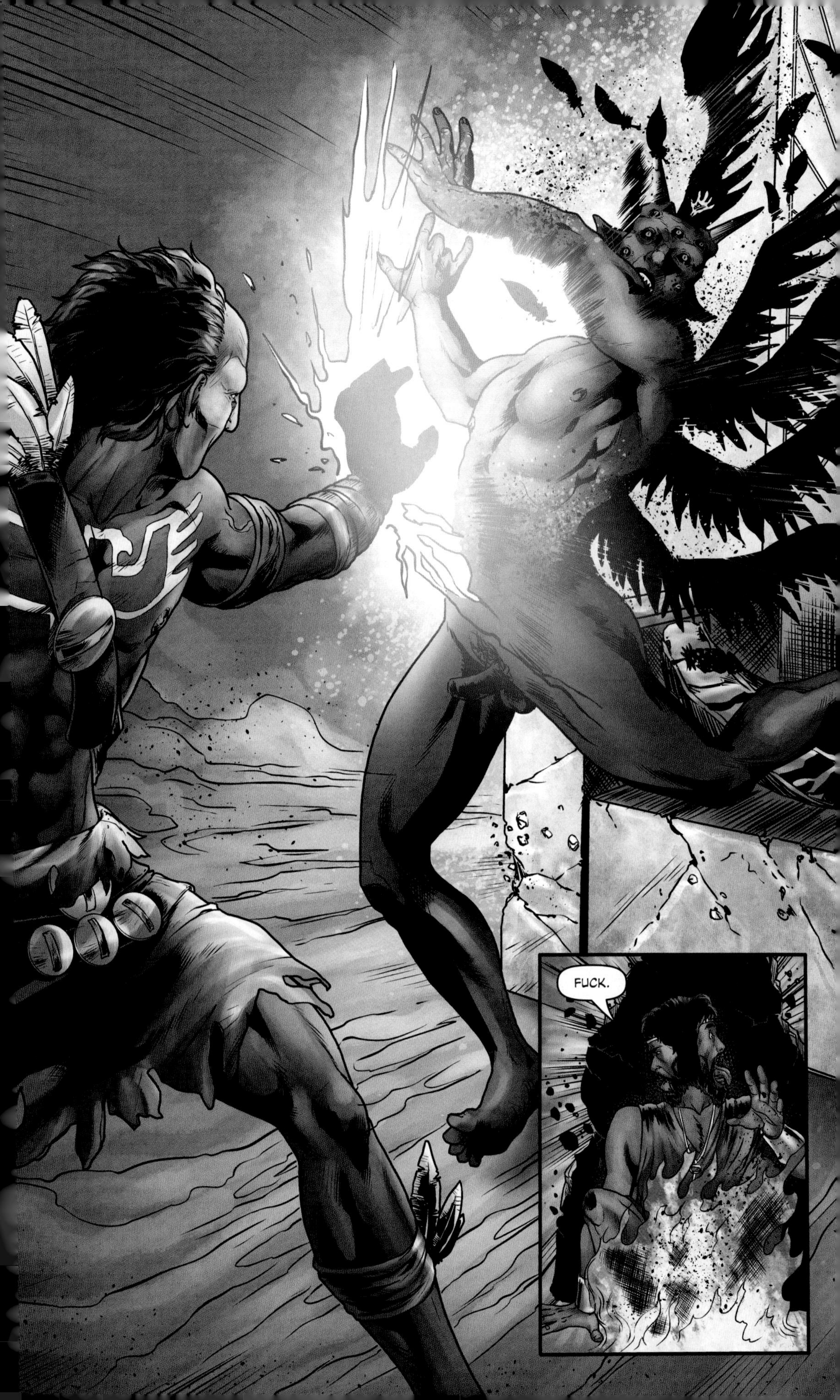
FUCK.

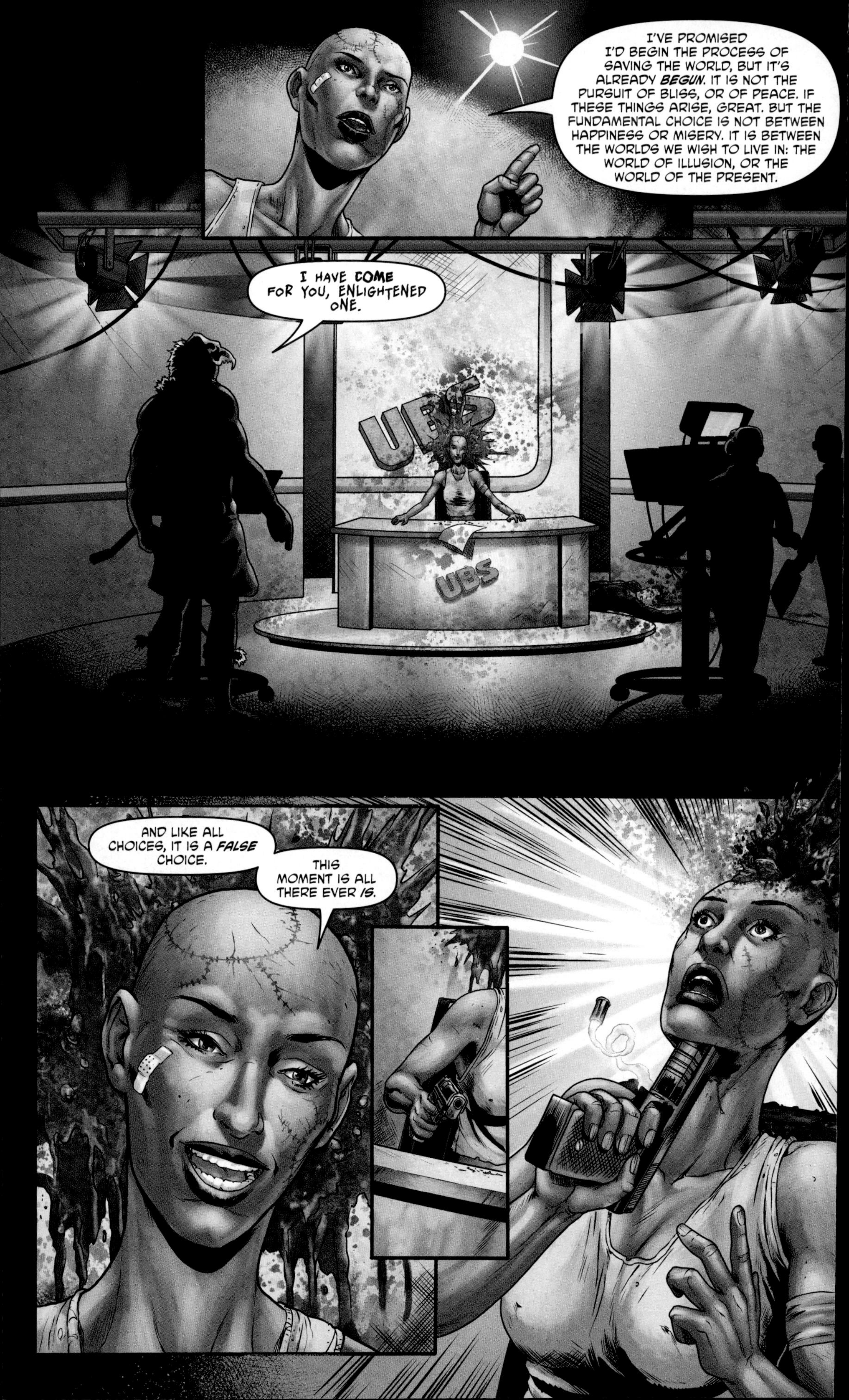
I'VE PROMISED I'D BEGIN THE PROCESS OF SAVING THE WORLD, BUT IT'S ALREADY *BEGUN*. IT IS NOT THE PURSUIT OF BLISS, OR OF PEACE. IF THESE THINGS ARISE, GREAT. BUT THE FUNDAMENTAL CHOICE IS NOT BETWEEN HAPPINESS OR MISERY. IT IS BETWEEN THE WORLDS WE WISH TO LIVE IN: THE WORLD OF ILLUSION, OR THE WORLD OF THE PRESENT.
I HAVE **COME** FOR YOU, ENLIGHTENED ONE.
UBS
UBS
AND LIKE ALL CHOICES, IT IS A *FALSE* CHOICE.
THIS MOMENT IS ALL THERE EVER *IS*.

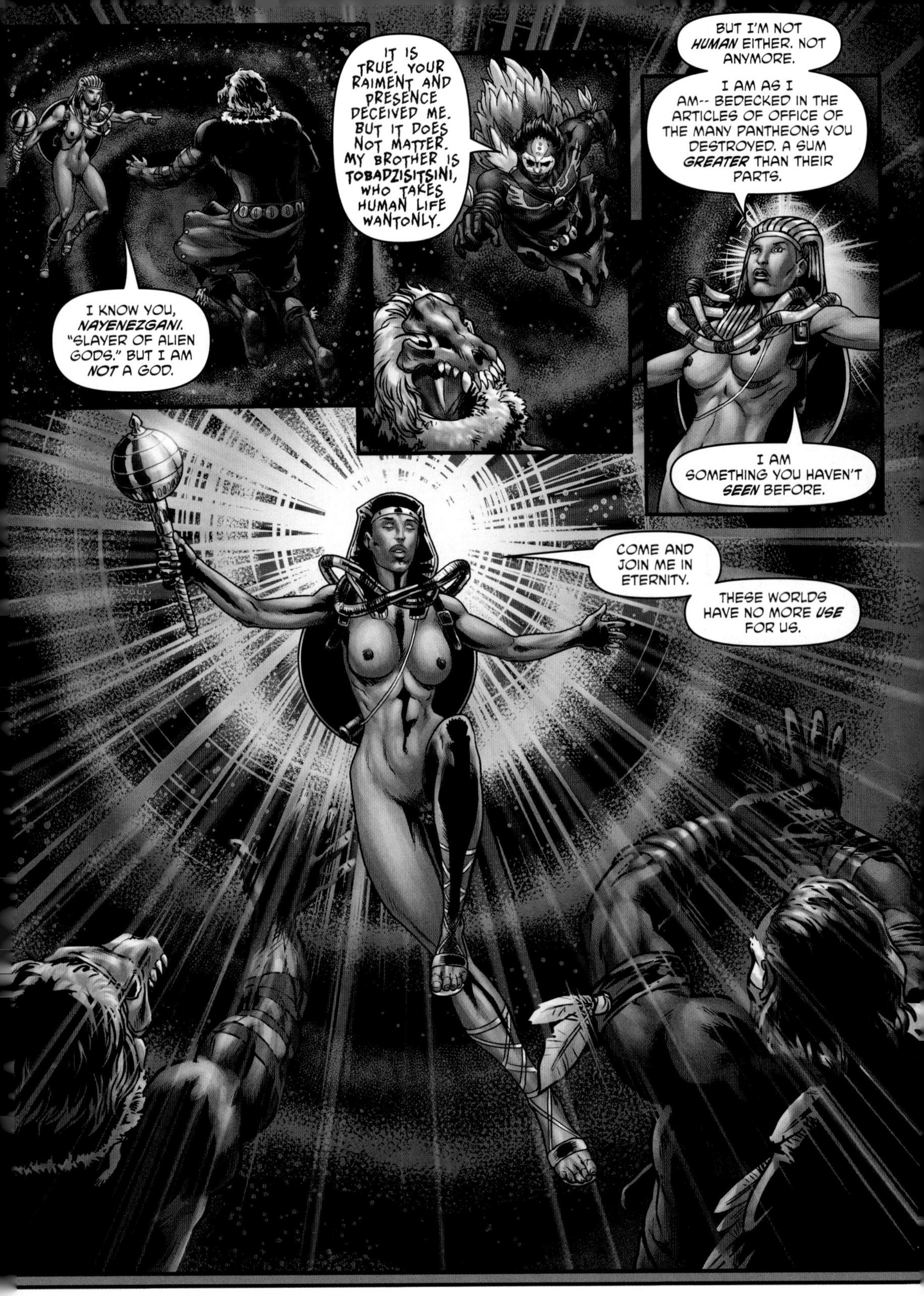
I KNOW YOU, *NAYENEZGANI*. "SLAYER OF ALIEN GODS." BUT I AM *NOT* A GOD.
IT IS TRUE. YOUR RAIMENT AND PRESENCE DECEIVED ME. BUT IT DOES NOT MATTER. MY BROTHER IS **TOBADZISITSINI**, WHO TAKES HUMAN LIFE WANTONLY.
BUT I'M NOT *HUMAN* EITHER. NOT ANYMORE.
I AM AS I AM-- BEDECKED IN THE ARTICLES OF OFFICE OF THE MANY PANTHEONS YOU DESTROYED. A SUM *GREATER* THAN THEIR PARTS.
I AM SOMETHING YOU HAVEN'T *SEEN* BEFORE.
COME AND JOIN ME IN ETERNITY.
THESE WORLDS HAVE NO MORE *USE* FOR US.

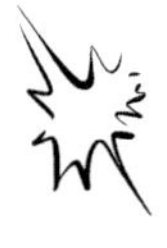

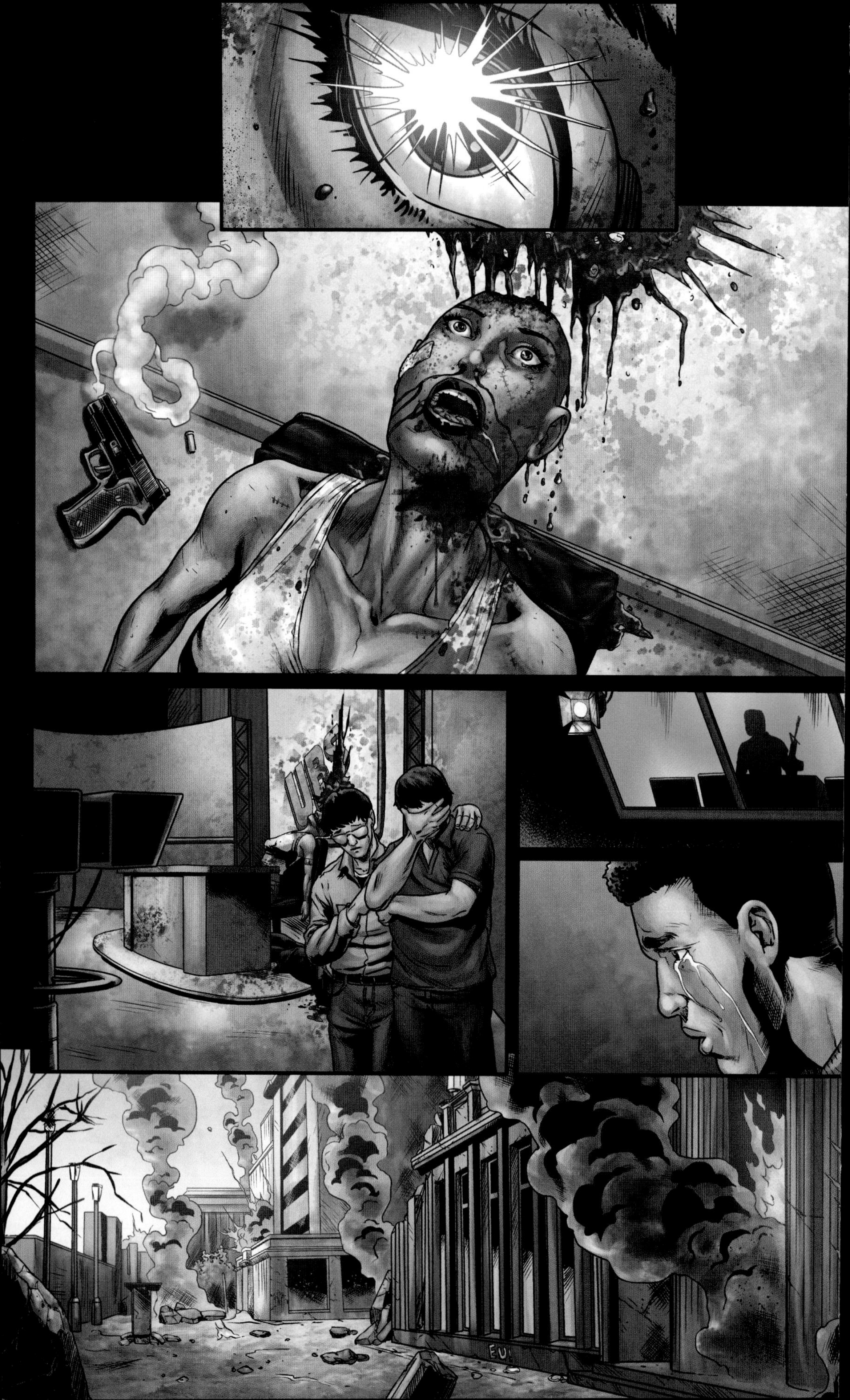
EU!

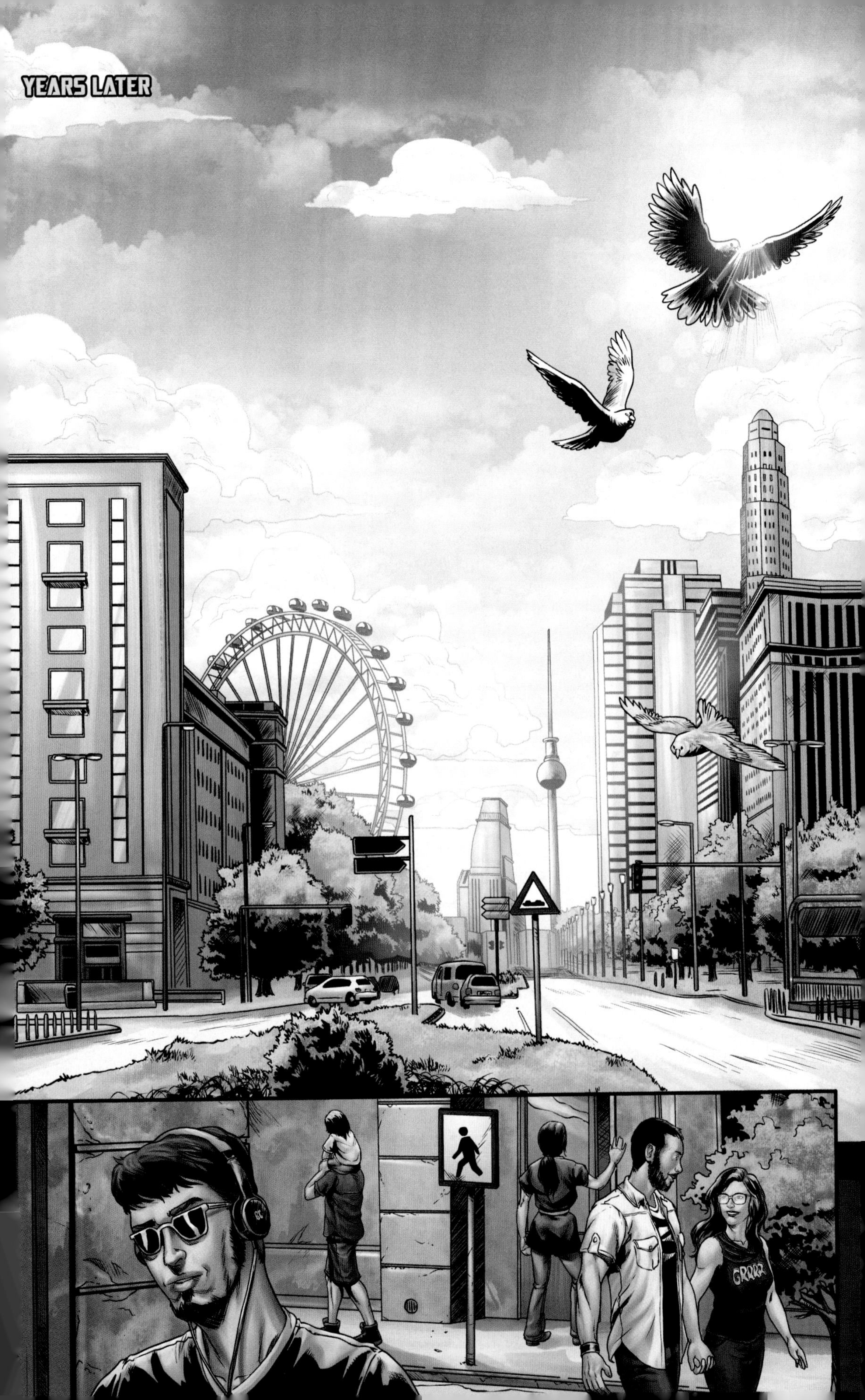
YEARS LATER

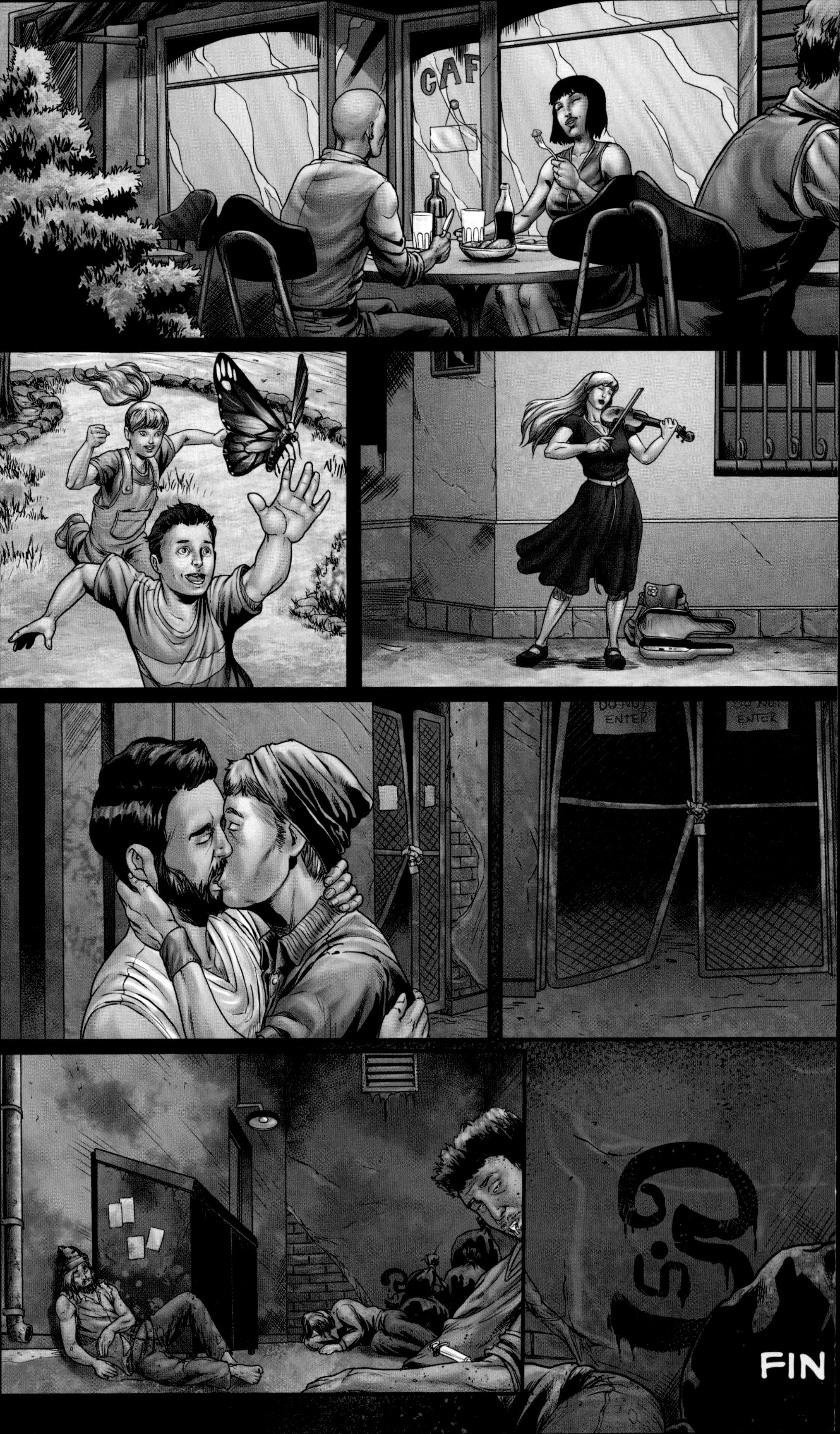
CAF
DO NOT ENTER
DO NOT ENTER
FIN

INTERLUDE

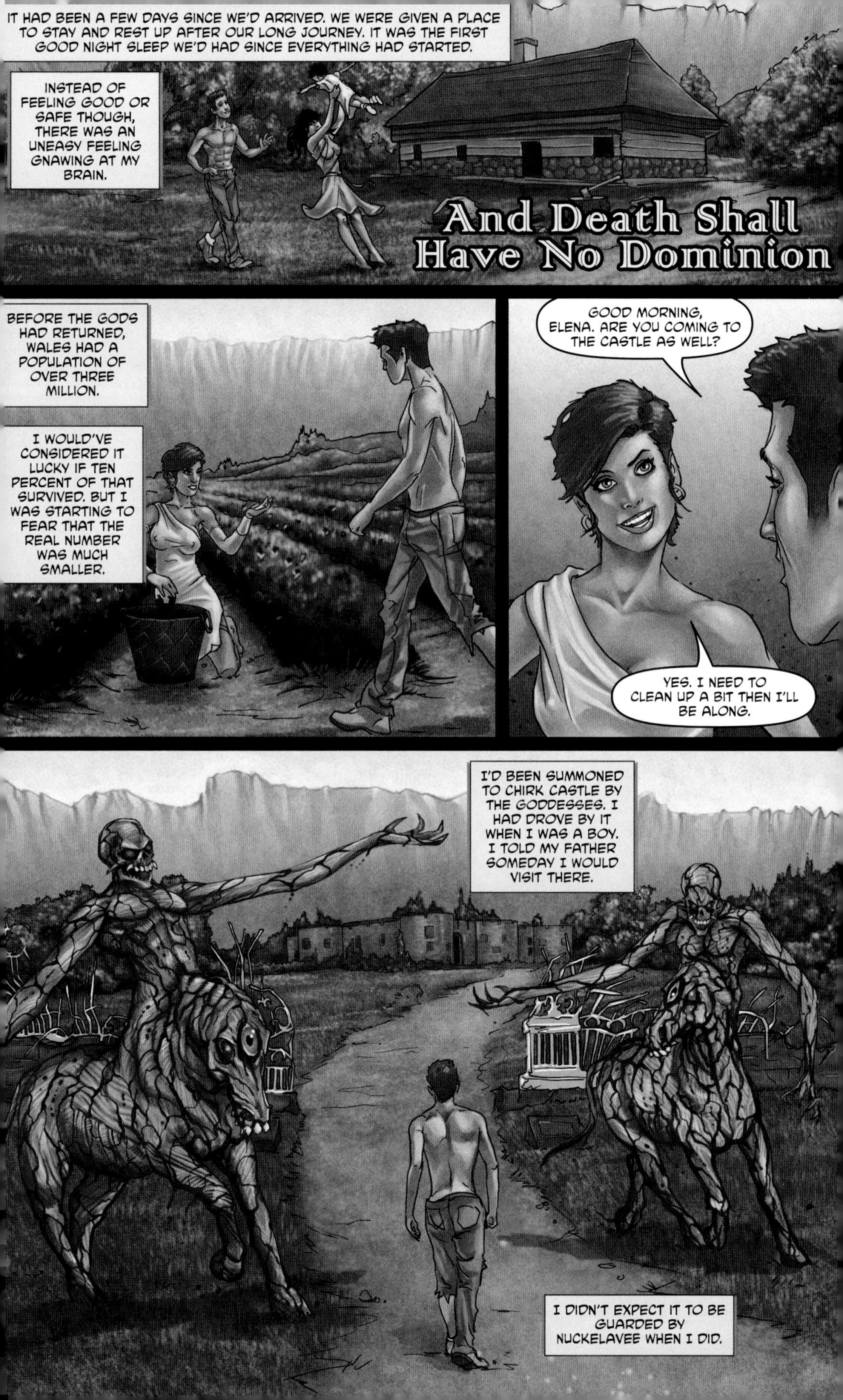
IT HAD BEEN A FEW DAYS SINCE WE'D ARRIVED. WE WERE GIVEN A PLACE TO STAY AND REST UP AFTER OUR LONG JOURNEY. IT WAS THE FIRST GOOD NIGHT SLEEP WE'D HAD SINCE EVERYTHING HAD STARTED.
INSTEAD OF FEELING GOOD OR SAFE THOUGH, THERE WAS AN UNEASY FEELING GNAWING AT MY BRAIN.
And Death Shall Have No Dominion
BEFORE THE GODS HAD RETURNED, WALES HAD A POPULATION OF OVER THREE MILLION.
I WOULD'VE CONSIDERED IT LUCKY IF TEN PERCENT OF THAT SURVIVED. BUT I WAS STARTING TO FEAR THAT THE REAL NUMBER WAS MUCH SMALLER.
GOOD MORNING, ELENA. ARE YOU COMING TO THE CASTLE AS WELL?
YES. I NEED TO CLEAN UP A BIT THEN I'LL BE ALONG.
I'D BEEN SUMMONED TO CHIRK CASTLE BY THE GODDESSES. I HAD DROVE BY IT WHEN I WAS A BOY. I TOLD MY FATHER SOMEDAY I WOULD VISIT THERE.
I DIDN'T EXPECT IT TO BE GUARDED BY NUCKELAVEE WHEN I DID.

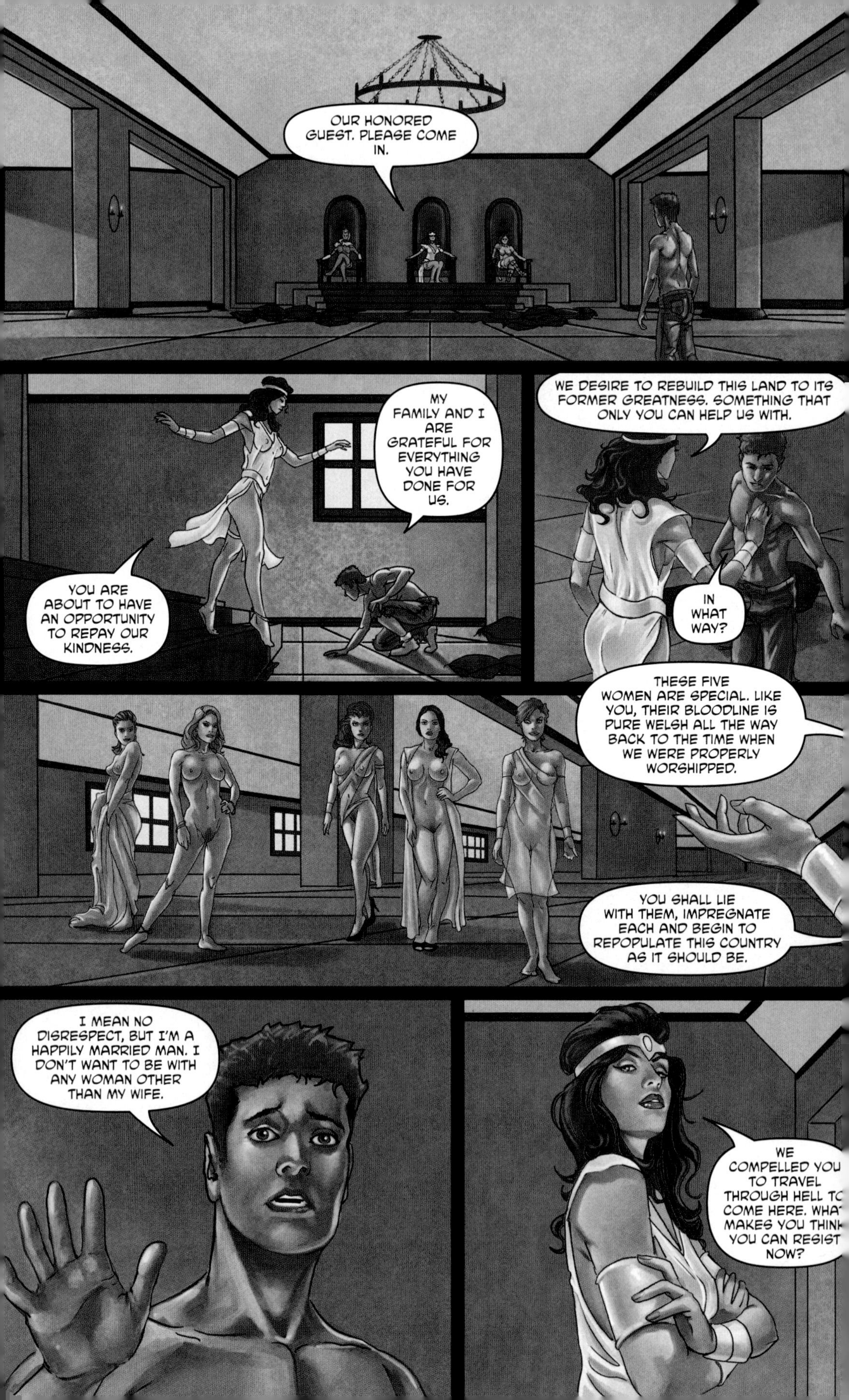
OUR HONORED GUEST. PLEASE COME IN.
MY FAMILY AND I ARE GRATEFUL FOR EVERYTHING YOU HAVE DONE FOR US.
YOU ARE ABOUT TO HAVE AN OPPORTUNITY TO REPAY OUR KINDNESS.
WE DESIRE TO REBUILD THIS LAND TO ITS FORMER GREATNESS. SOMETHING THAT ONLY YOU CAN HELP US WITH.
IN WHAT WAY?
THESE FIVE WOMEN ARE SPECIAL. LIKE YOU, THEIR BLOODLINE IS PURE WELSH ALL THE WAY BACK TO THE TIME WHEN WE WERE PROPERLY WORSHIPPED.
YOU SHALL LIE WITH THEM, IMPREGNATE EACH AND BEGIN TO REPOPULATE THIS COUNTRY AS IT SHOULD BE.
I MEAN NO DISRESPECT, BUT I'M A HAPPILY MARRIED MAN. I DON'T WANT TO BE WITH ANY WOMAN OTHER THAN MY WIFE.
WE COMPELLED YOU TO TRAVEL THROUGH HELL TO COME HERE. WHAT MAKES YOU THINK YOU CAN RESIST NOW?

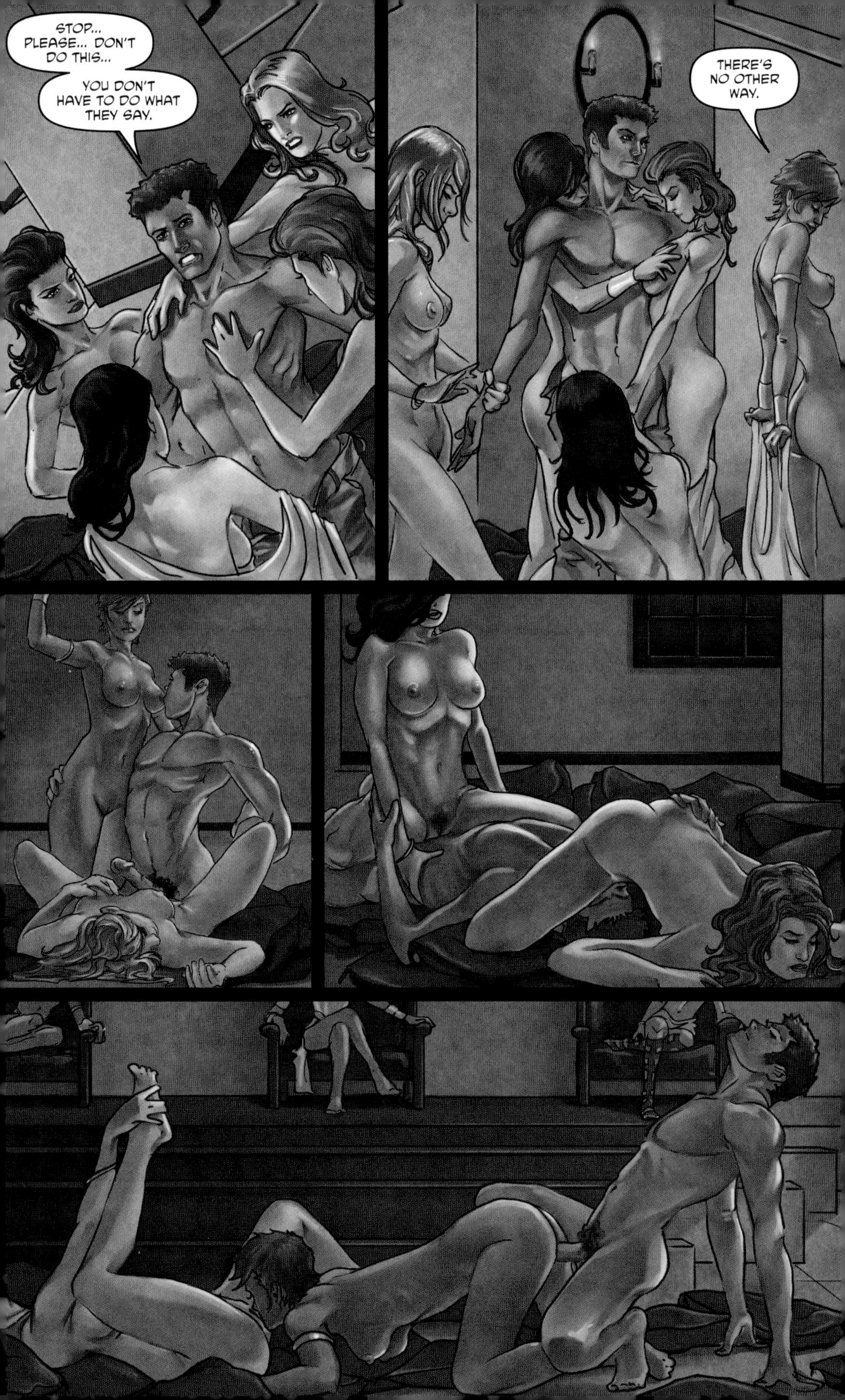
STOP... PLEASE... DON'T DO THIS...
YOU DON'T HAVE TO DO WHAT THEY SAY.
THERE'S NO OTHER WAY.

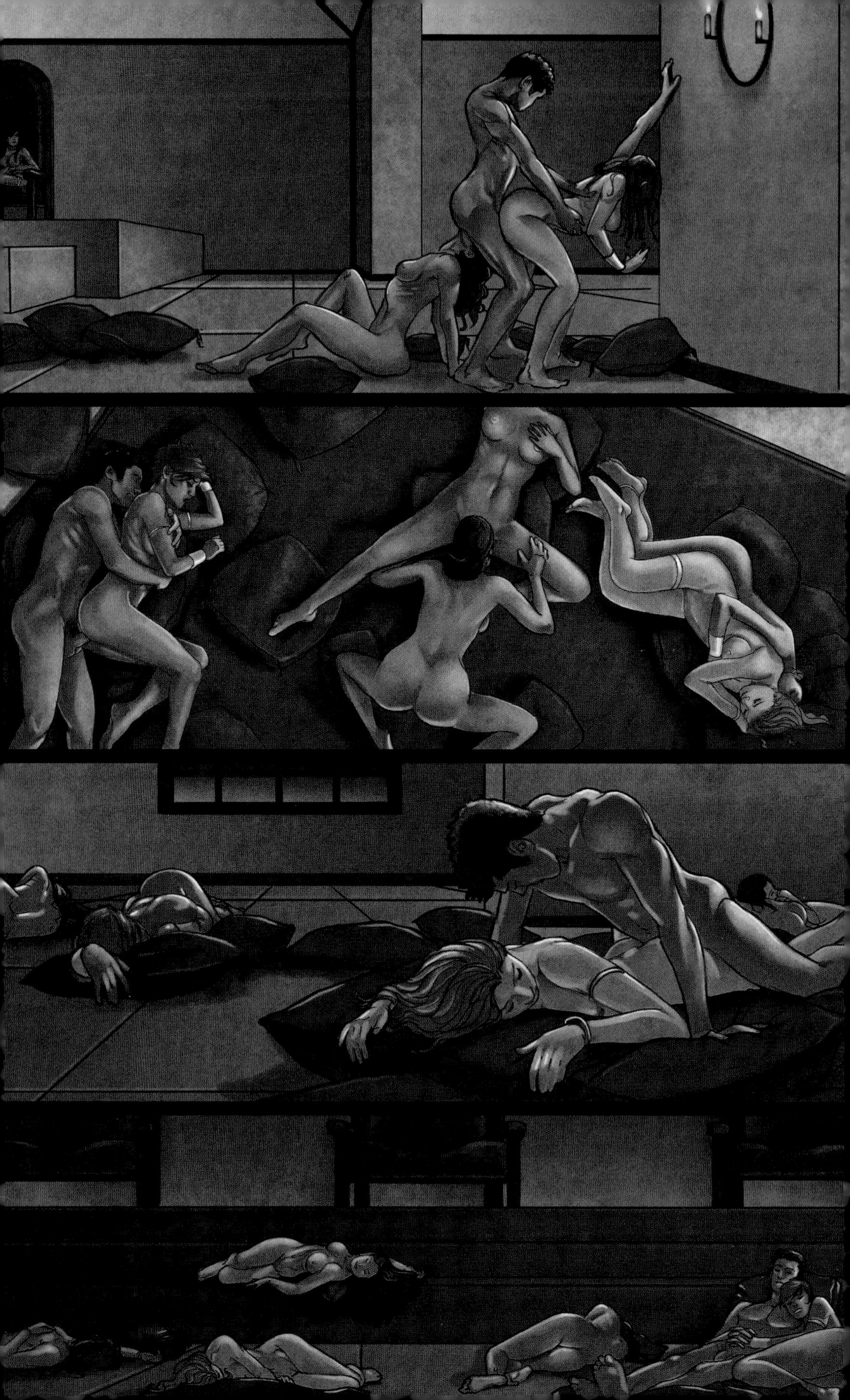

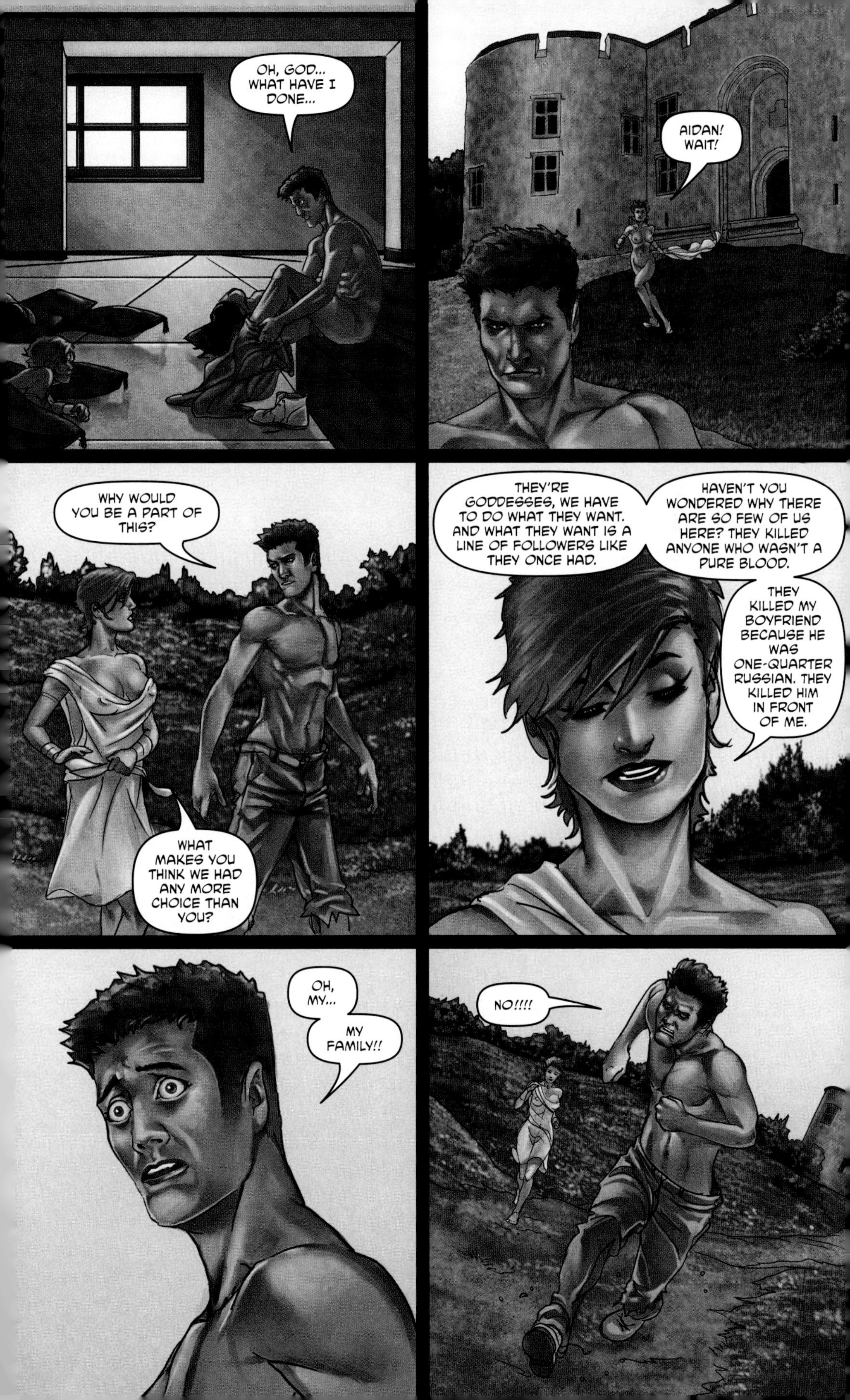
OH, GOD... WHAT HAVE I DONE...
AIDAN! WAIT!
WHY WOULD YOU BE A PART OF THIS?
WHAT MAKES YOU THINK WE HAD ANY MORE CHOICE THAN YOU?
THEY'RE GODDESSES, WE HAVE TO DO WHAT THEY WANT. AND WHAT THEY WANT IS A LINE OF FOLLOWERS LIKE THEY ONCE HAD.
HAVEN'T YOU WONDERED WHY THERE ARE SO FEW OF US HERE? THEY KILLED ANYONE WHO WASN'T A PURE BLOOD.
THEY KILLED MY BOYFRIEND BECAUSE HE WAS ONE-QUARTER RUSSIAN. THEY KILLED HIM IN FRONT OF ME.
OH, MY...
MY FAMILY!!
NO!!!!

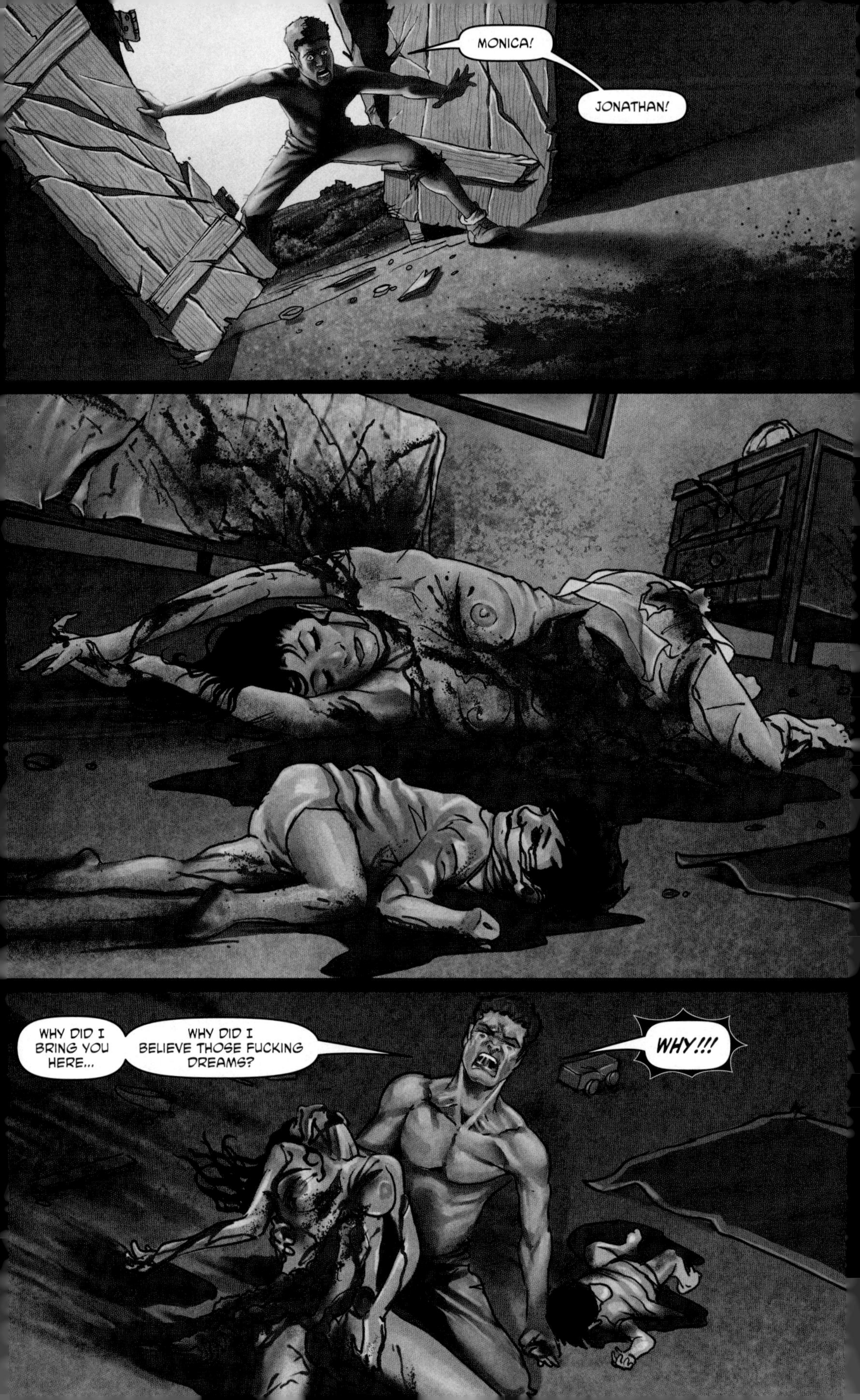
MONICA!
JONATHAN!
WHY DID I BRING YOU HERE...
WHY DID I BELIEVE THOSE FUCKING DREAMS?
WHY!!!

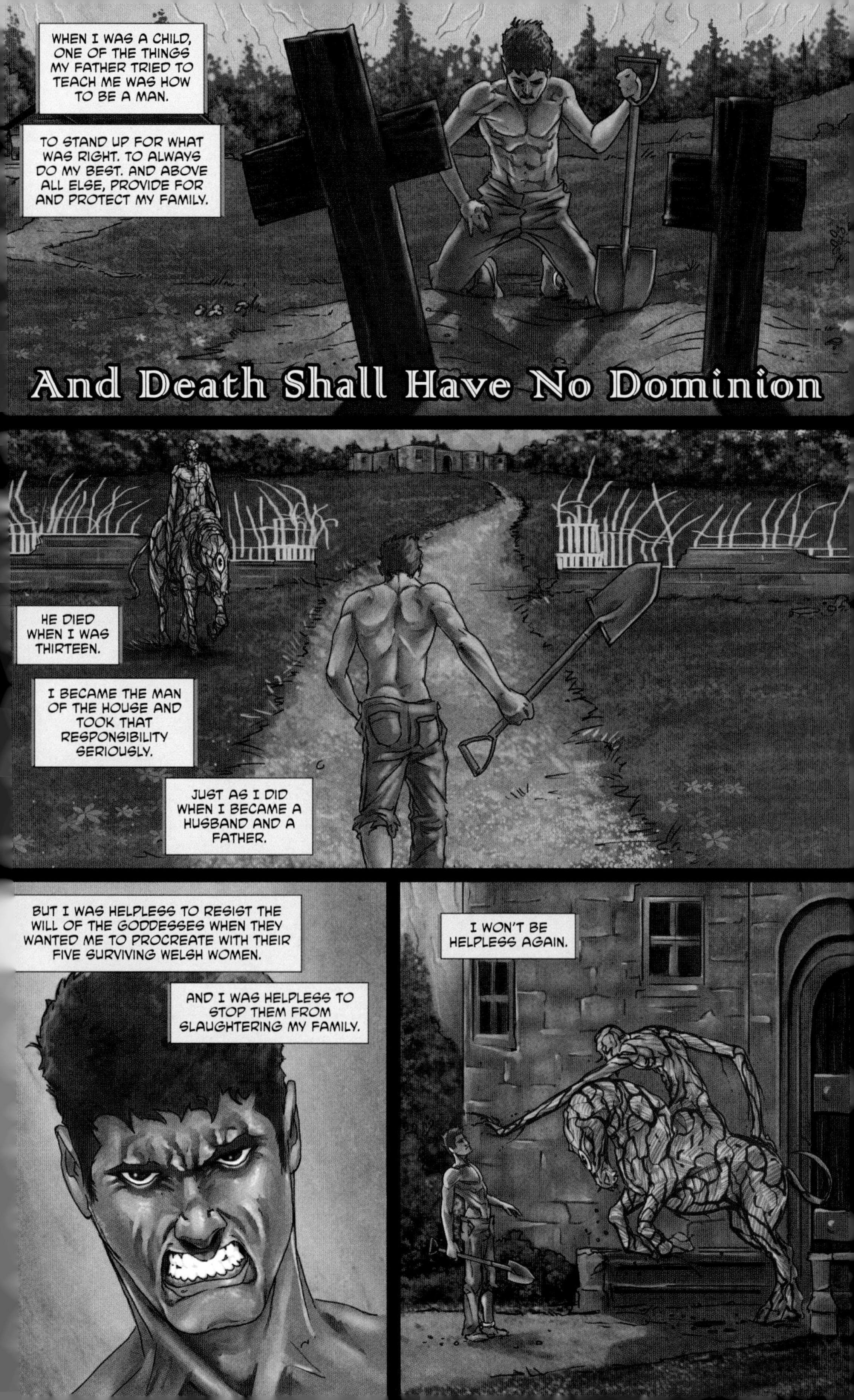

WHEN I WAS A CHILD, ONE OF THE THINGS MY FATHER TRIED TO TEACH ME WAS HOW TO BE A MAN.
TO STAND UP FOR WHAT WAS RIGHT. TO ALWAYS DO MY BEST. AND ABOVE ALL ELSE, PROVIDE FOR AND PROTECT MY FAMILY.
And Death Shall Have No Dominion
HE DIED WHEN I WAS THIRTEEN.
I BECAME THE MAN OF THE HOUSE AND TOOK THAT RESPONSIBILITY SERIOUSLY.
JUST AS I DID WHEN I BECAME A HUSBAND AND A FATHER.
BUT I WAS HELPLESS TO RESIST THE WILL OF THE GODDESSES WHEN THEY WANTED ME TO PROCREATE WITH THEIR FIVE SURVIVING WELSH WOMEN.
AND I WAS HELPLESS TO STOP THEM FROM SLAUGHTERING MY FAMILY.
I WON'T BE HELPLESS AGAIN.

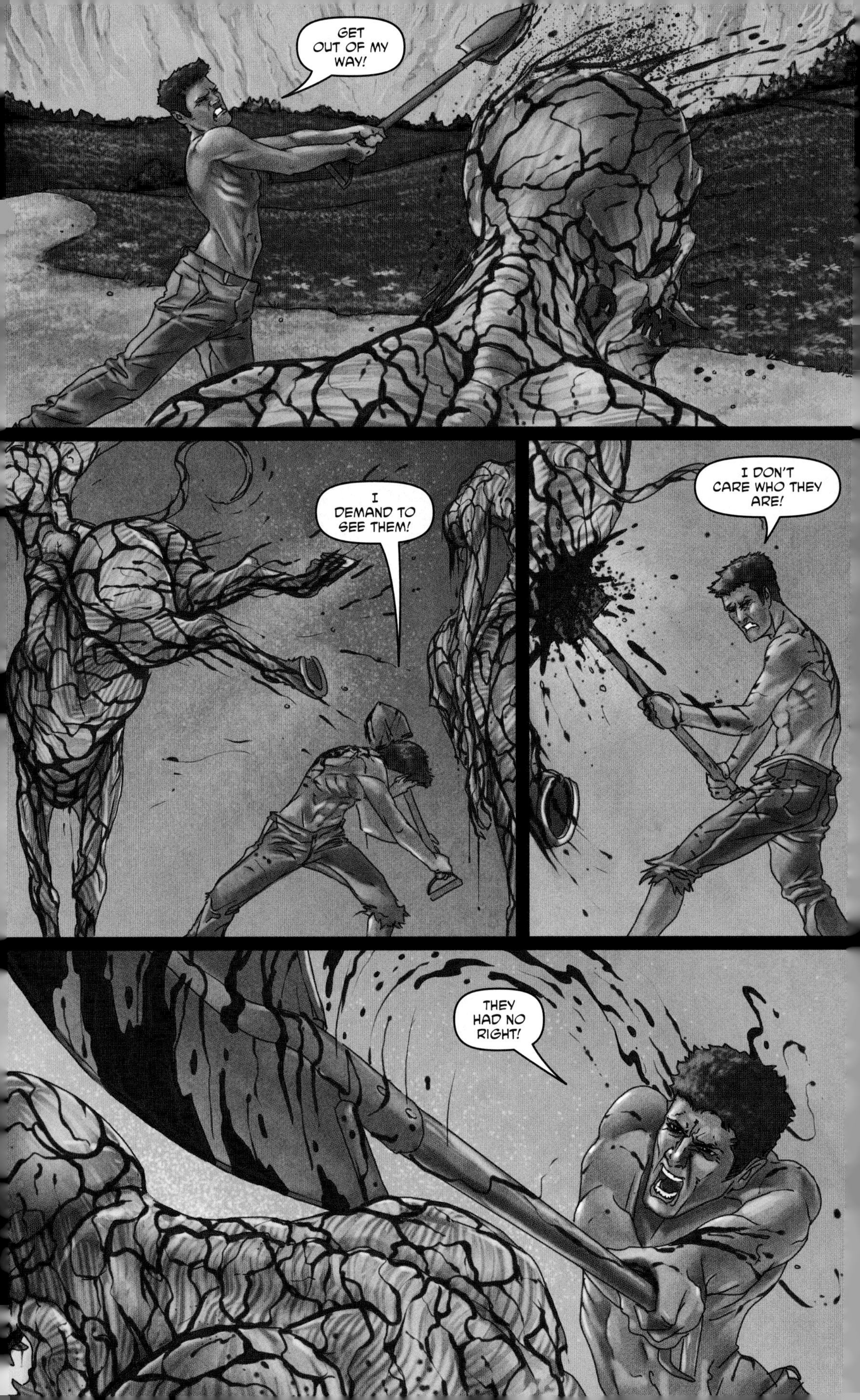
GET OUT OF MY WAY!
I DEMAND TO SEE THEM!
I DON'T CARE WHO THEY ARE!
THEY HAD NO RIGHT!

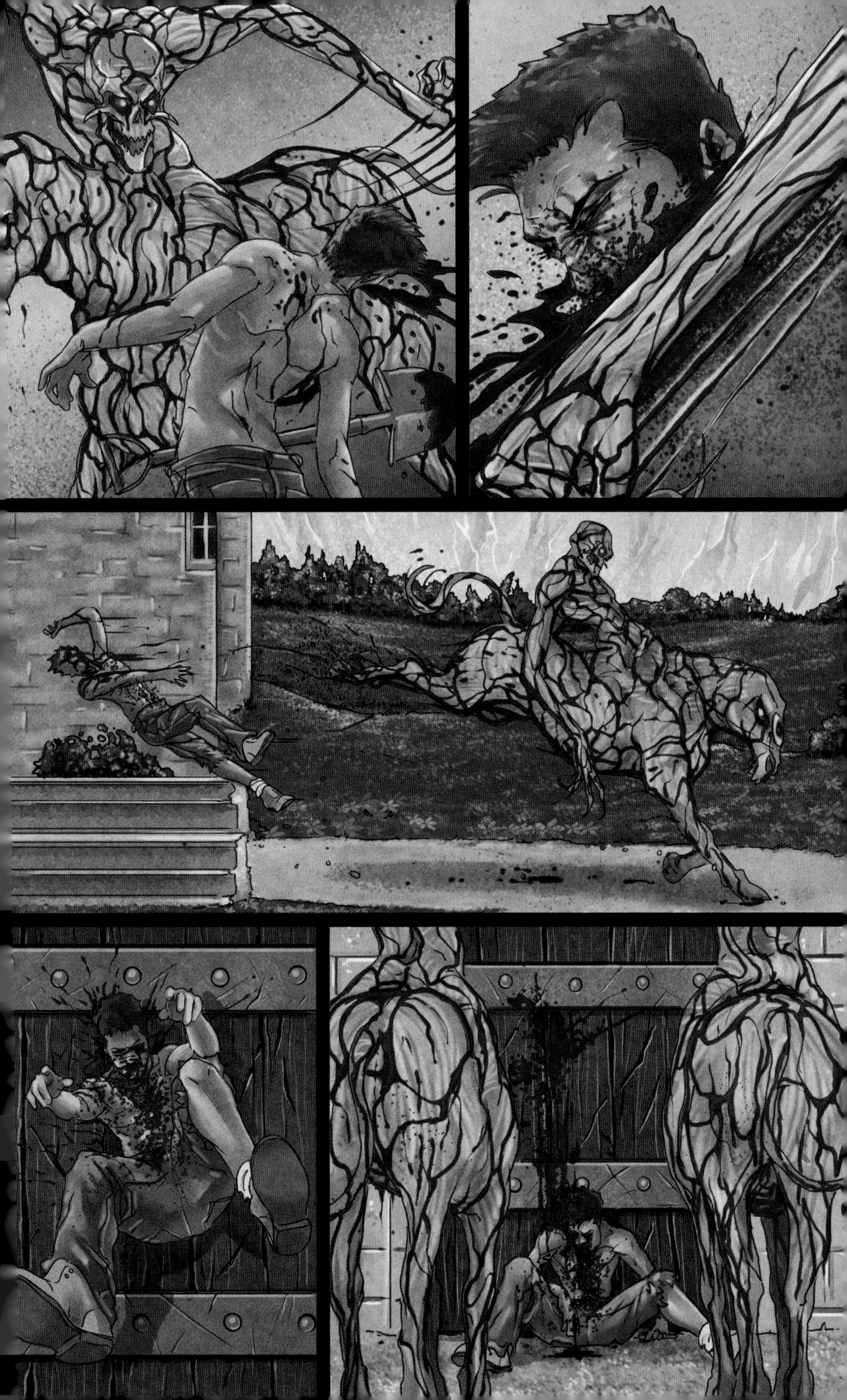

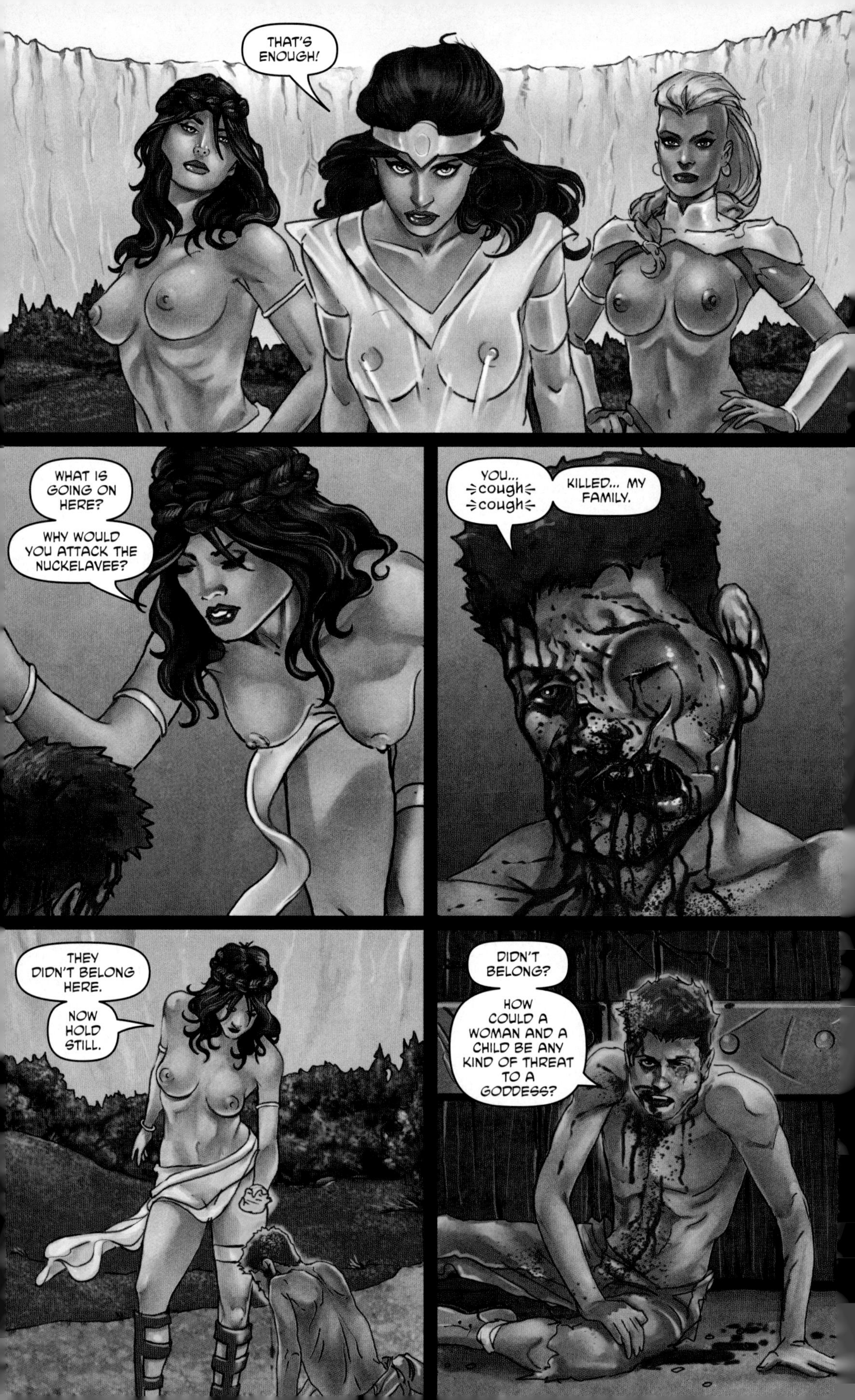
THAT'S ENOUGH!
WHAT IS GOING ON HERE?
WHY WOULD YOU ATTACK THE NUCKELAVEE?
YOU... =cough= =cough=
KILLED... MY FAMILY.
THEY DIDN'T BELONG HERE.
NOW HOLD STILL.
DIDN'T BELONG?
HOW COULD A WOMAN AND A CHILD BE ANY KIND OF THREAT TO A GODDESS?

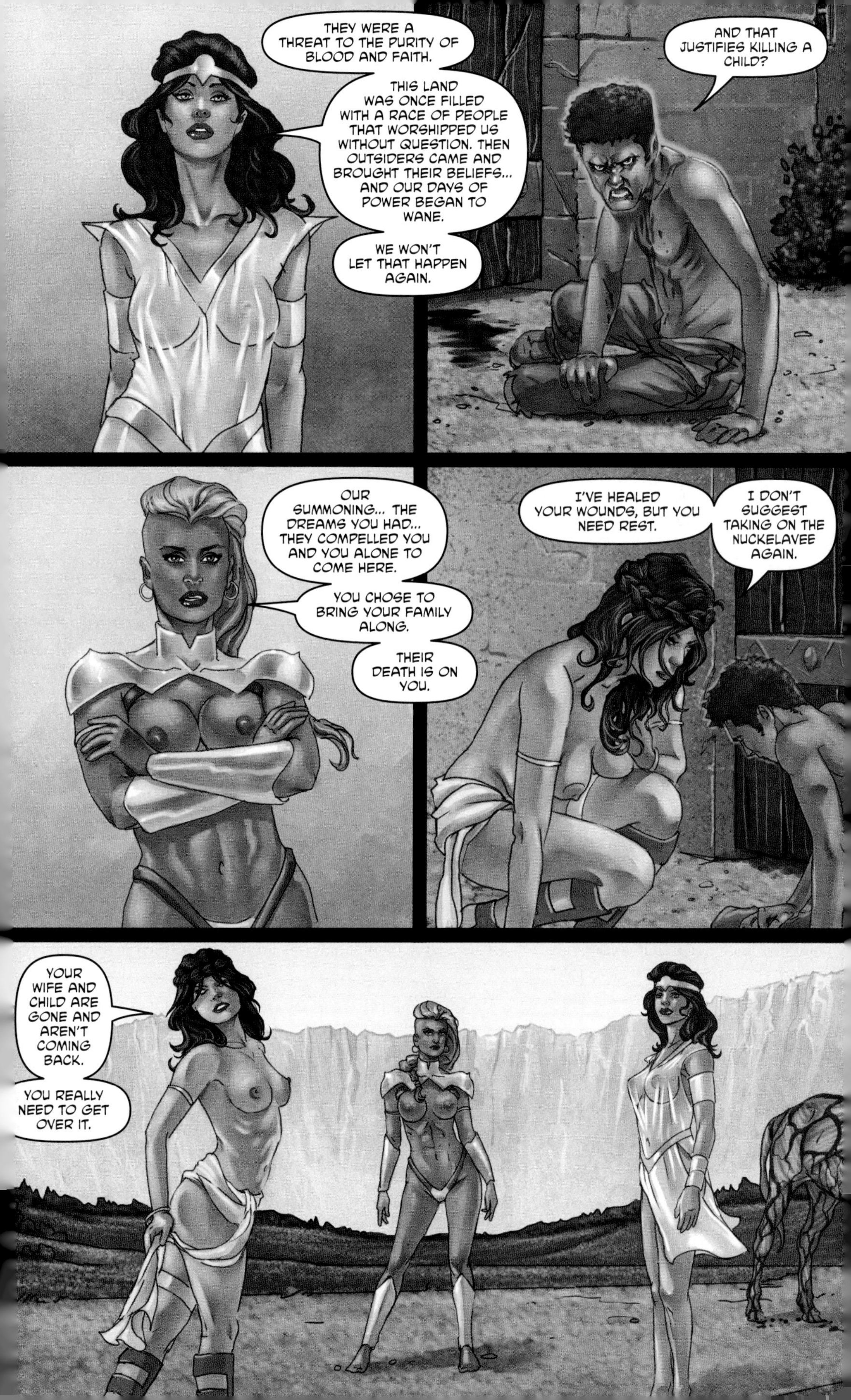
THEY WERE A THREAT TO THE PURITY OF BLOOD AND FAITH.
THIS LAND WAS ONCE FILLED WITH A RACE OF PEOPLE THAT WORSHIPPED US WITHOUT QUESTION. THEN OUTSIDERS CAME AND BROUGHT THEIR BELIEFS... AND OUR DAYS OF POWER BEGAN TO WANE.
WE WON'T LET THAT HAPPEN AGAIN.
AND THAT JUSTIFIES KILLING A CHILD?
OUR SUMMONING... THE DREAMS YOU HAD... THEY COMPELLED YOU AND YOU ALONE TO COME HERE.
YOU CHOSE TO BRING YOUR FAMILY ALONG.
THEIR DEATH IS ON YOU.
I'VE HEALED YOUR WOUNDS, BUT YOU NEED REST.
I DON'T SUGGEST TAKING ON THE NUCKELAVEE AGAIN.
YOUR WIFE AND CHILD ARE GONE AND AREN'T COMING BACK.
YOU REALLY NEED TO GET OVER IT.

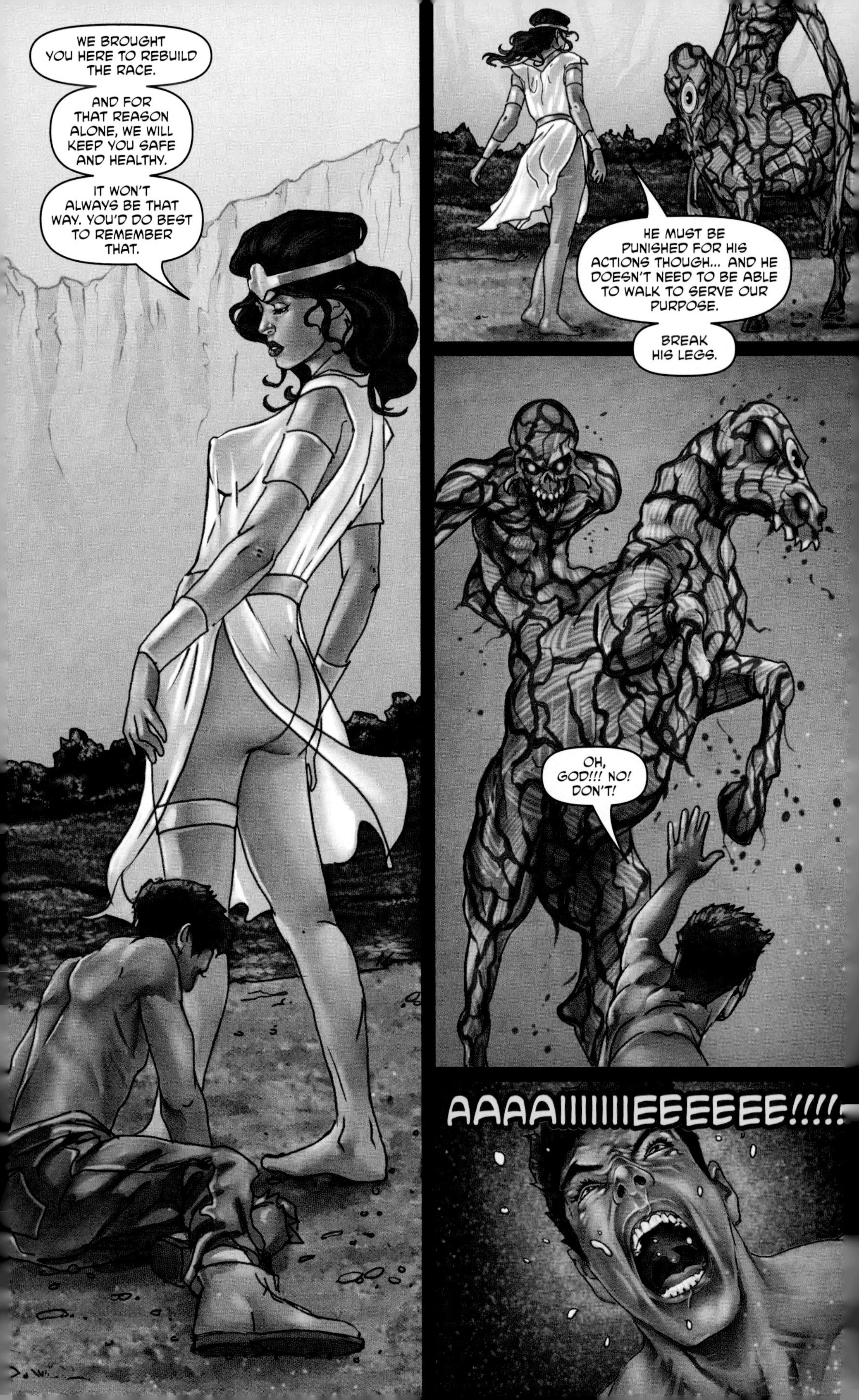

WE BROUGHT YOU HERE TO REBUILD THE RACE.
AND FOR THAT REASON ALONE, WE WILL KEEP YOU SAFE AND HEALTHY.
IT WON'T ALWAYS BE THAT WAY. YOU'D DO BEST TO REMEMBER THAT.
HE MUST BE PUNISHED FOR HIS ACTIONS THOUGH... AND HE DOESN'T NEED TO BE ABLE TO WALK TO SERVE OUR PURPOSE.
BREAK HIS LEGS.
OH, GOD!!! NO! DON'T!
AAAAIIIIIIIEEEEEE!!!!

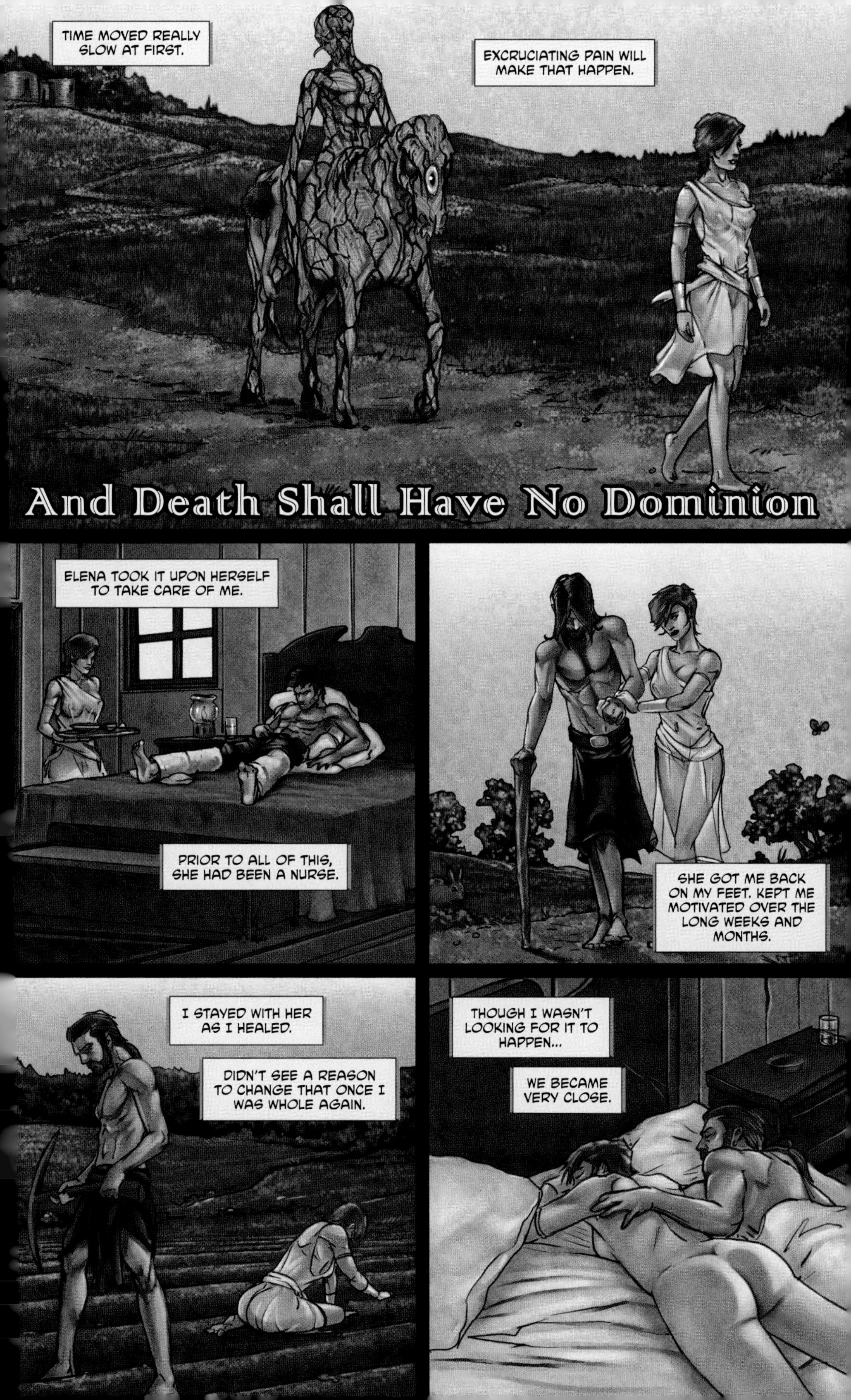
TIME MOVED REALLY SLOW AT FIRST.
EXCRUCIATING PAIN WILL MAKE THAT HAPPEN.
And Death Shall Have No Dominion
ELENA TOOK IT UPON HERSELF TO TAKE CARE OF ME.
PRIOR TO ALL OF THIS, SHE HAD BEEN A NURSE.
SHE GOT ME BACK ON MY FEET. KEPT ME MOTIVATED OVER THE LONG WEEKS AND MONTHS.
I STAYED WITH HER AS I HEALED.
DIDN'T SEE A REASON TO CHANGE THAT ONCE I WAS WHOLE AGAIN.
THOUGH I WASN'T LOOKING FOR IT TO HAPPEN...
WE BECAME VERY CLOSE.

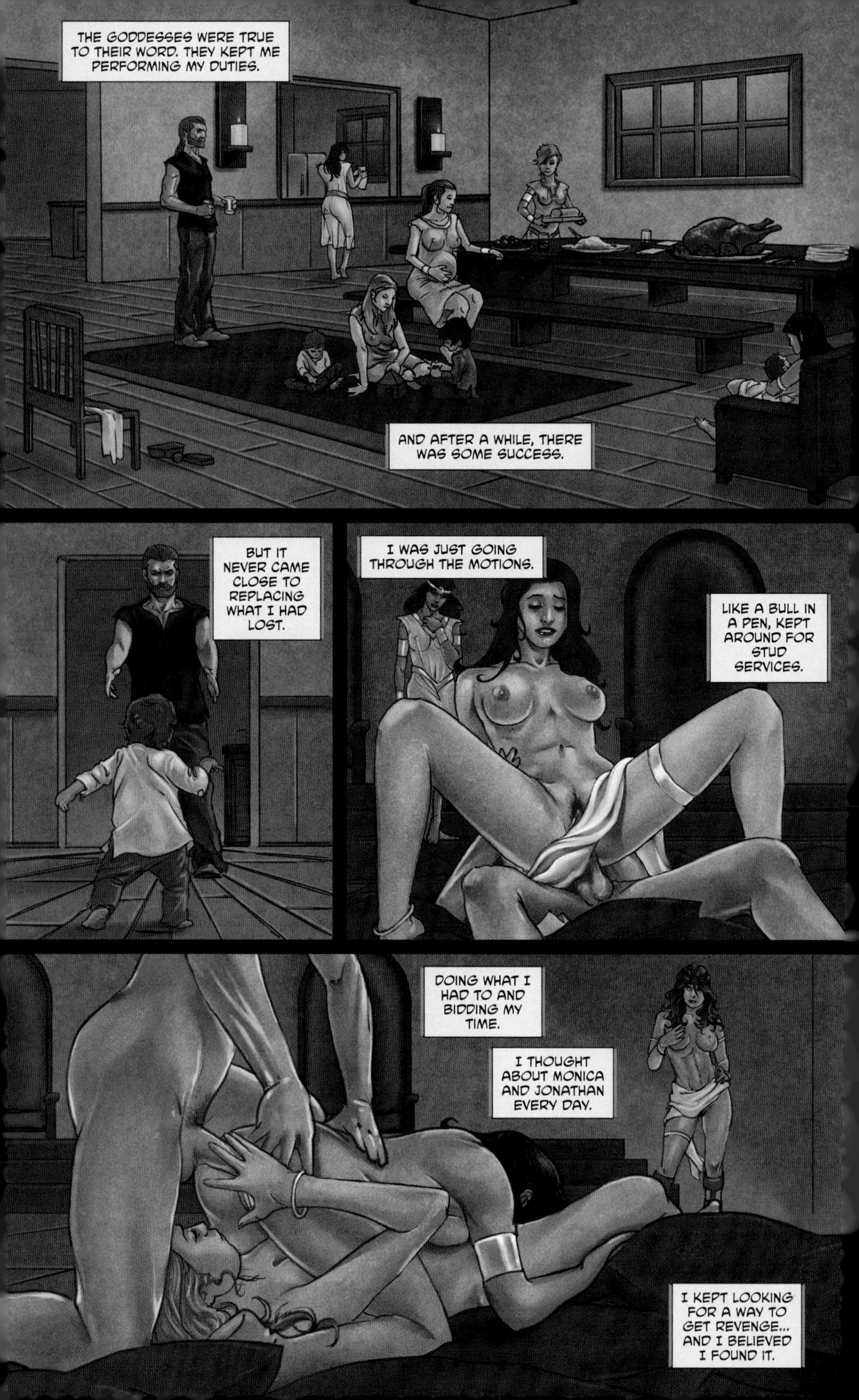
THE GODDESSES WERE TRUE TO THEIR WORD. THEY KEPT ME PERFORMING MY DUTIES.
AND AFTER A WHILE, THERE WAS SOME SUCCESS.
BUT IT NEVER CAME CLOSE TO REPLACING WHAT I HAD LOST.
I WAS JUST GOING THROUGH THE MOTIONS.
LIKE A BULL IN A PEN, KEPT AROUND FOR STUD SERVICES.
DOING WHAT I HAD TO AND BIDDING MY TIME.
I THOUGHT ABOUT MONICA AND JONATHAN EVERY DAY.
I KEPT LOOKING FOR A WAY TO GET REVENGE... AND I BELIEVED I FOUND IT.

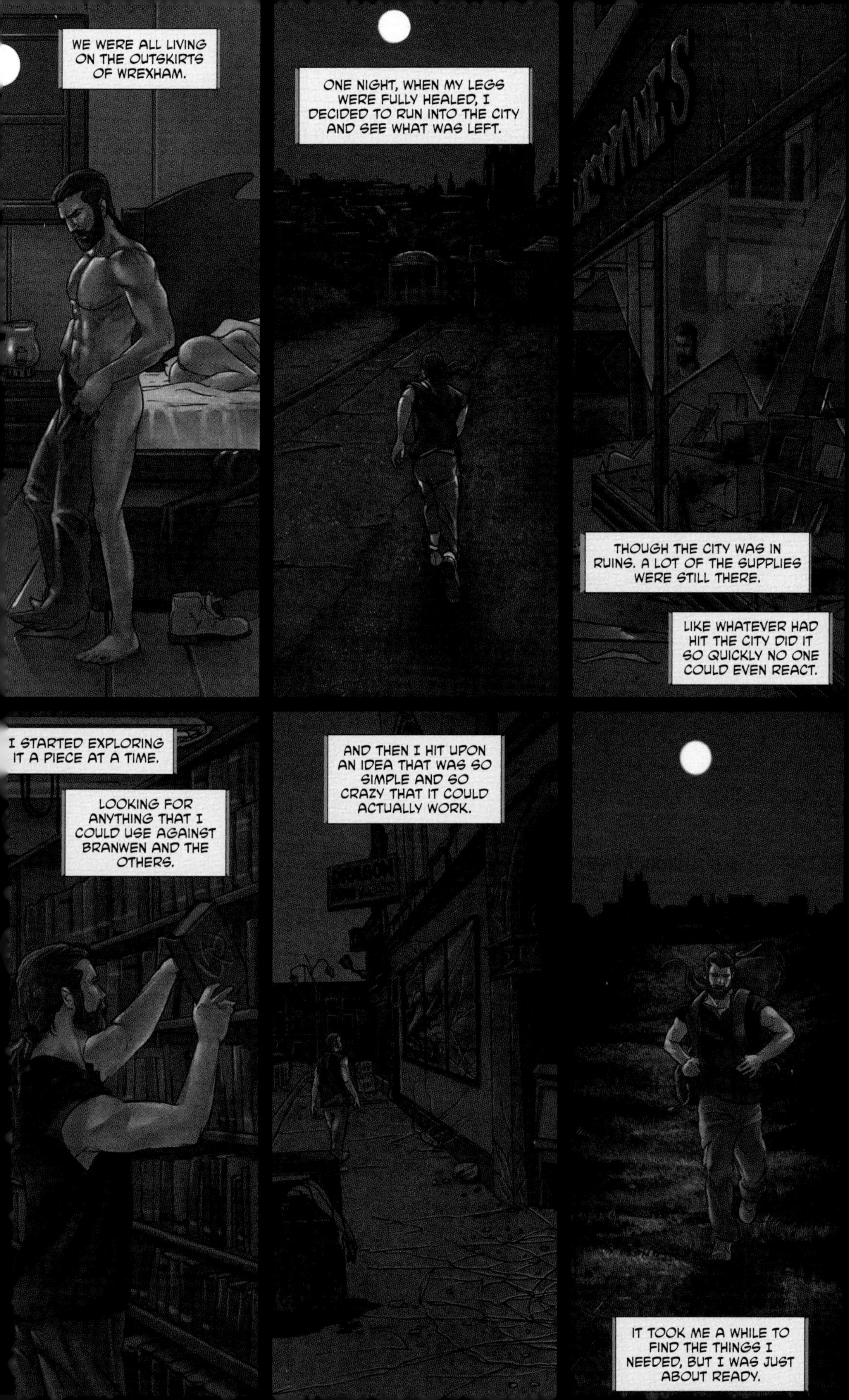
WE WERE ALL LIVING ON THE OUTSKIRTS OF WREXHAM.
ONE NIGHT, WHEN MY LEGS WERE FULLY HEALED, I DECIDED TO RUN INTO THE CITY AND SEE WHAT WAS LEFT.
THOUGH THE CITY WAS IN RUINS. A LOT OF THE SUPPLIES WERE STILL THERE.
LIKE WHATEVER HAD HIT THE CITY DID IT SO QUICKLY NO ONE COULD EVEN REACT.
I STARTED EXPLORING IT A PIECE AT A TIME.
LOOKING FOR ANYTHING THAT I COULD USE AGAINST BRANWEN AND THE OTHERS.
AND THEN I HIT UPON AN IDEA THAT WAS SO SIMPLE AND SO CRAZY THAT IT COULD ACTUALLY WORK.
IT TOOK ME A WHILE TO FIND THE THINGS I NEEDED, BUT I WAS JUST ABOUT READY.

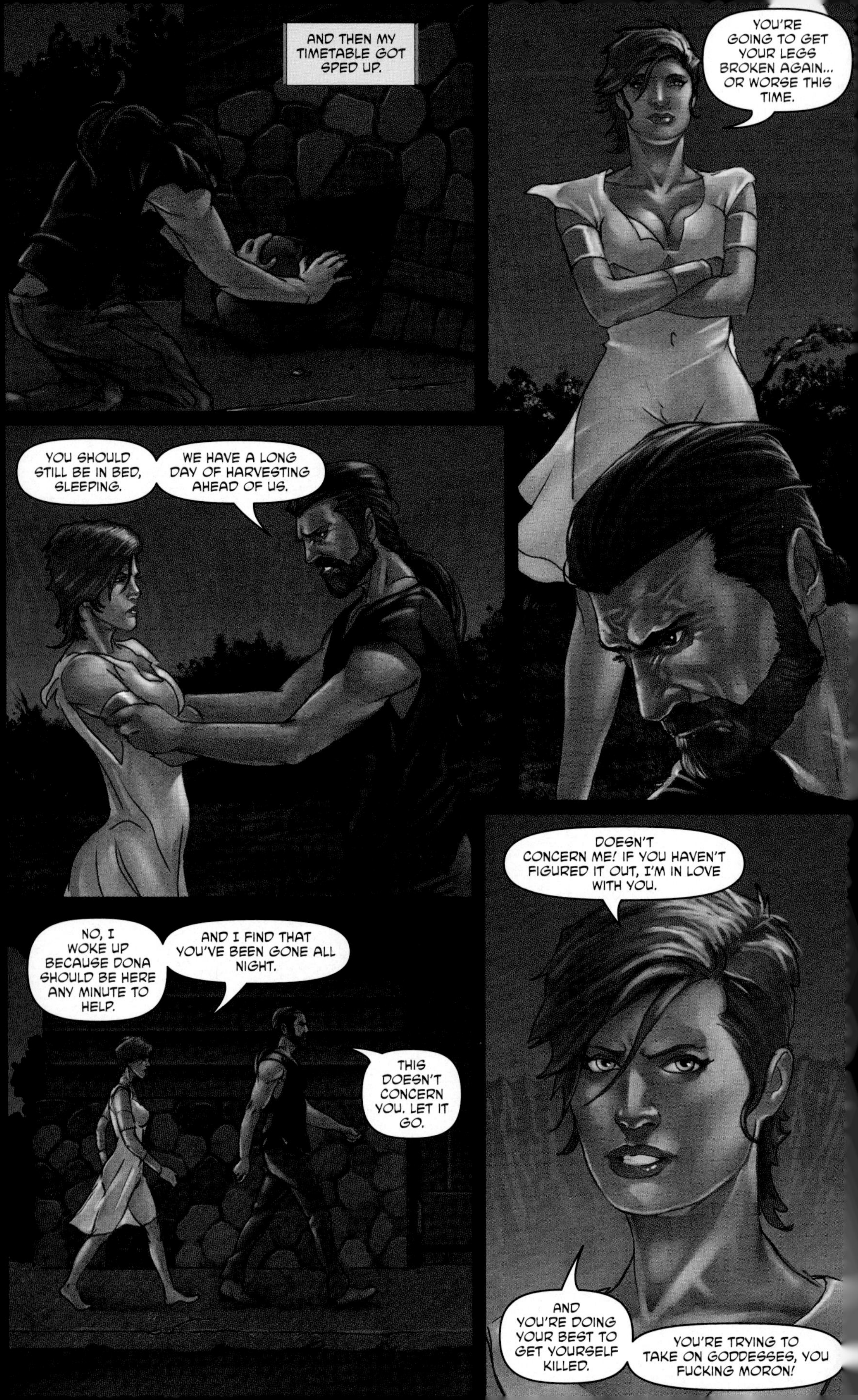
AND THEN MY TIMETABLE GOT SPED UP.
YOU'RE GOING TO GET YOUR LEGS BROKEN AGAIN... OR WORSE THIS TIME.
YOU SHOULD STILL BE IN BED, SLEEPING.
WE HAVE A LONG DAY OF HARVESTING AHEAD OF US.
NO, I WOKE UP BECAUSE DONA SHOULD BE HERE ANY MINUTE TO HELP.
AND I FIND THAT YOU'VE BEEN GONE ALL NIGHT.
THIS DOESN'T CONCERN YOU. LET IT GO.
DOESN'T CONCERN ME! IF YOU HAVEN'T FIGURED IT OUT, I'M IN LOVE WITH YOU.
AND YOU'RE DOING YOUR BEST TO GET YOURSELF KILLED.
YOU'RE TRYING TO TAKE ON GODDESSES, YOU FUCKING MORON!

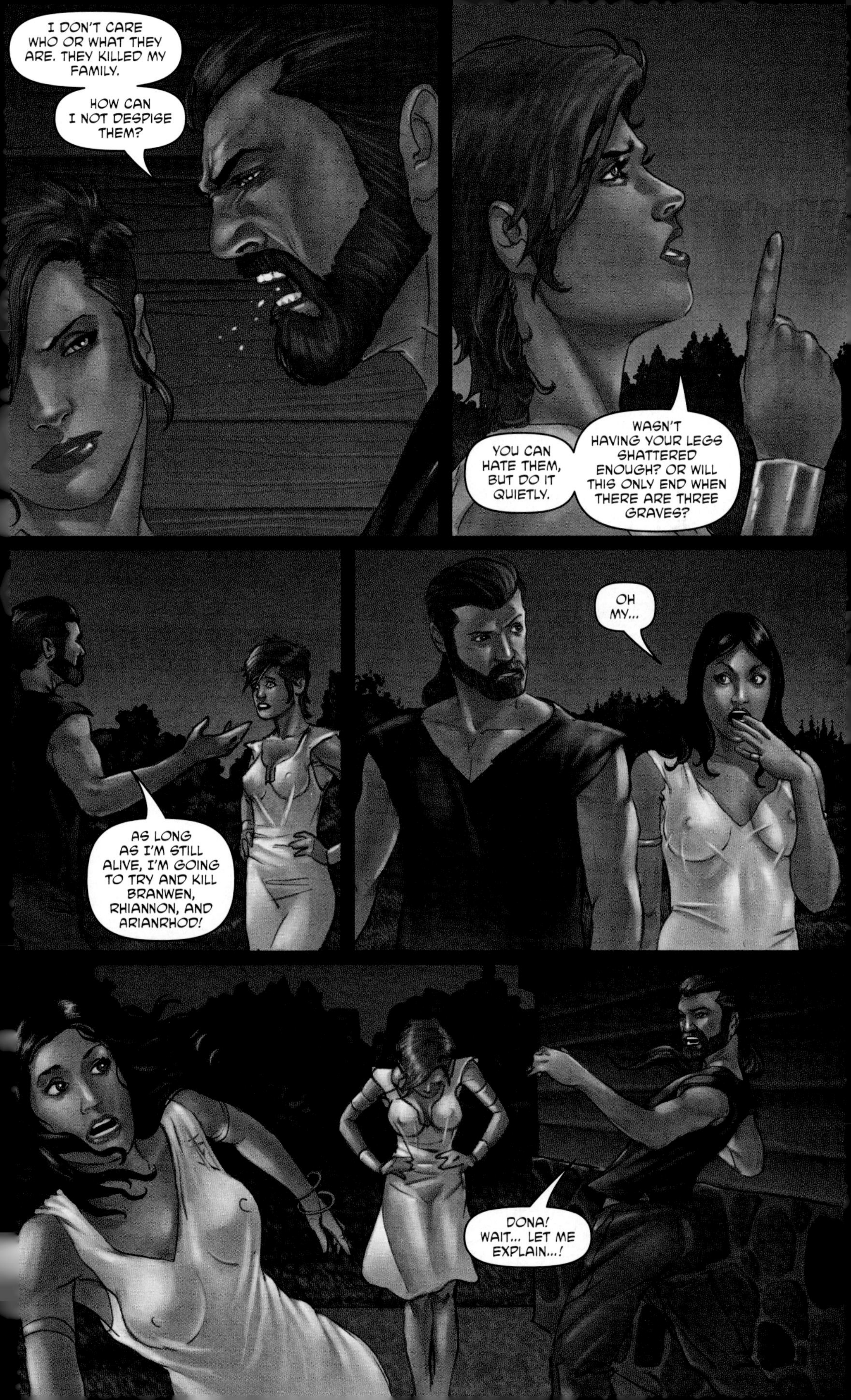

I DON'T CARE WHO OR WHAT THEY ARE. THEY KILLED MY FAMILY.
HOW CAN I NOT DESPISE THEM?
YOU CAN HATE THEM, BUT DO IT QUIETLY.
WASN'T HAVING YOUR LEGS SHATTERED ENOUGH? OR WILL THIS ONLY END WHEN THERE ARE THREE GRAVES?
AS LONG AS I'M STILL ALIVE, I'M GOING TO TRY AND KILL BRANWEN, RHIANNON, AND ARIANRHOD!
OH MY...
DONA! WAIT... LET ME EXPLAIN...!

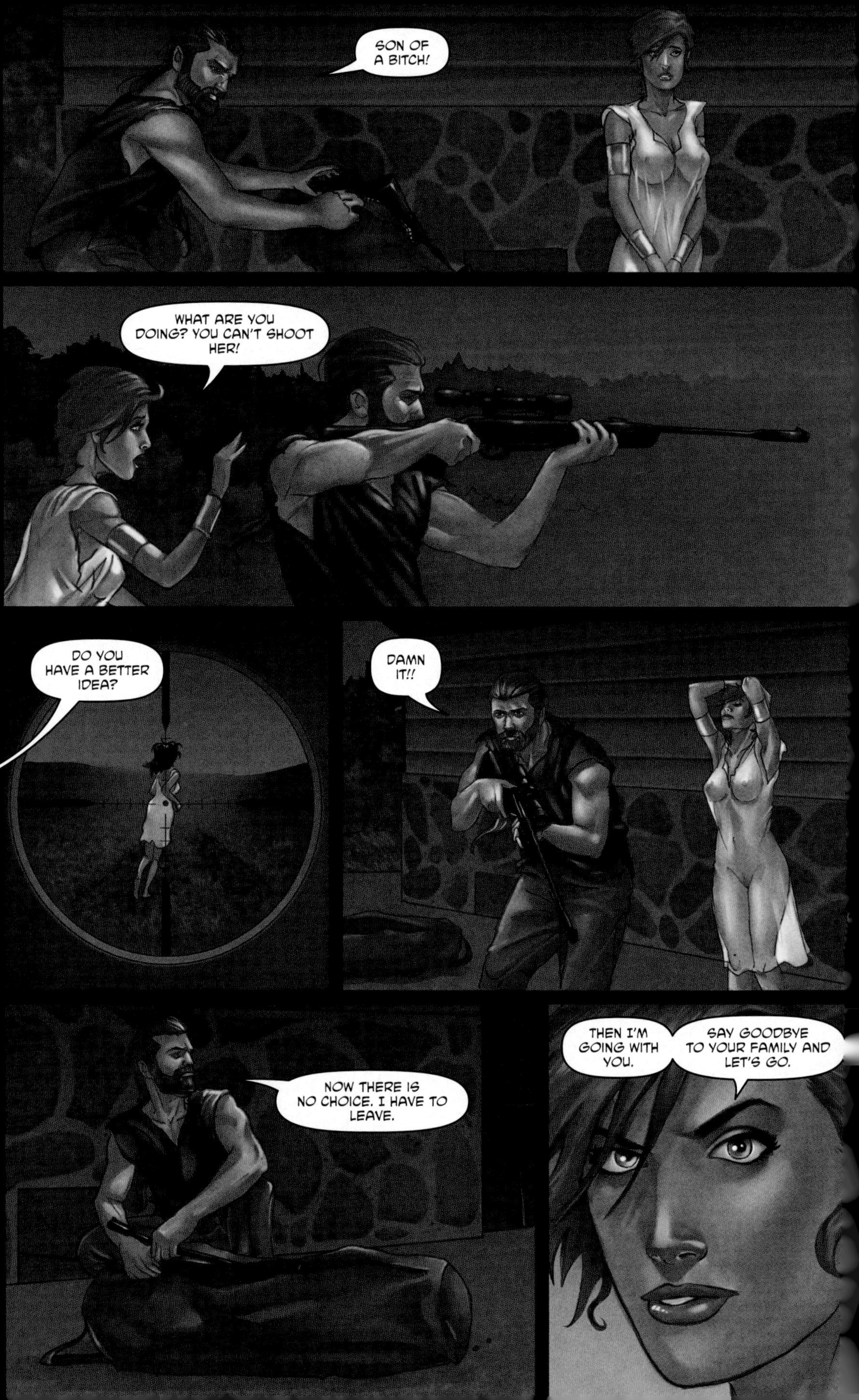
SON OF A BITCH!
WHAT ARE YOU DOING? YOU CAN'T SHOOT HER!
DO YOU HAVE A BETTER IDEA?
DAMN IT!!
NOW THERE IS NO CHOICE. I HAVE TO LEAVE.
THEN I'M GOING WITH YOU.
SAY GOODBYE TO YOUR FAMILY AND LET'S GO.

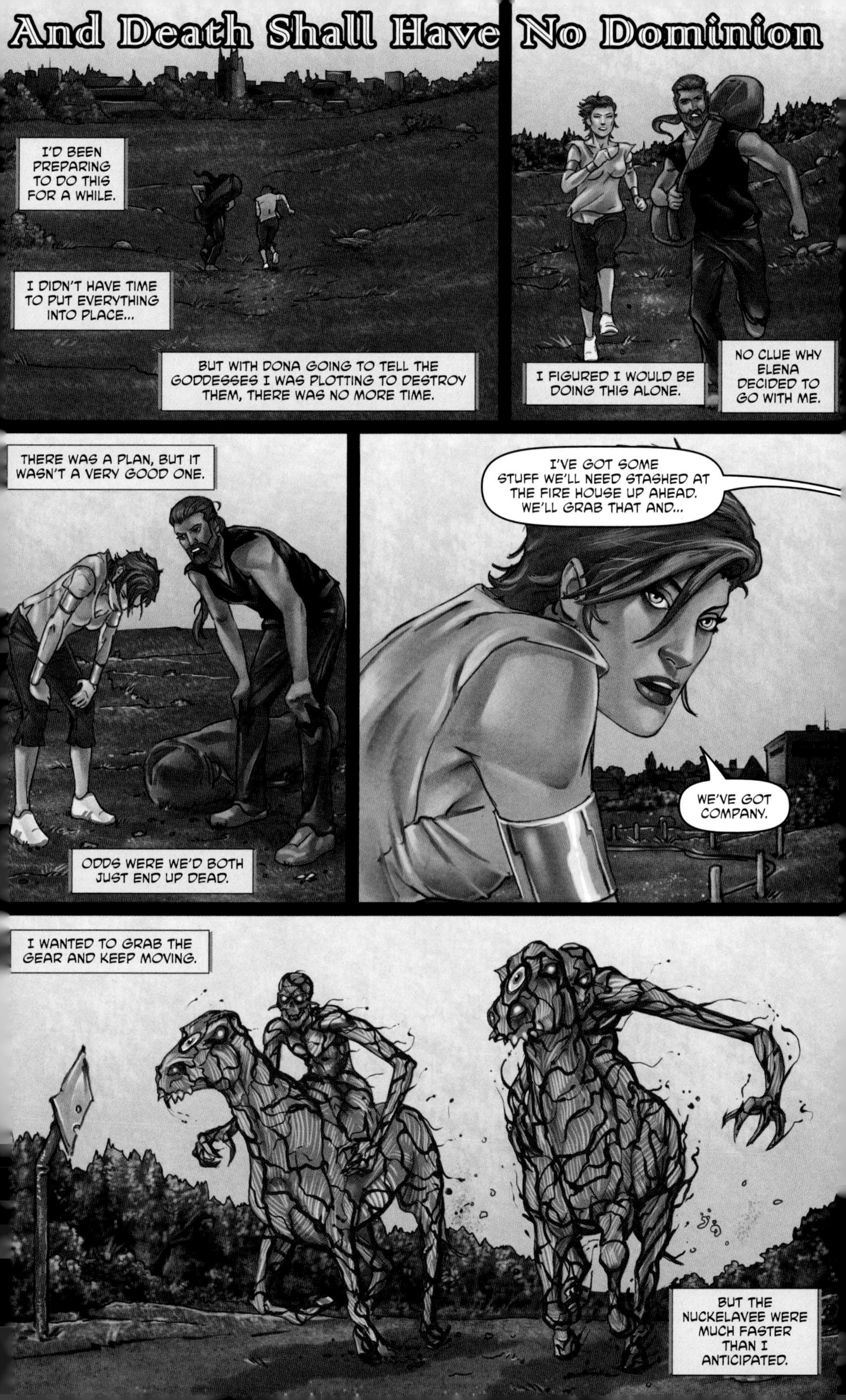
And Death Shall Have No Dominion
I'D BEEN PREPARING TO DO THIS FOR A WHILE.
I DIDN'T HAVE TIME TO PUT EVERYTHING INTO PLACE...
BUT WITH DONA GOING TO TELL THE GODDESSES I WAS PLOTTING TO DESTROY THEM, THERE WAS NO MORE TIME.
I FIGURED I WOULD BE DOING THIS ALONE.
NO CLUE WHY ELENA DECIDED TO GO WITH ME.
THERE WAS A PLAN, BUT IT WASN'T A VERY GOOD ONE.
ODDS WERE WE'D BOTH JUST END UP DEAD.
I'VE GOT SOME STUFF WE'LL NEED STASHED AT THE FIRE HOUSE UP AHEAD. WE'LL GRAB THAT AND...
WE'VE GOT COMPANY.
I WANTED TO GRAB THE GEAR AND KEEP MOVING.
BUT THE NUCKELAVEE WERE MUCH FASTER THAN I ANTICIPATED.

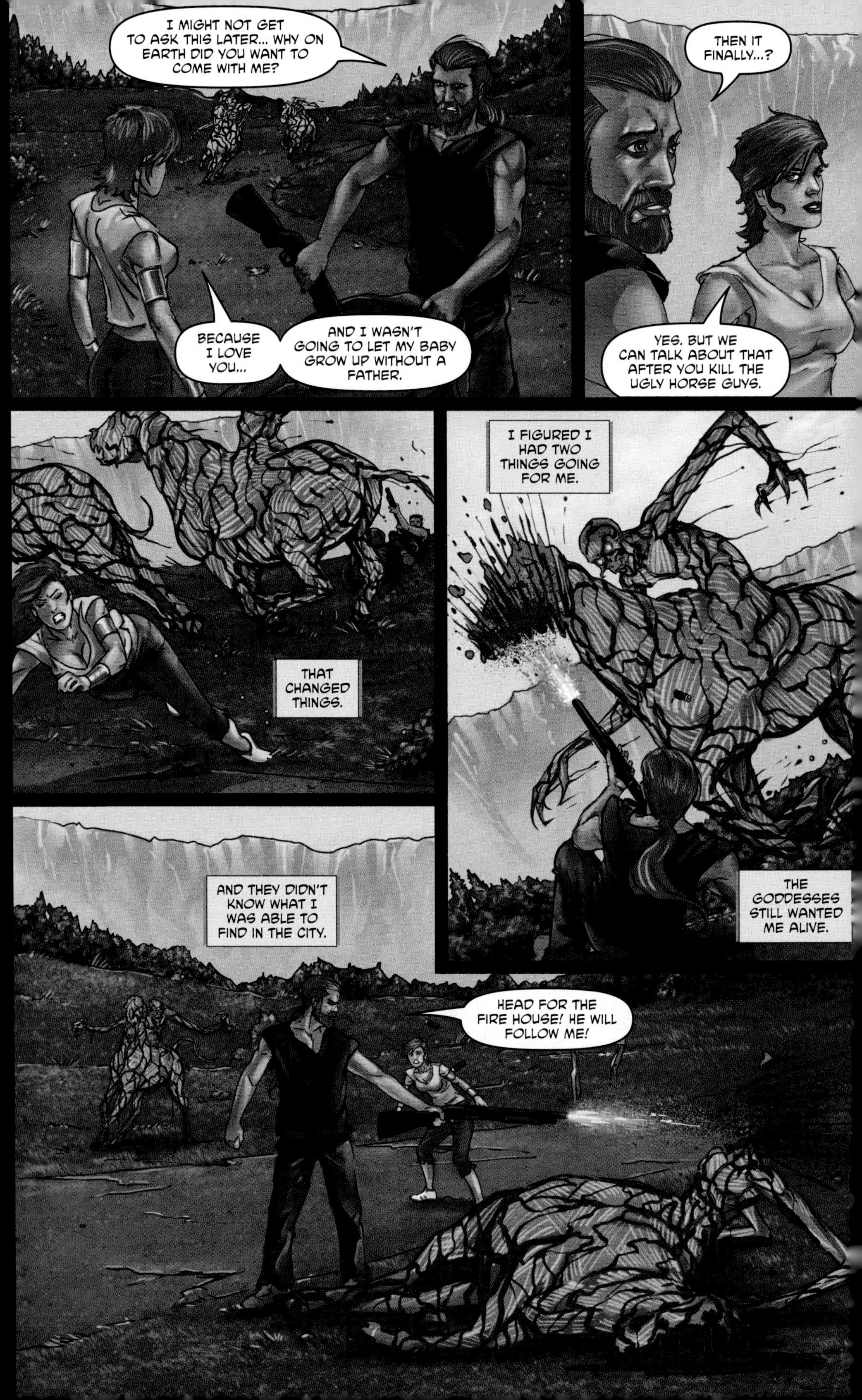
I MIGHT NOT GET TO ASK THIS LATER... WHY ON EARTH DID YOU WANT TO COME WITH ME?
BECAUSE I LOVE YOU...
AND I WASN'T GOING TO LET MY BABY GROW UP WITHOUT A FATHER.
THEN IT FINALLY...?
YES. BUT WE CAN TALK ABOUT THAT AFTER YOU KILL THE UGLY HORSE GUYS.
THAT CHANGED THINGS.
I FIGURED I HAD TWO THINGS GOING FOR ME.
THE GODDESSES STILL WANTED ME ALIVE.
AND THEY DIDN'T KNOW WHAT I WAS ABLE TO FIND IN THE CITY.
HEAD FOR THE FIRE HOUSE! HE WILL FOLLOW ME!

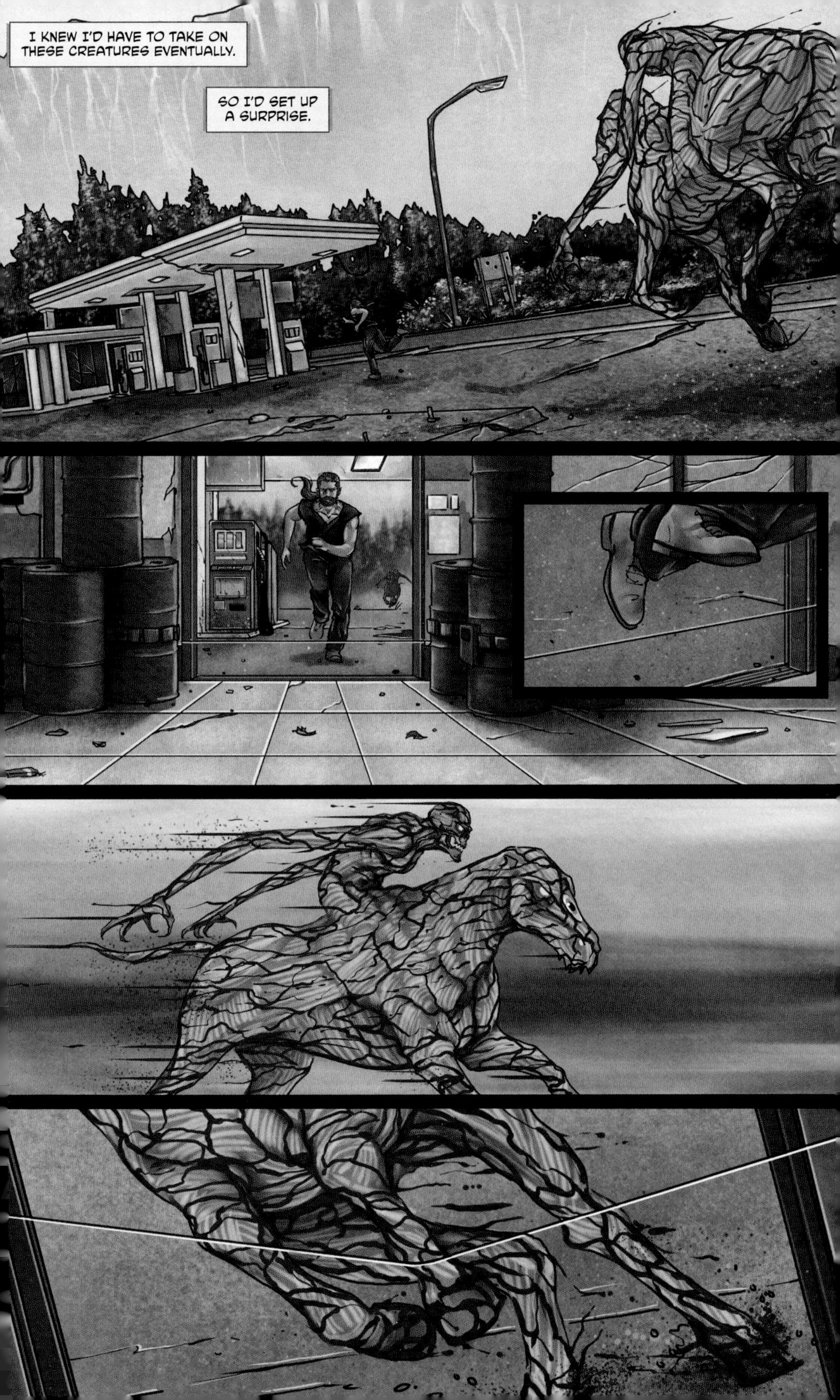
I KNEW I'D HAVE TO TAKE ON THESE CREATURES EVENTUALLY.
SO I'D SET UP A SURPRISE.

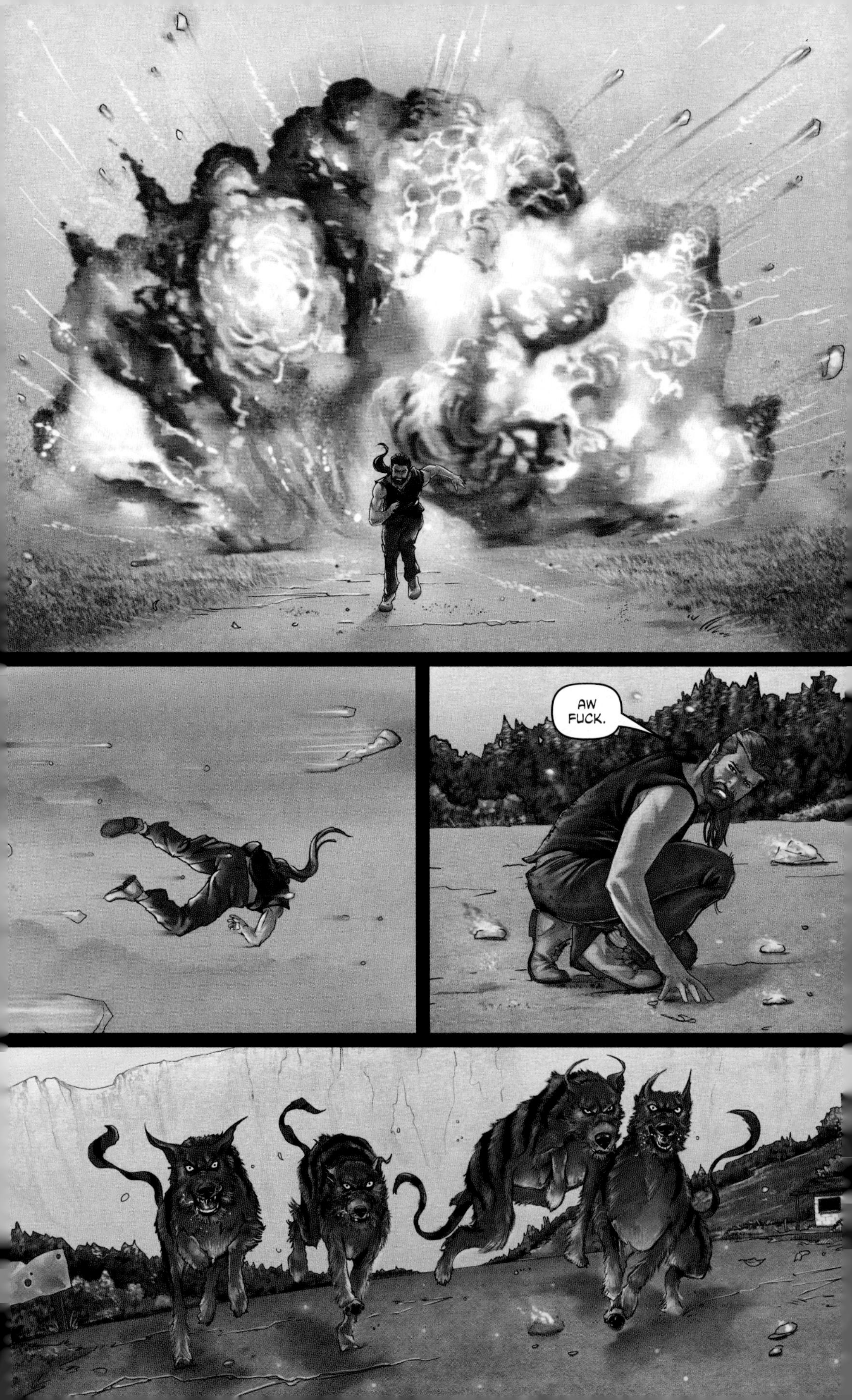
AW
FUCK.

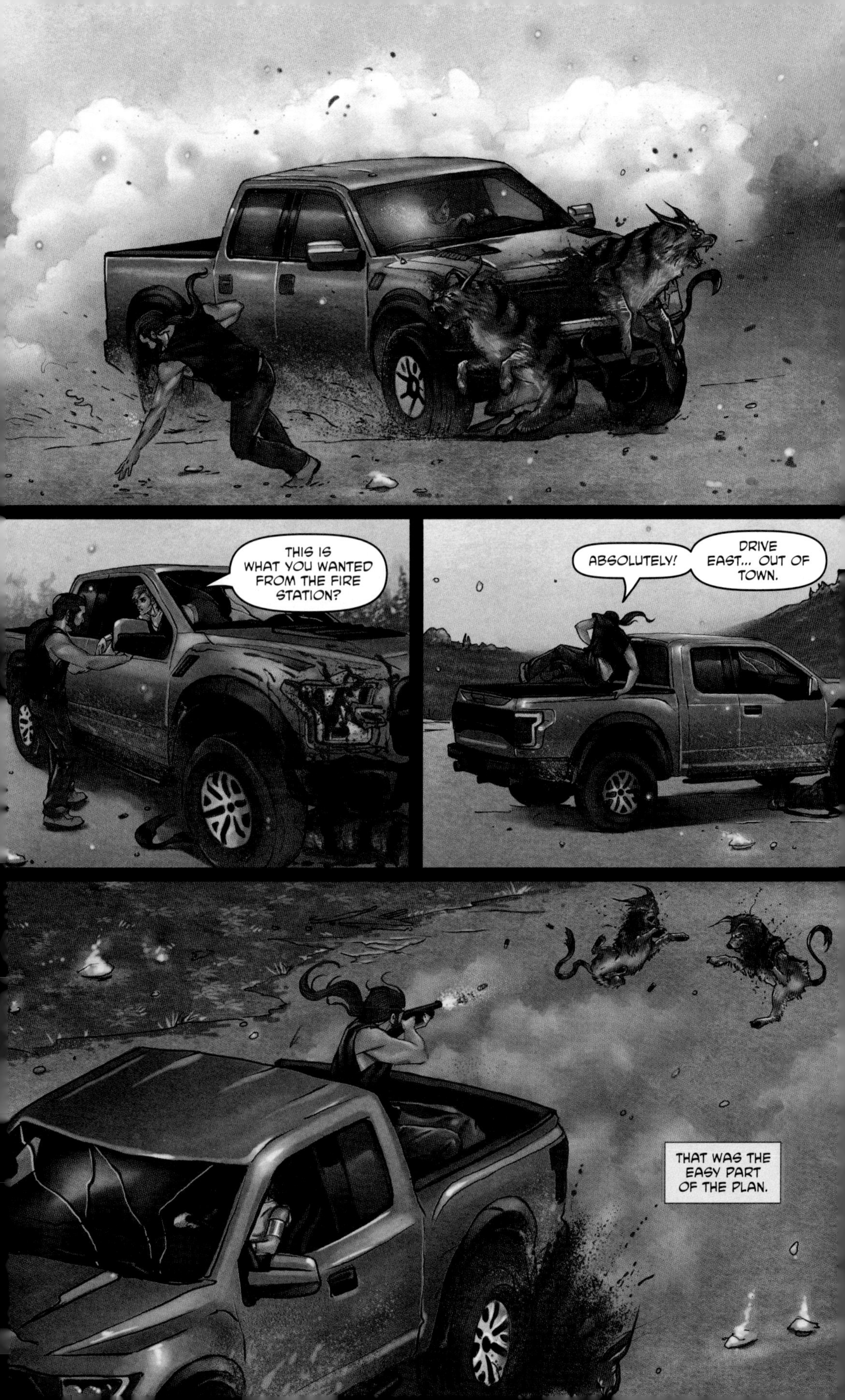
THIS IS WHAT YOU WANTED FROM THE FIRE STATION?
ABSOLUTELY!
DRIVE EAST... OUT OF TOWN.
THAT WAS THE EASY PART OF THE PLAN.

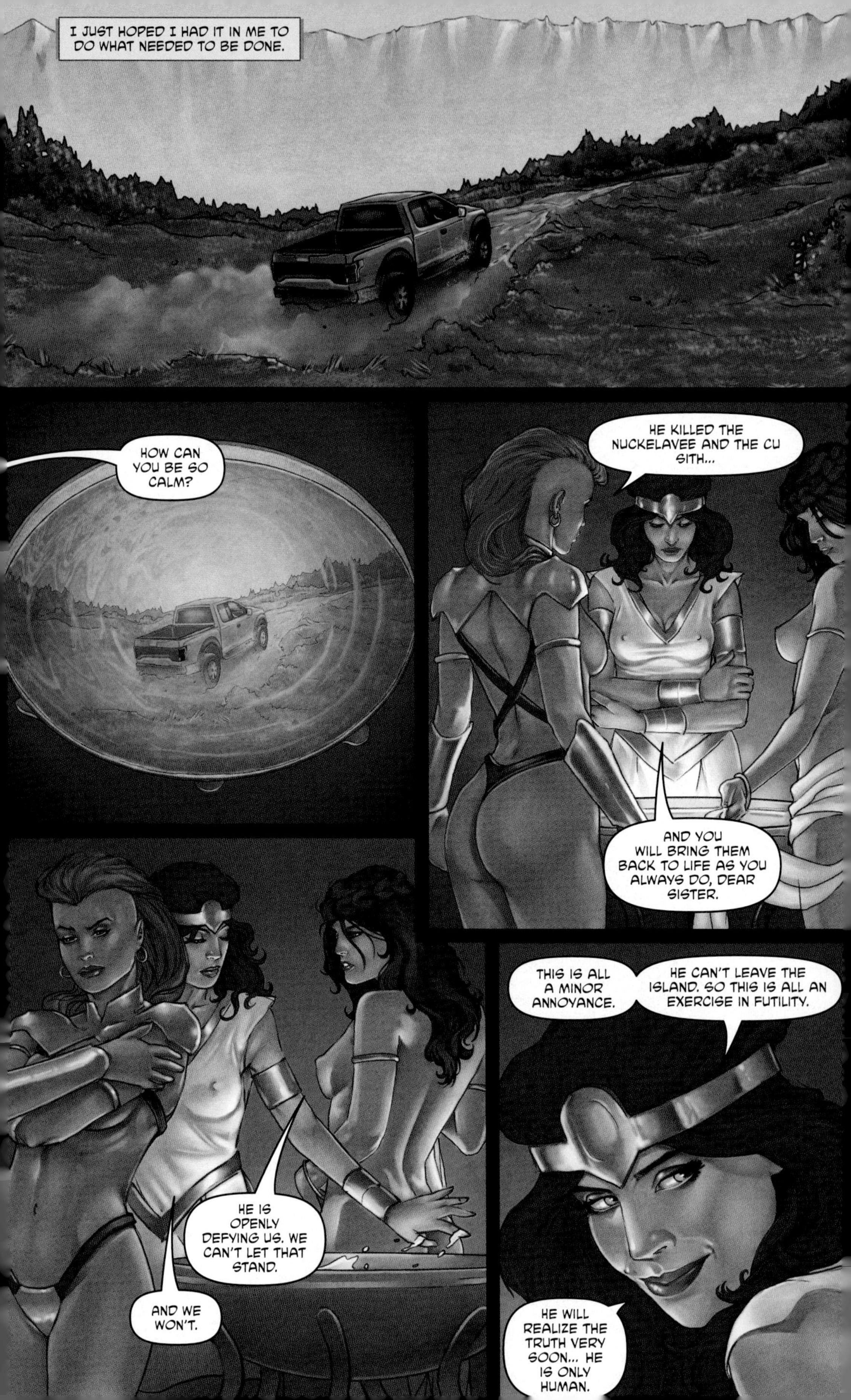
I JUST HOPED I HAD IT IN ME TO DO WHAT NEEDED TO BE DONE.
HOW CAN YOU BE SO CALM?
HE KILLED THE NUCKELAVEE AND THE CU SITH...
AND YOU WILL BRING THEM BACK TO LIFE AS YOU ALWAYS DO, DEAR SISTER.
HE IS OPENLY DEFYING US. WE CAN'T LET THAT STAND.
AND WE WON'T.
THIS IS ALL A MINOR ANNOYANCE.
HE CAN'T LEAVE THE ISLAND. SO THIS IS ALL AN EXERCISE IN FUTILITY.
HE WILL REALIZE THE TRUTH VERY SOON... HE IS ONLY HUMAN.

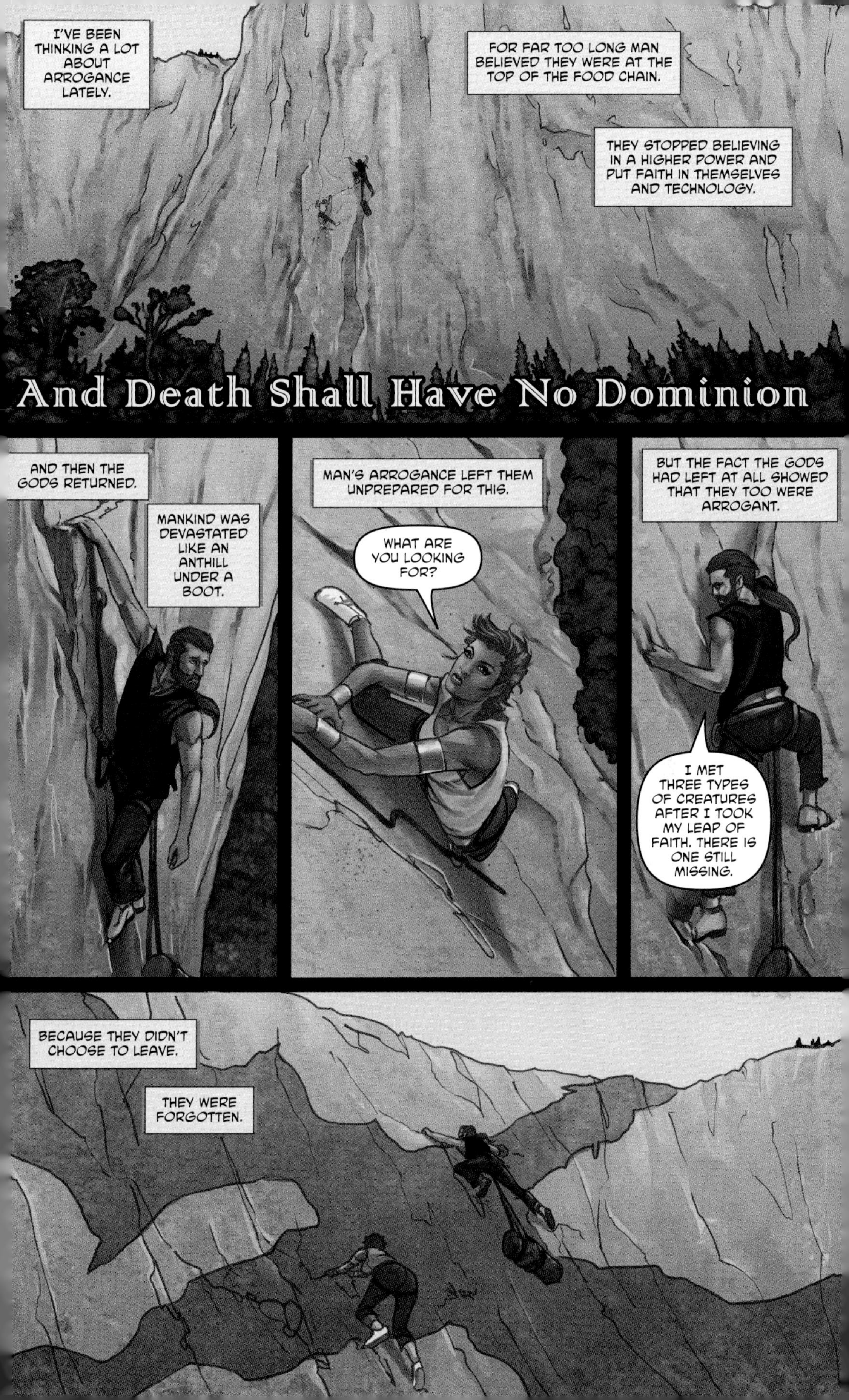
I'VE BEEN THINKING A LOT ABOUT ARROGANCE LATELY.
FOR FAR TOO LONG MAN BELIEVED THEY WERE AT THE TOP OF THE FOOD CHAIN.
THEY STOPPED BELIEVING IN A HIGHER POWER AND PUT FAITH IN THEMSELVES AND TECHNOLOGY.
And Death Shall Have No Dominion
AND THEN THE GODS RETURNED.
MANKIND WAS DEVASTATED LIKE AN ANTHILL UNDER A BOOT.
MAN'S ARROGANCE LEFT THEM UNPREPARED FOR THIS.
WHAT ARE YOU LOOKING FOR?
BUT THE FACT THE GODS HAD LEFT AT ALL SHOWED THAT THEY TOO WERE ARROGANT.
I MET THREE TYPES OF CREATURES AFTER I TOOK MY LEAP OF FAITH. THERE IS ONE STILL MISSING.
BECAUSE THEY DIDN'T CHOOSE TO LEAVE.
THEY WERE FORGOTTEN.

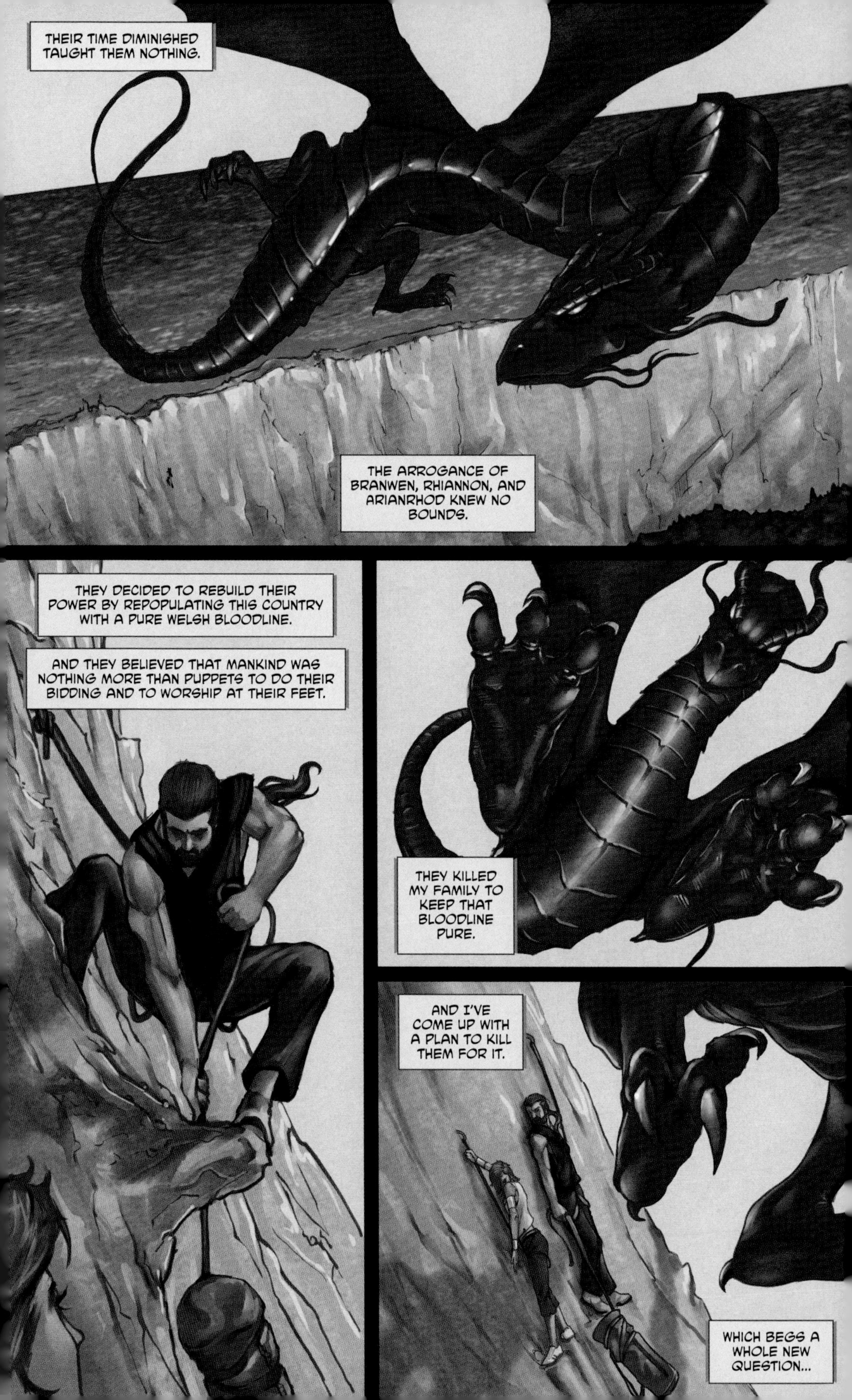
THEIR TIME DIMINISHED TAUGHT THEM NOTHING.
THE ARROGANCE OF BRANWEN, RHIANNON, AND ARIANRHOD KNEW NO BOUNDS.
THEY DECIDED TO REBUILD THEIR POWER BY REPOPULATING THIS COUNTRY WITH A PURE WELSH BLOODLINE.
AND THEY BELIEVED THAT MANKIND WAS NOTHING MORE THAN PUPPETS TO DO THEIR BIDDING AND TO WORSHIP AT THEIR FEET.
THEY KILLED MY FAMILY TO KEEP THAT BLOODLINE PURE.
AND I'VE COME UP WITH A PLAN TO KILL THEM FOR IT.
WHICH BEGS A WHOLE NEW QUESTION...

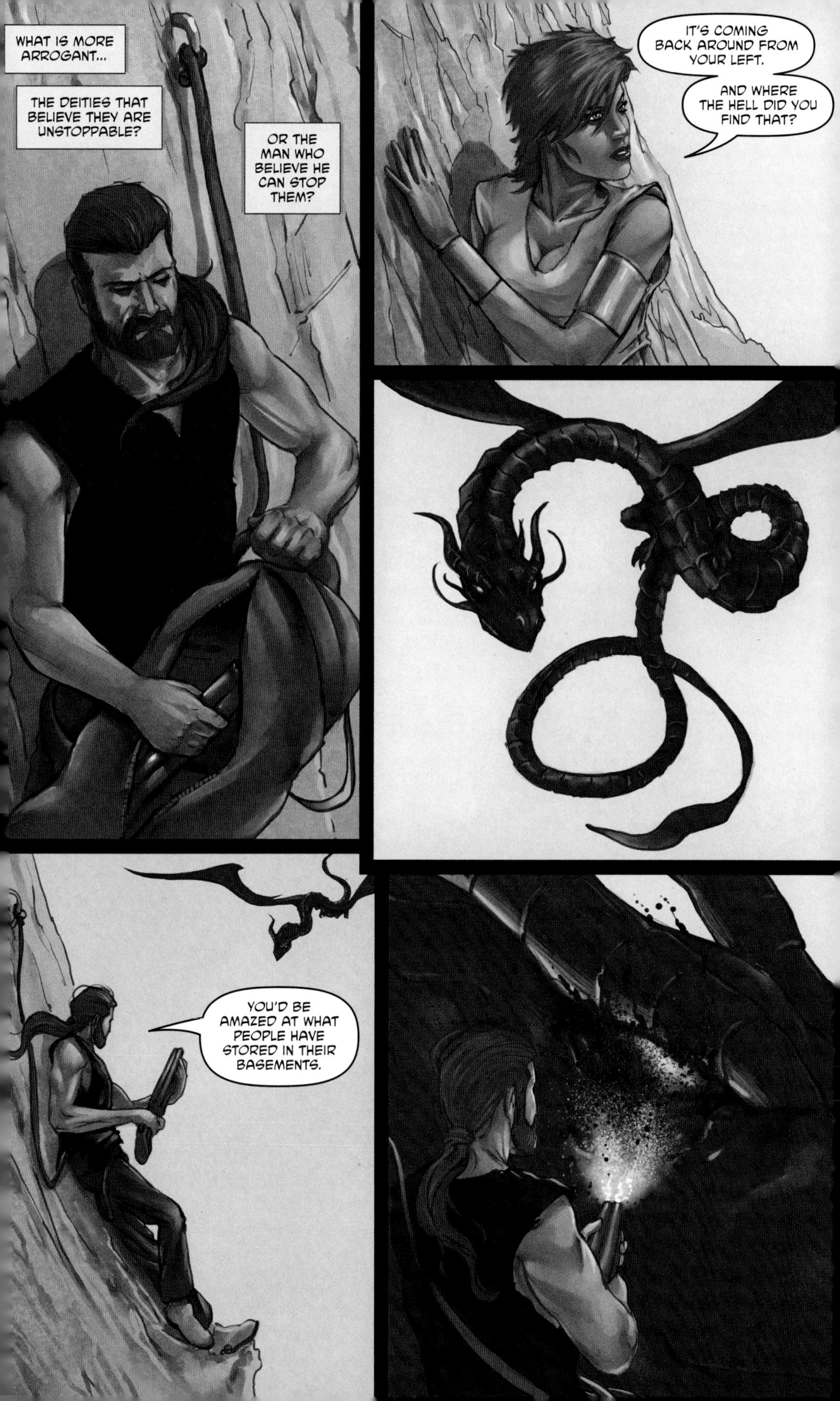
WHAT IS MORE ARROGANT...
THE DEITIES THAT BELIEVE THEY ARE UNSTOPPABLE?
OR THE MAN WHO BELIEVE HE CAN STOP THEM?
IT'S COMING BACK AROUND FROM YOUR LEFT.
AND WHERE THE HELL DID YOU FIND THAT?
YOU'D BE AMAZED AT WHAT PEOPLE HAVE STORED IN THEIR BASEMENTS.

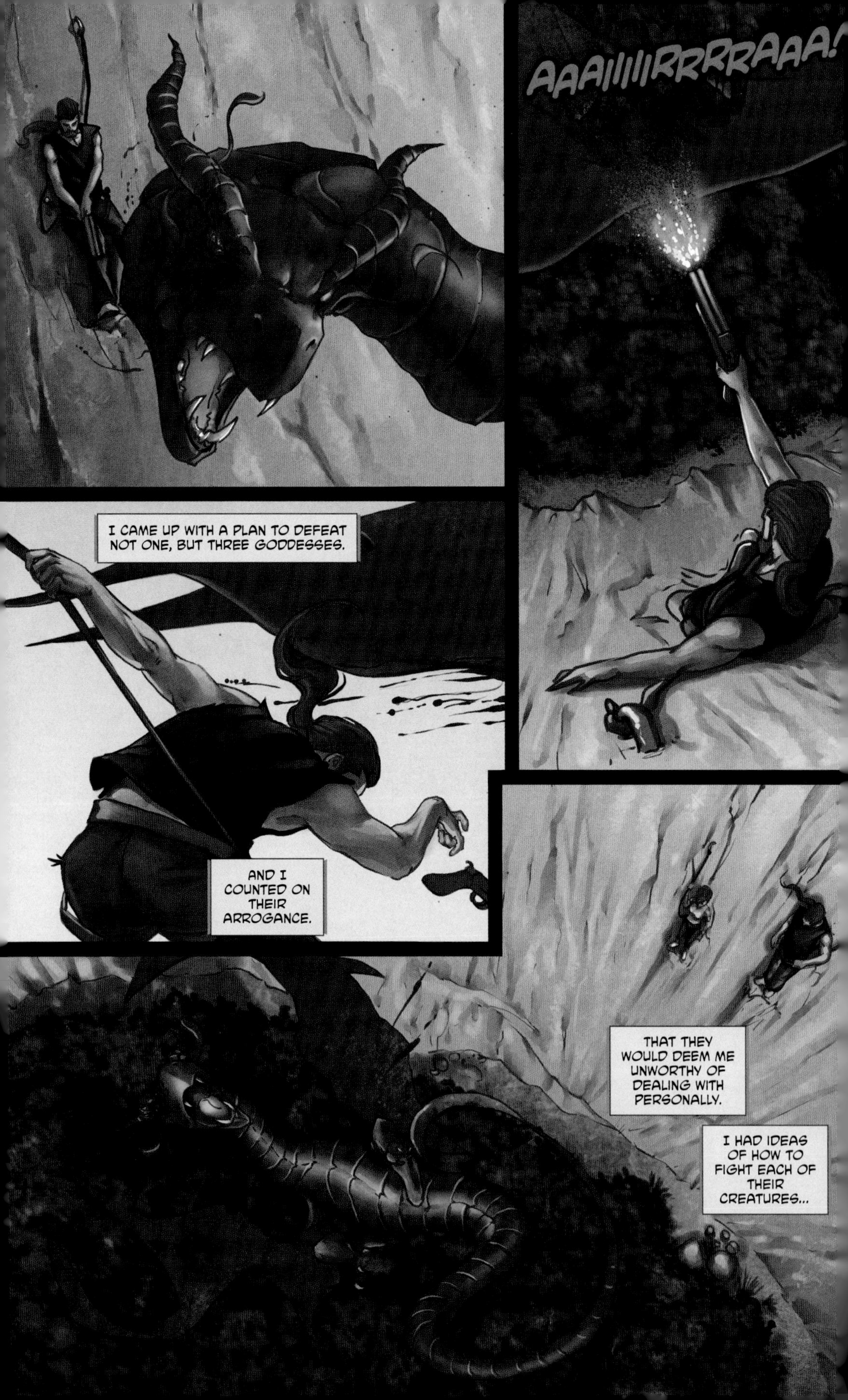
AAAIIIIIIRRRRAAA!
I CAME UP WITH A PLAN TO DEFEAT NOT ONE, BUT THREE GODDESSES.
AND I COUNTED ON THEIR ARROGANCE.
THAT THEY WOULD DEEM ME UNWORTHY OF DEALING WITH PERSONALLY.
I HAD IDEAS OF HOW TO FIGHT EACH OF THEIR CREATURES...

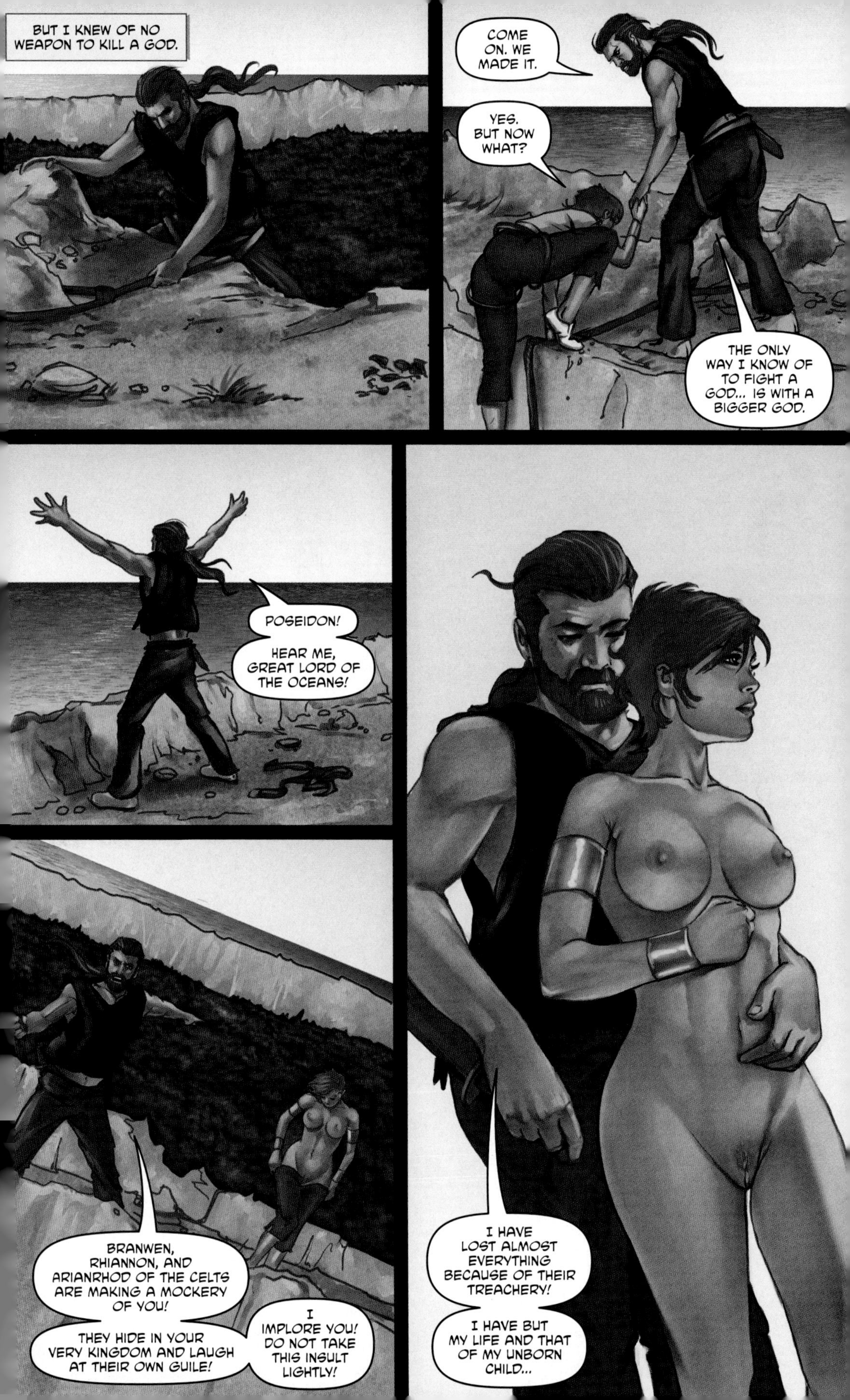

BUT I KNEW OF NO WEAPON TO KILL A GOD.
COME ON. WE MADE IT.
YES. BUT NOW WHAT?
THE ONLY WAY I KNOW OF TO FIGHT A GOD... IS WITH A BIGGER GOD.
POSEIDON!
HEAR ME, GREAT LORD OF THE OCEANS!
BRANWEN, RHIANNON, AND ARIANRHOD OF THE CELTS ARE MAKING A MOCKERY OF YOU!
THEY HIDE IN YOUR VERY KINGDOM AND LAUGH AT THEIR OWN GUILE!
I IMPLORE YOU! DO NOT TAKE THIS INSULT LIGHTLY!
I HAVE LOST ALMOST EVERYTHING BECAUSE OF THEIR TREACHERY!
I HAVE BUT MY LIFE AND THAT OF MY UNBORN CHILD...

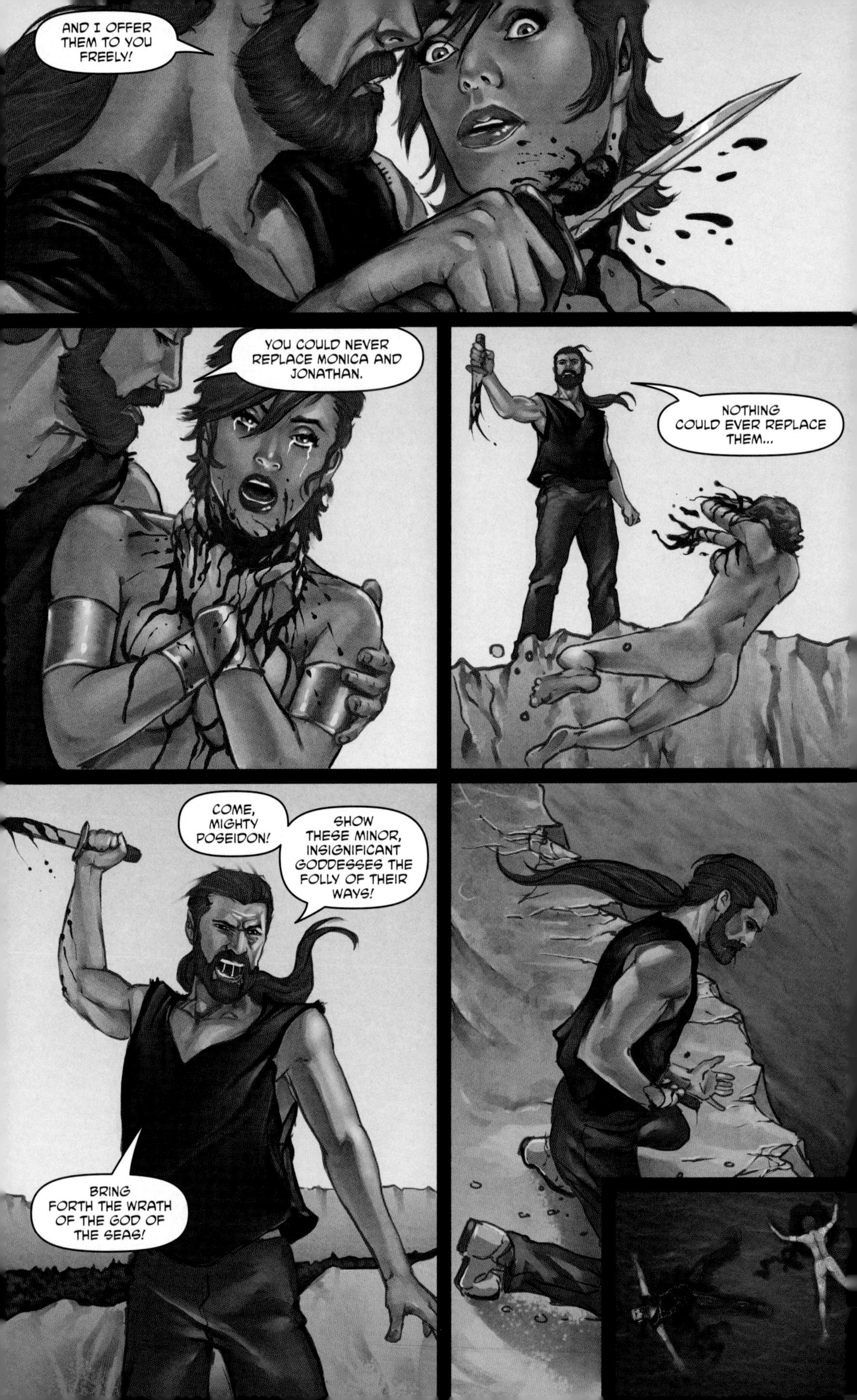
AND I OFFER THEM TO YOU FREELY!
YOU COULD NEVER REPLACE MONICA AND JONATHAN.
NOTHING COULD EVER REPLACE THEM...
COME, MIGHTY POSEIDON!
SHOW THESE MINOR, INSIGNIFICANT GODDESSES THE FOLLY OF THEIR WAYS!
BRING FORTH THE WRATH OF THE GOD OF THE SEAS!

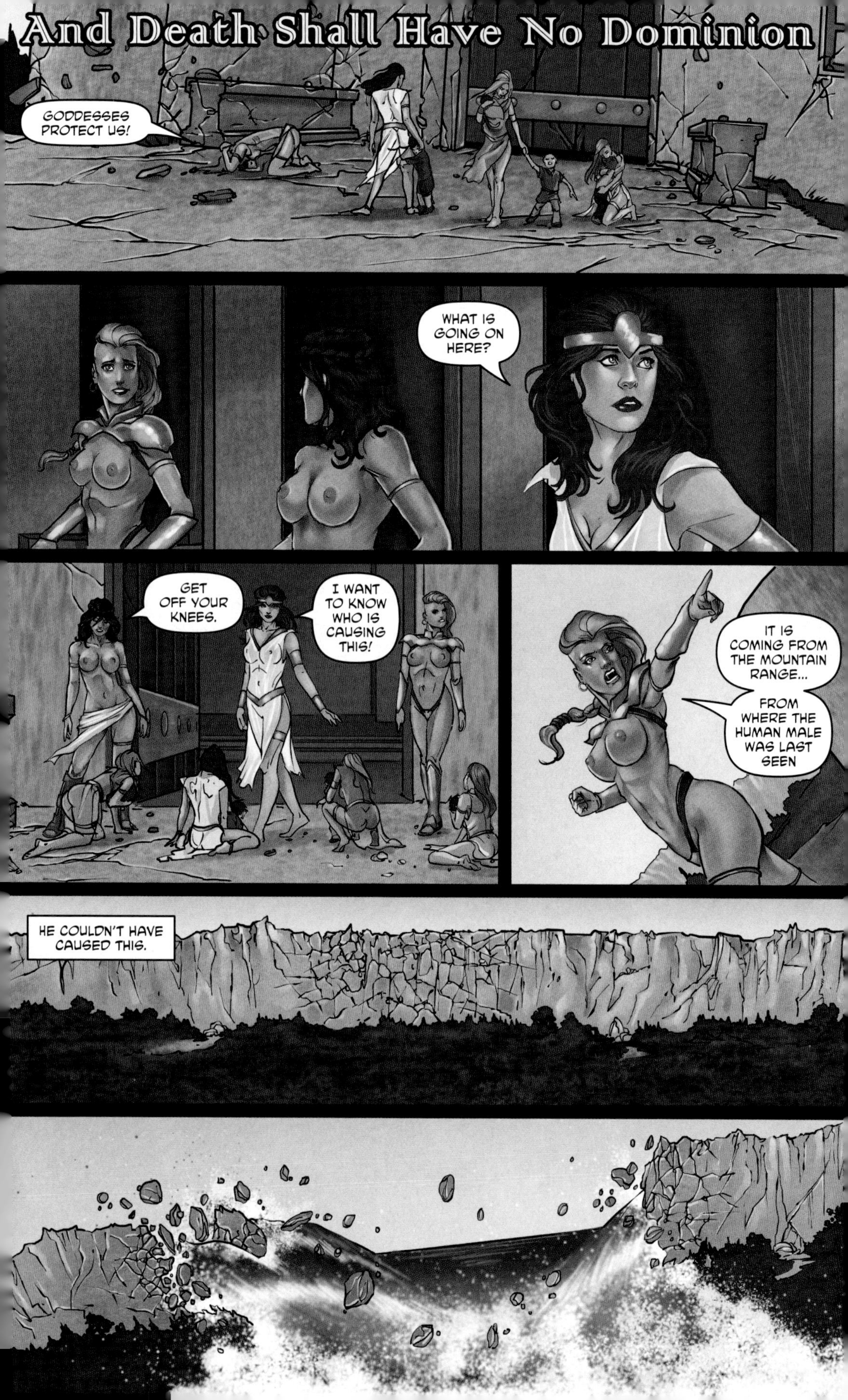
And Death Shall Have No Dominion
GODDESSES PROTECT US!
WHAT IS GOING ON HERE?
GET OFF YOUR KNEES.
I WANT TO KNOW WHO IS CAUSING THIS!
IT IS COMING FROM THE MOUNTAIN RANGE...
FROM WHERE THE HUMAN MALE WAS LAST SEEN
HE COULDN'T HAVE CAUSED THIS.

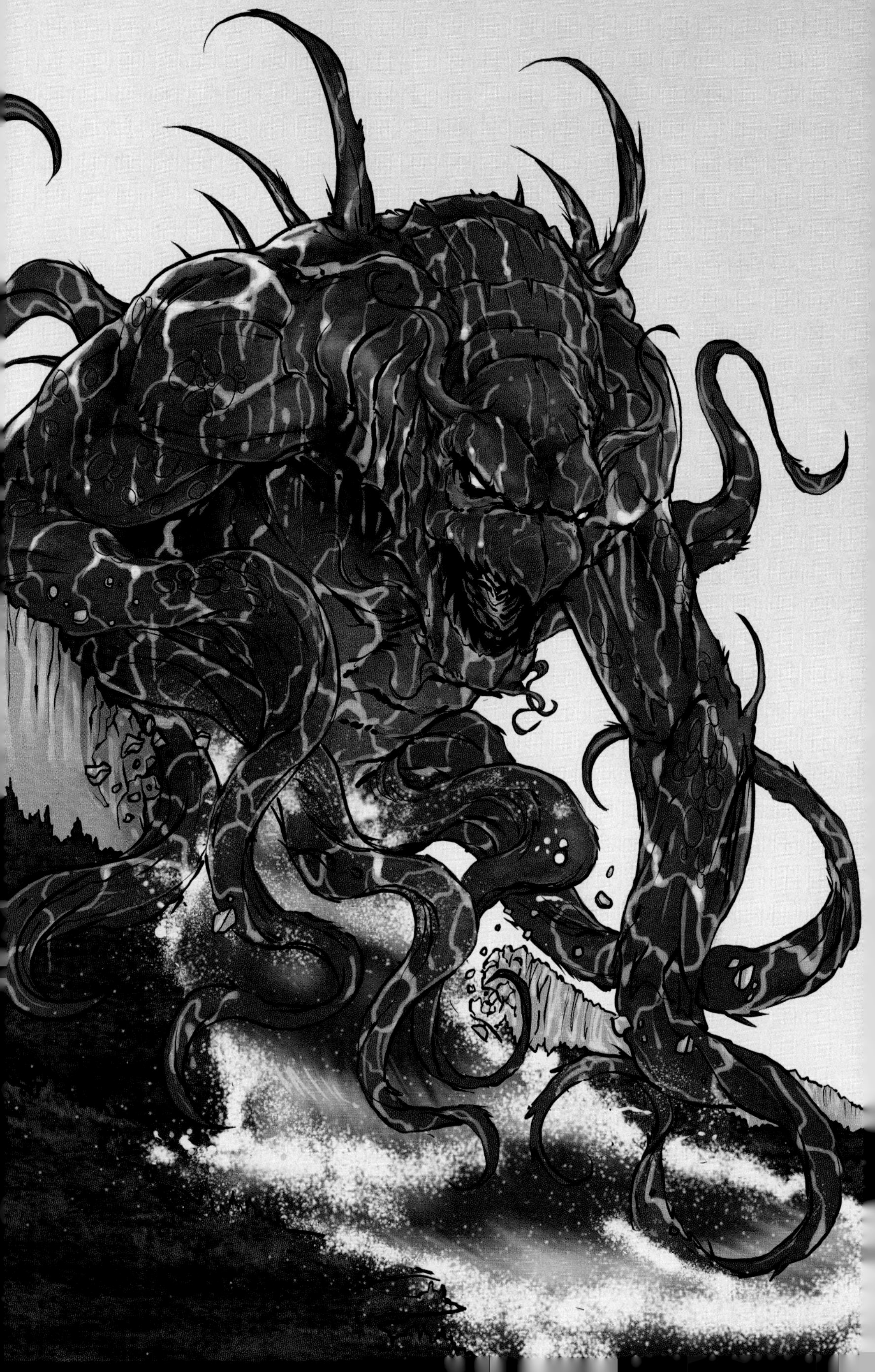

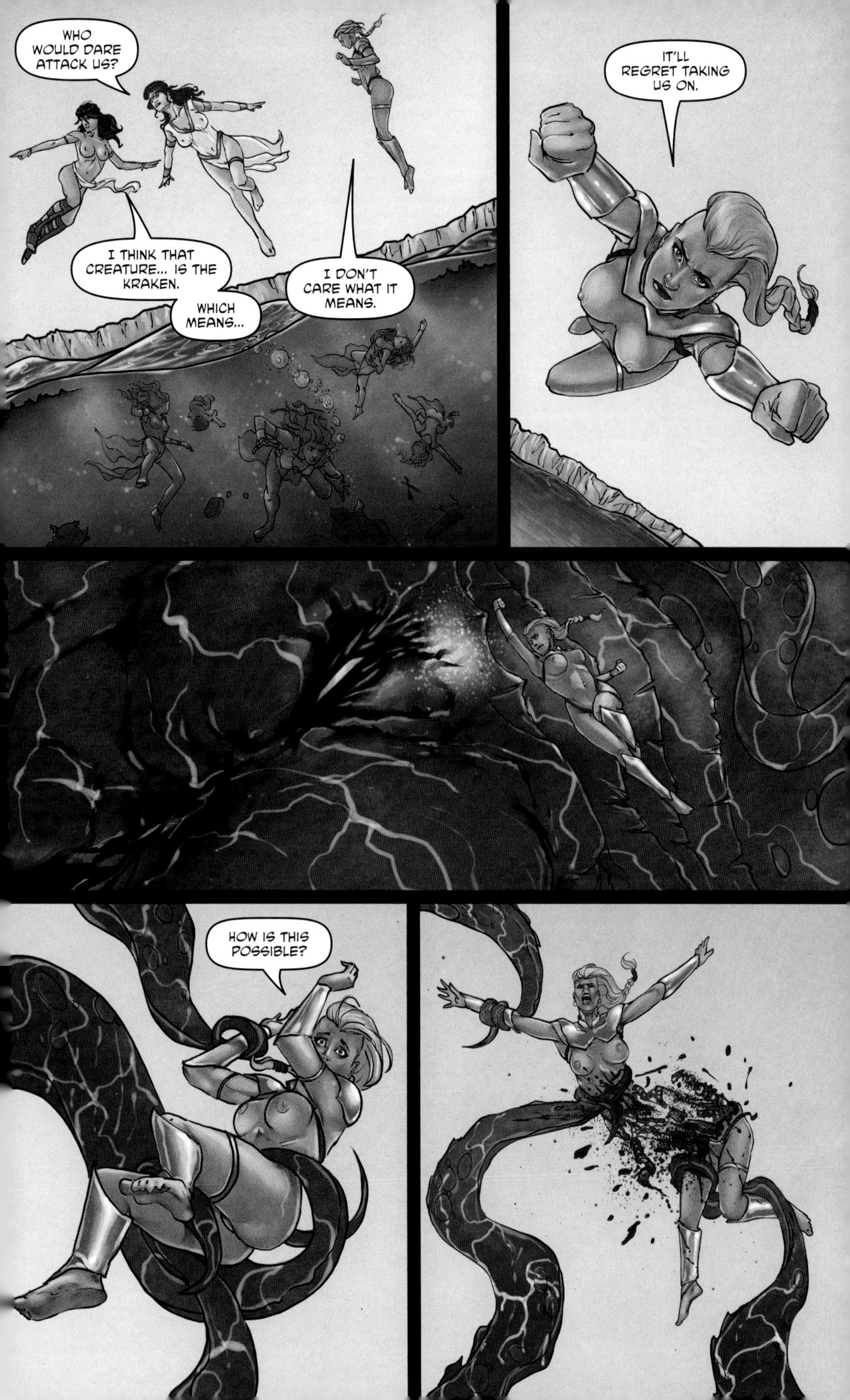
WHO WOULD DARE ATTACK US?
I THINK THAT CREATURE... IS THE KRAKEN.
WHICH MEANS...
I DON'T CARE WHAT IT MEANS.
IT'LL REGRET TAKING US ON.
HOW IS THIS POSSIBLE?

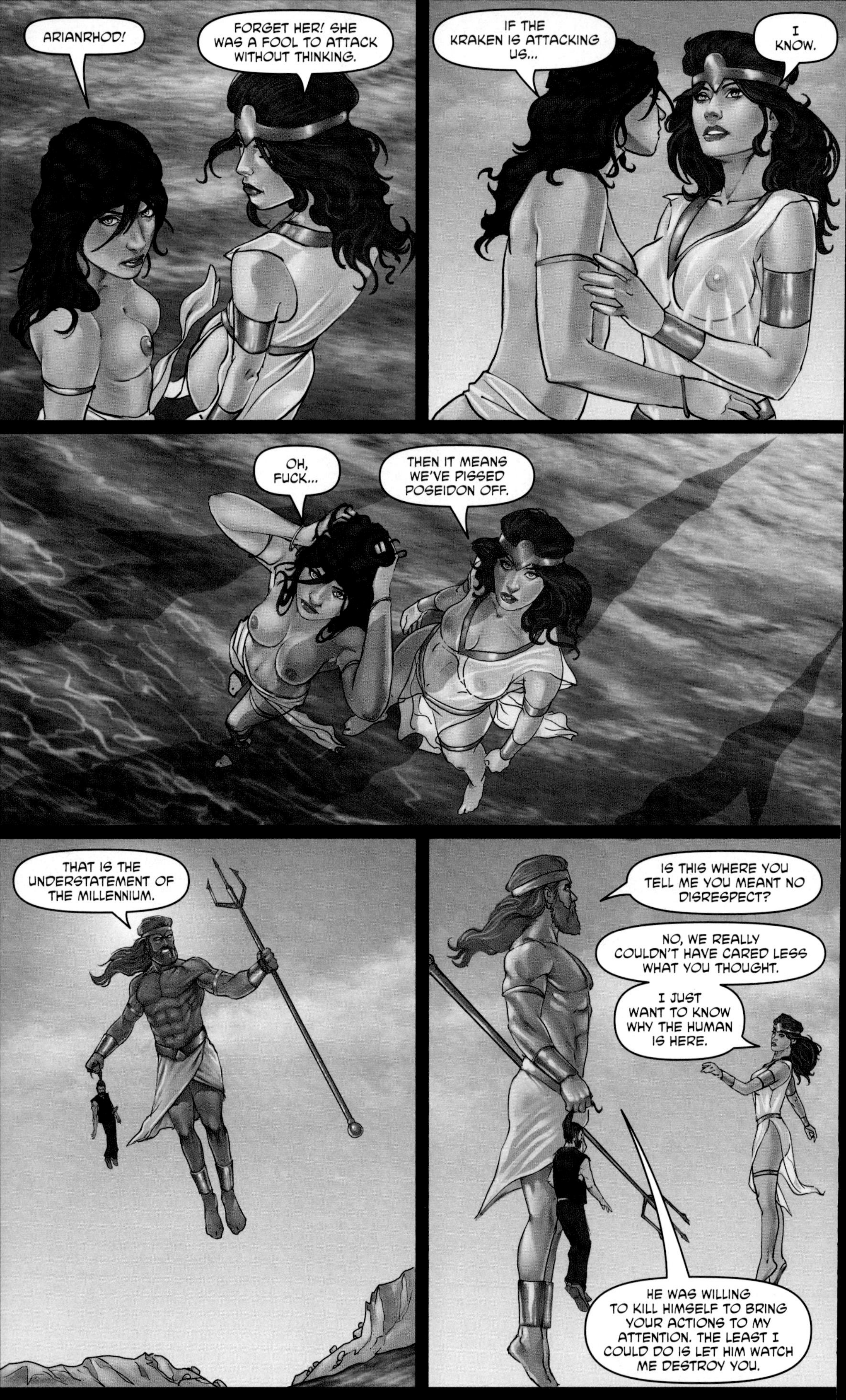
ARIANRHOD!
FORGET HER! SHE WAS A FOOL TO ATTACK WITHOUT THINKING.
IF THE KRAKEN IS ATTACKING US...
I KNOW.
OH, FUCK...
THEN IT MEANS WE'VE PISSED POSEIDON OFF.
THAT IS THE UNDERSTATEMENT OF THE MILLENNIUM.
IS THIS WHERE YOU TELL ME YOU MEANT NO DISRESPECT?
NO, WE REALLY COULDN'T HAVE CARED LESS WHAT YOU THOUGHT.
I JUST WANT TO KNOW WHY THE HUMAN IS HERE.
HE WAS WILLING TO KILL HIMSELF TO BRING YOUR ACTIONS TO MY ATTENTION. THE LEAST I COULD DO IS LET HIM WATCH ME DESTROY YOU.

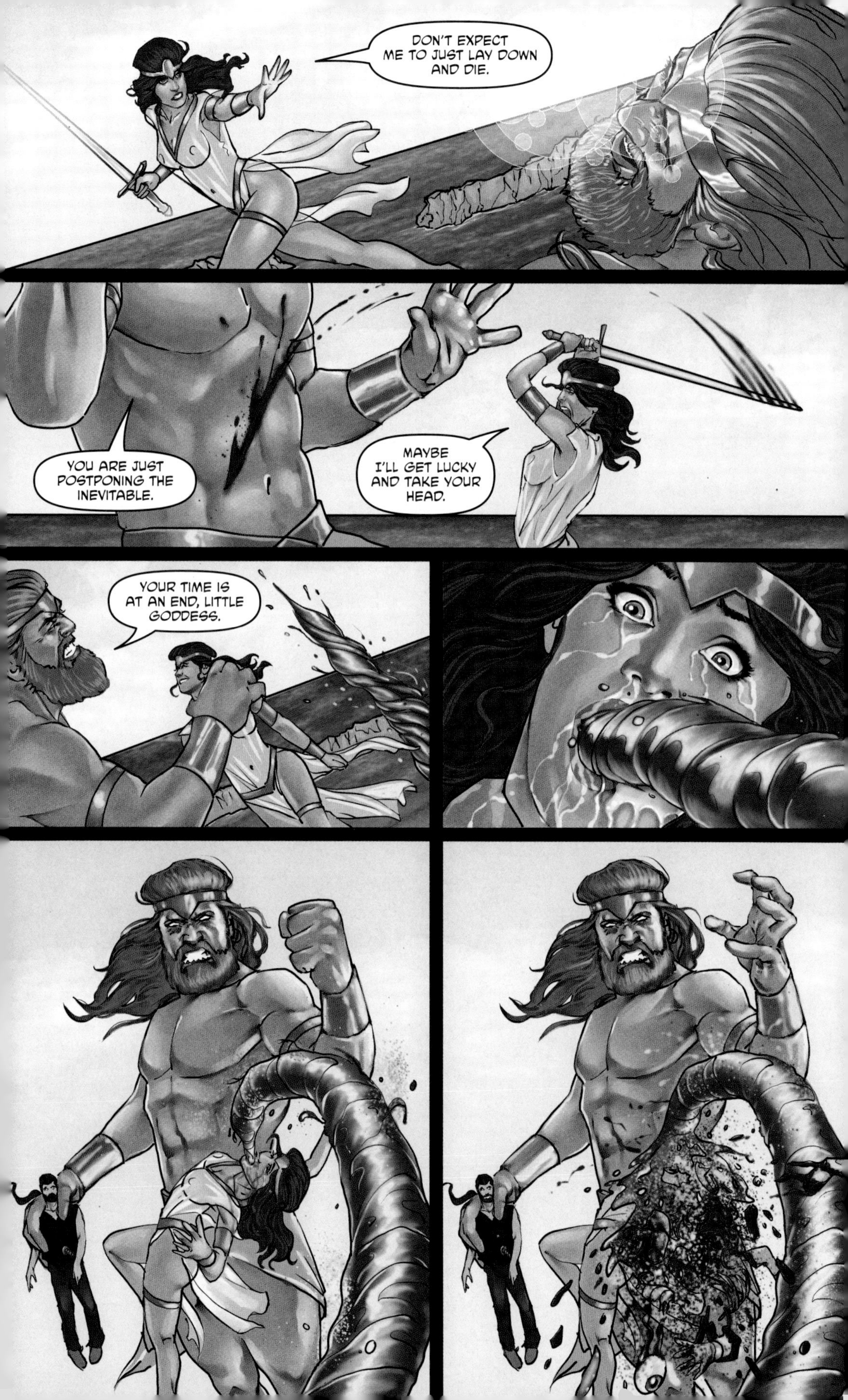
DON'T EXPECT ME TO JUST LAY DOWN AND DIE.
YOU ARE JUST POSTPONING THE INEVITABLE.
MAYBE I'LL GET LUCKY AND TAKE YOUR HEAD.
YOUR TIME IS AT AN END, LITTLE GODDESS.

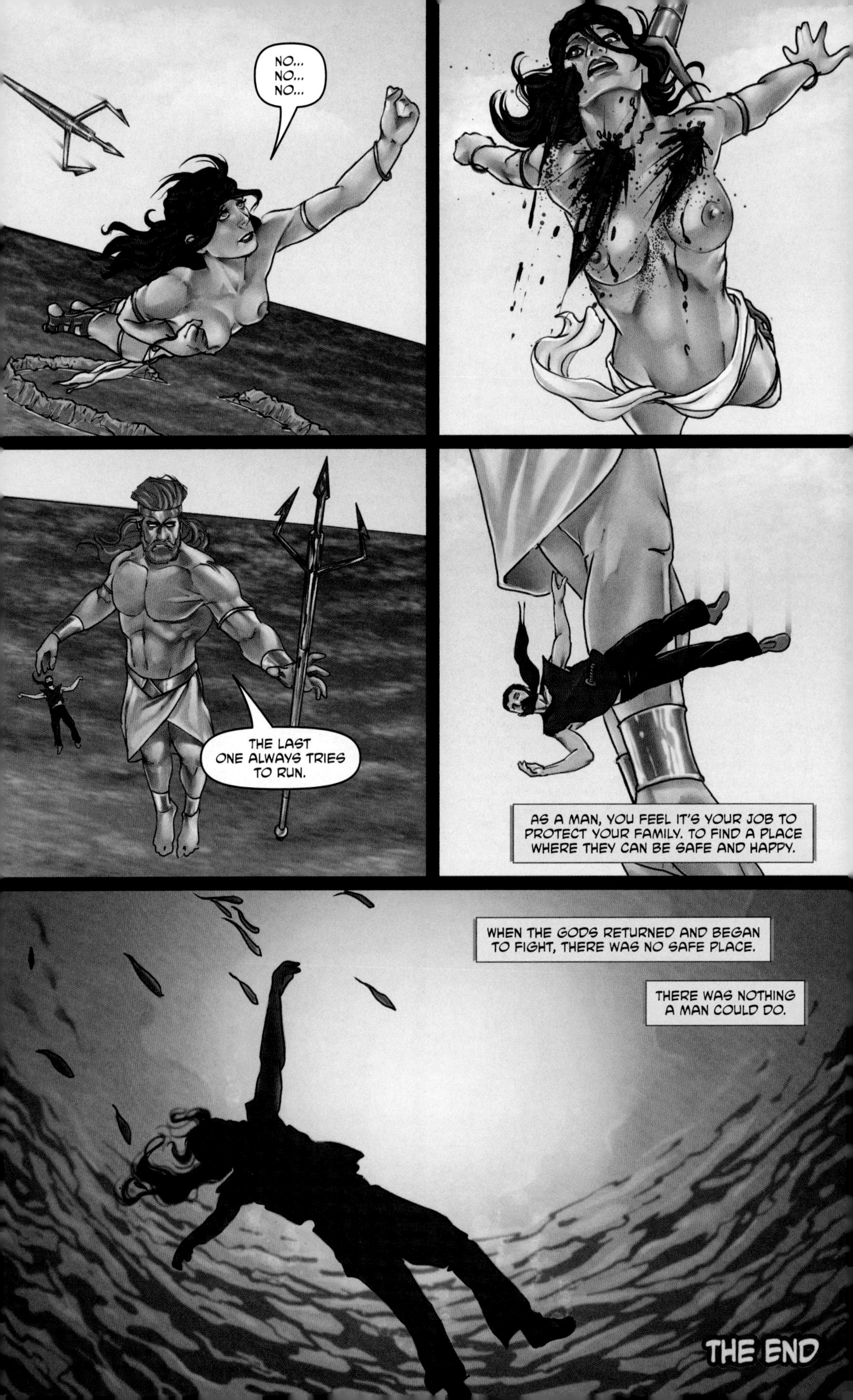
NO... NO... NO...
THE LAST ONE ALWAYS TRIES TO RUN.
AS A MAN, YOU FEEL IT'S YOUR JOB TO PROTECT YOUR FAMILY. TO FIND A PLACE WHERE THEY CAN BE SAFE AND HAPPY.
WHEN THE GODS RETURNED AND BEGAN TO FIGHT, THERE WAS NO SAFE PLACE.
THERE WAS NOTHING A MAN COULD DO.
THE END

GALLERY

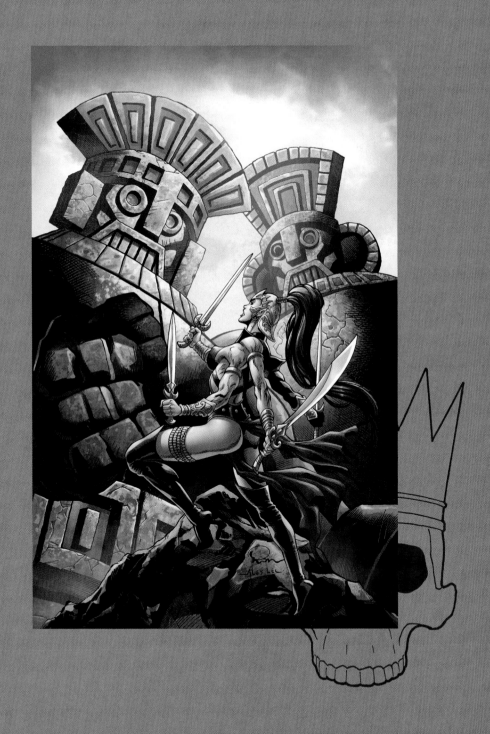

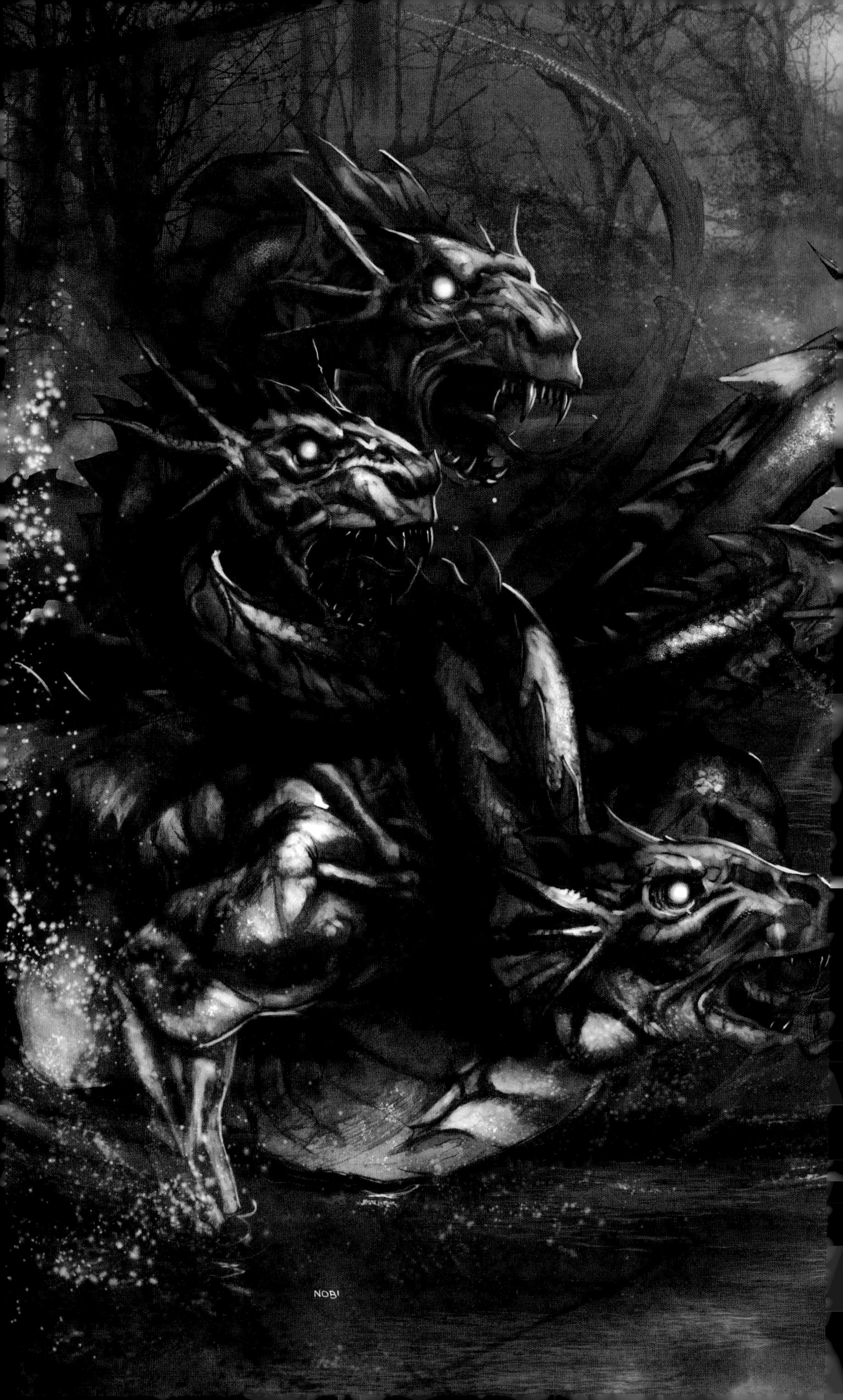
NOBI

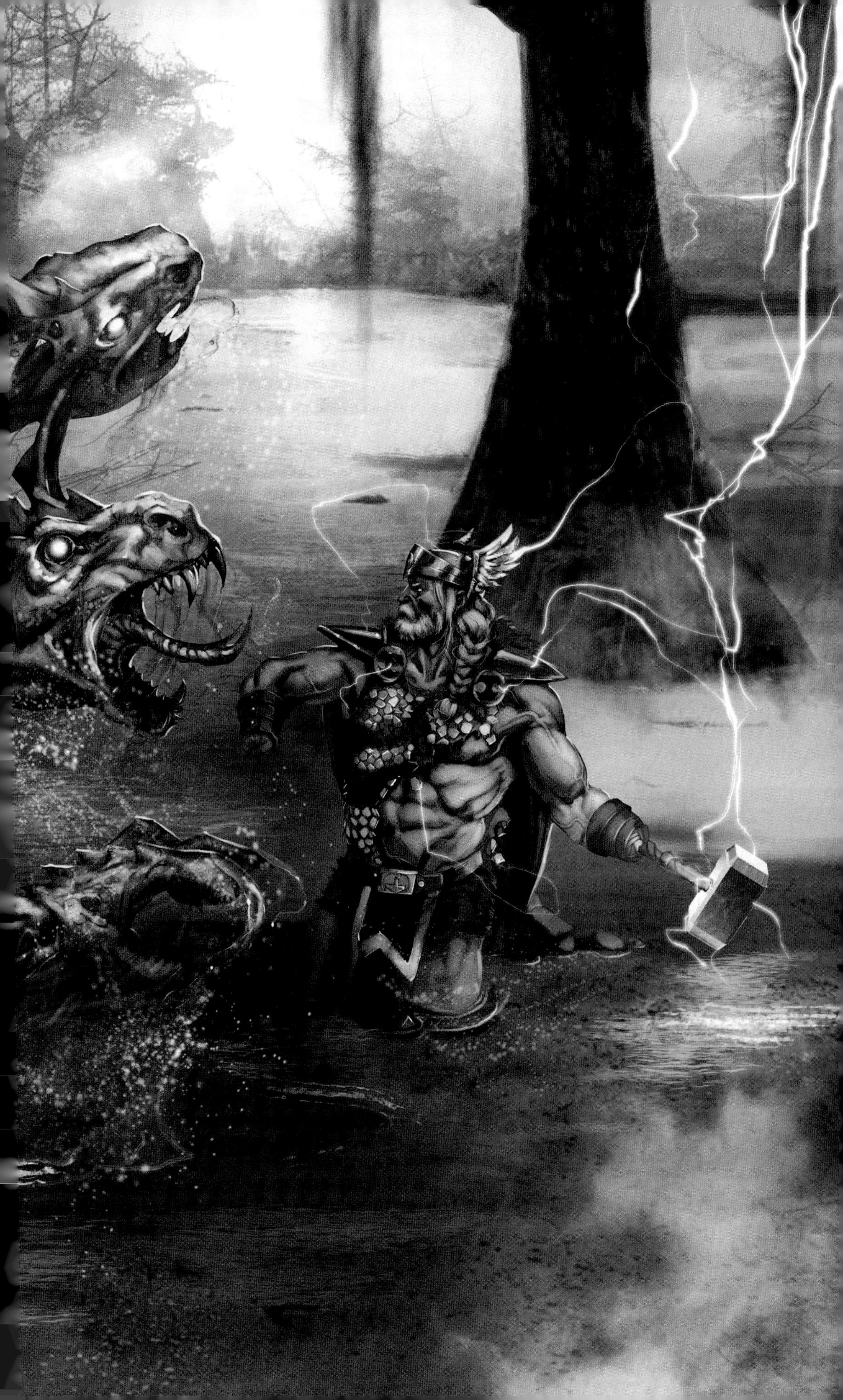

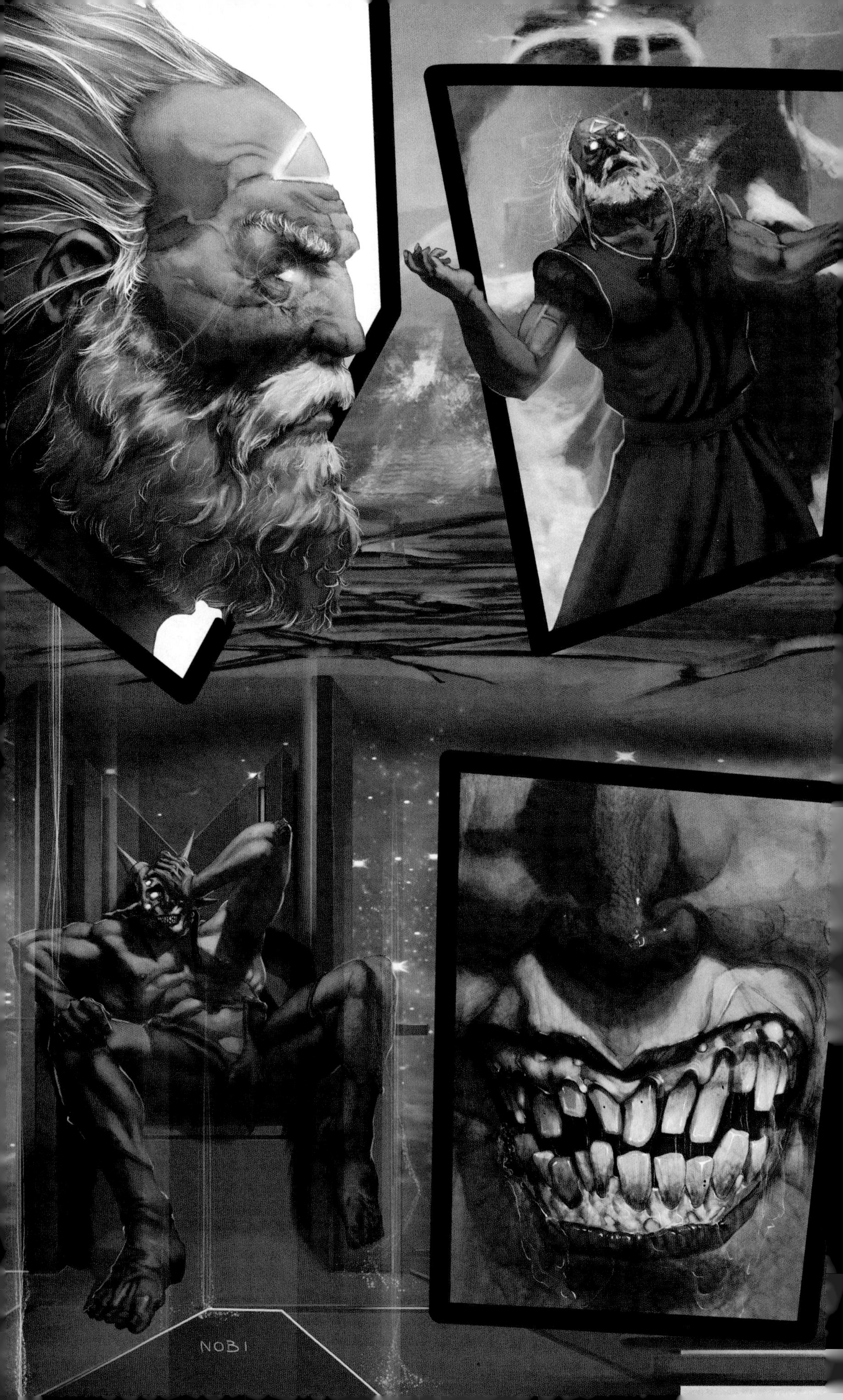
NOBI

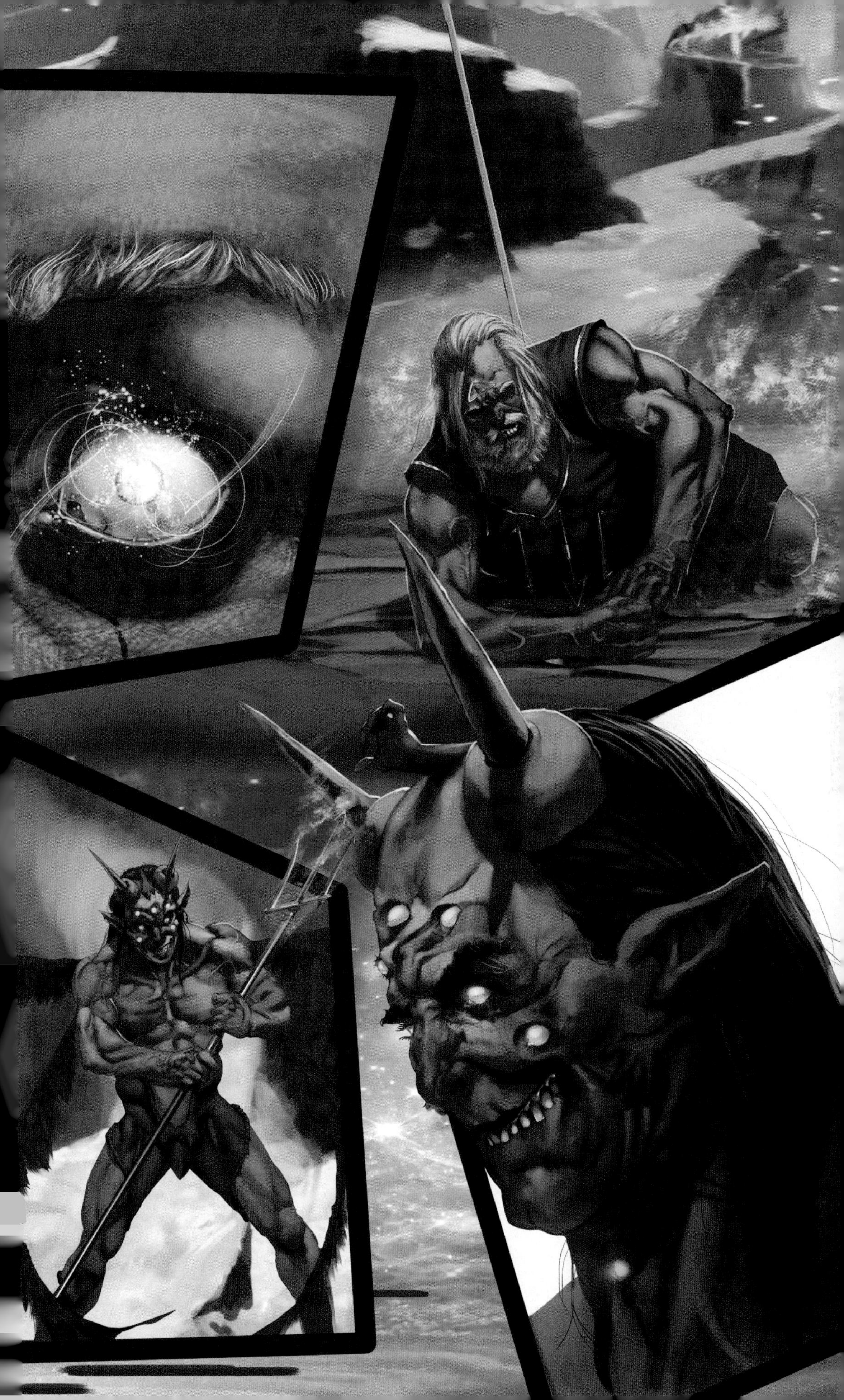

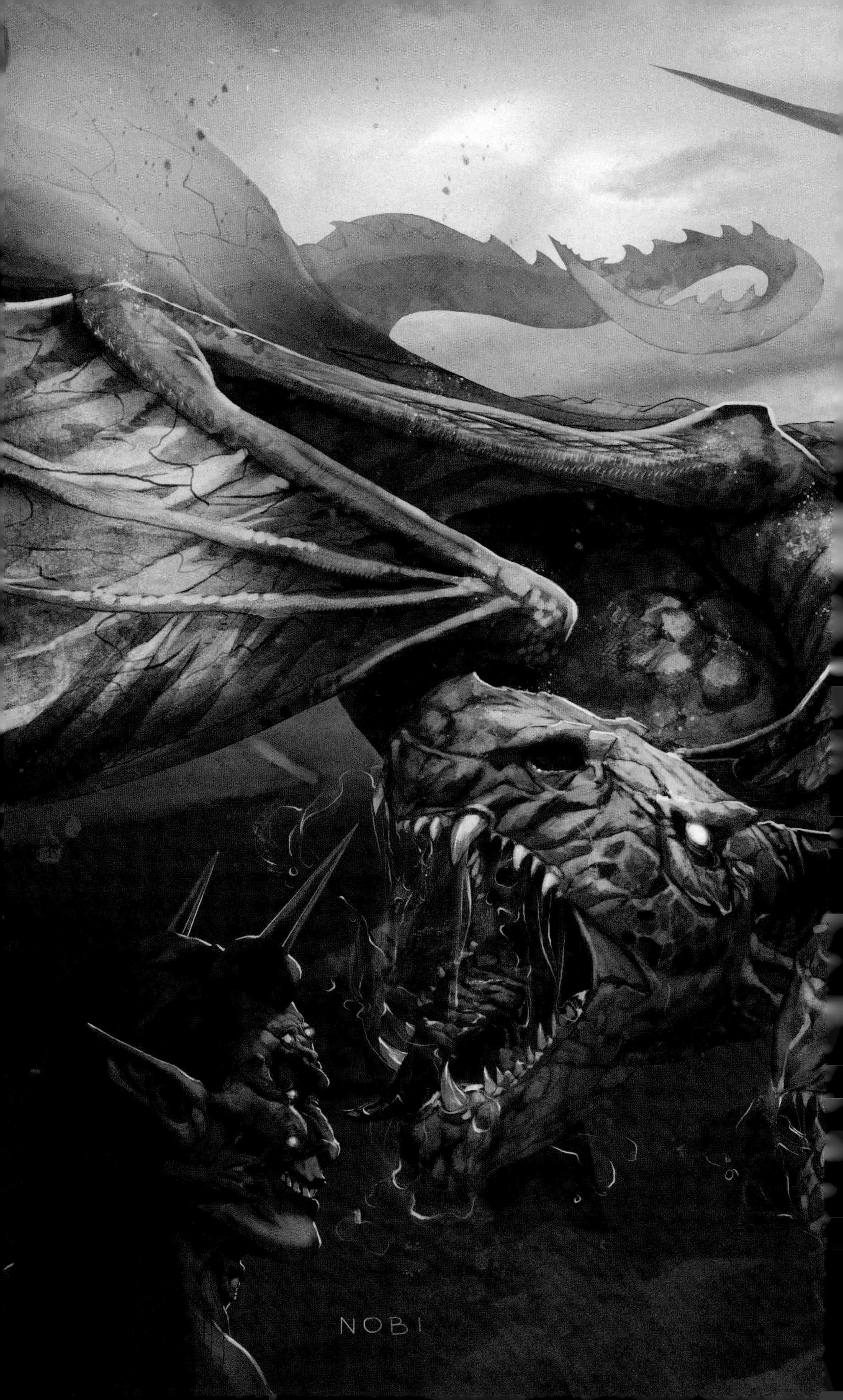
NOBI

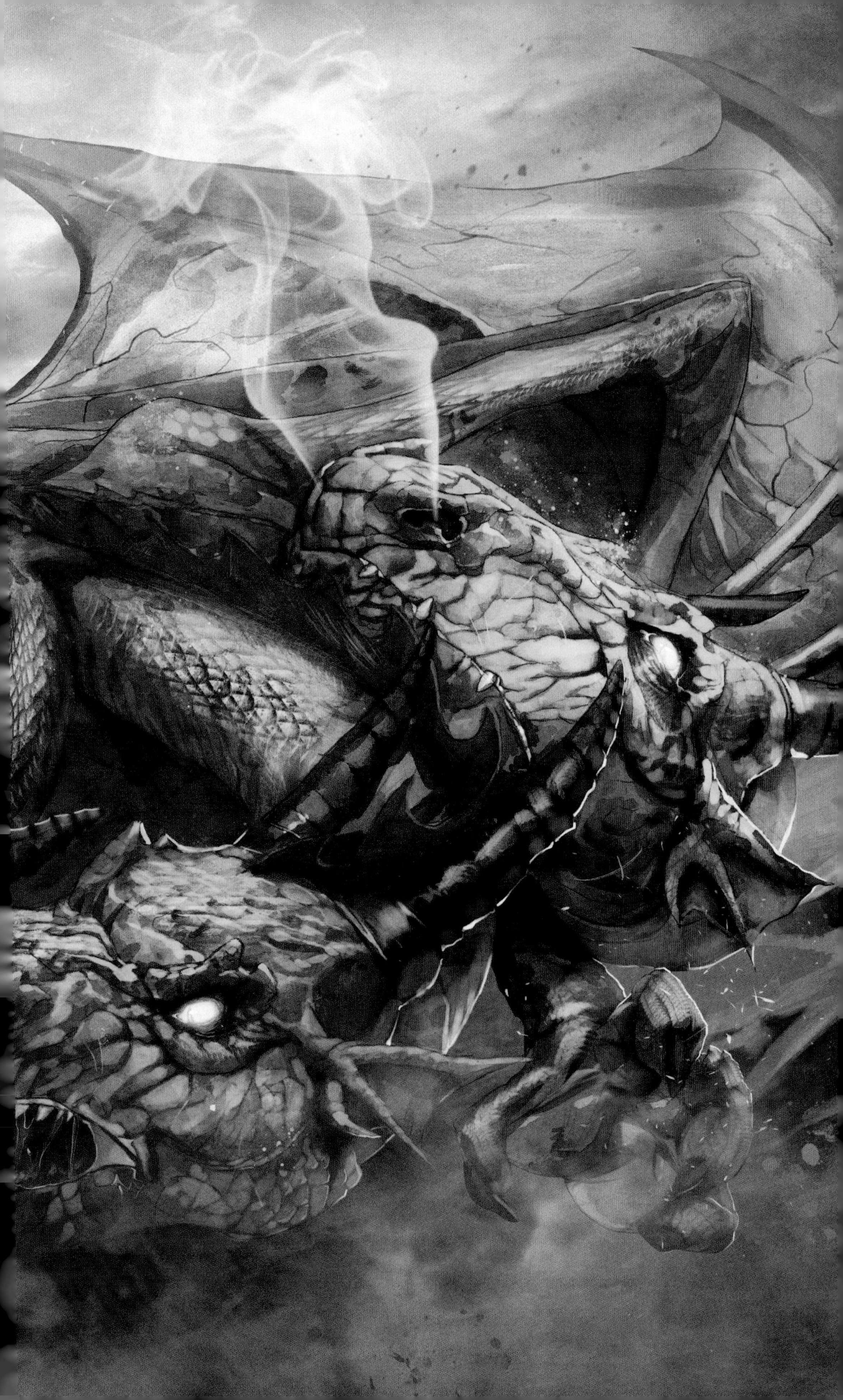

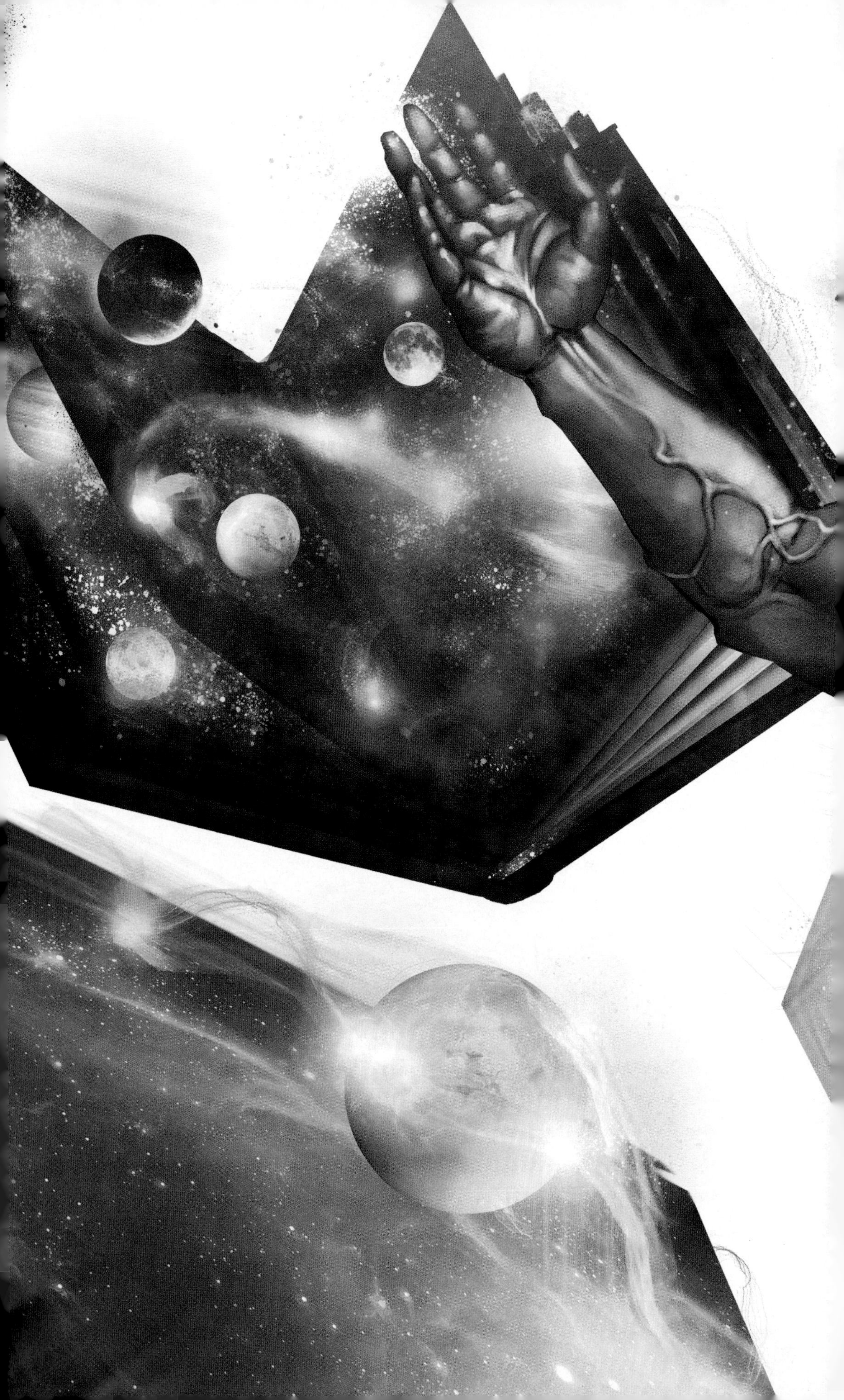

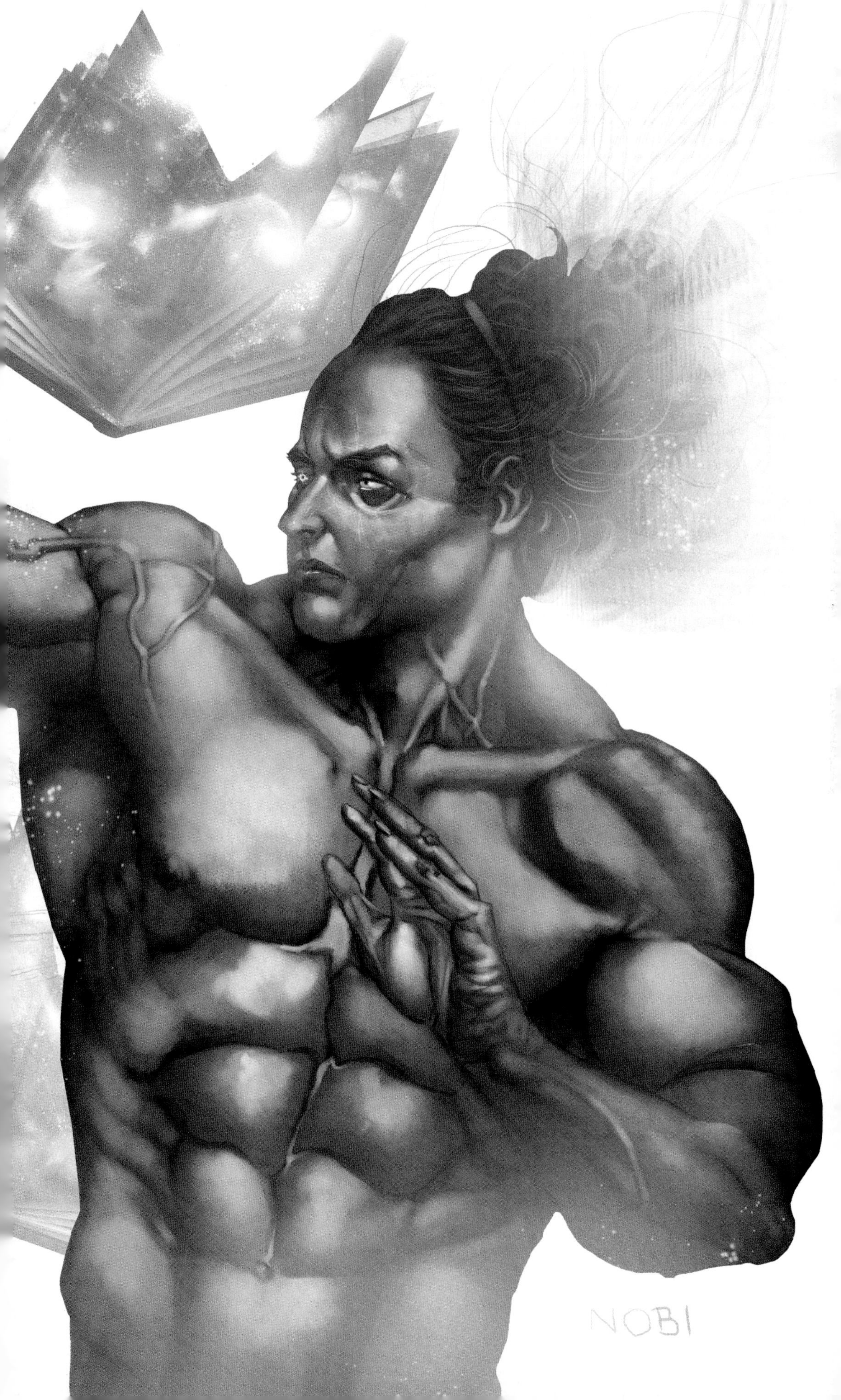
NOBI

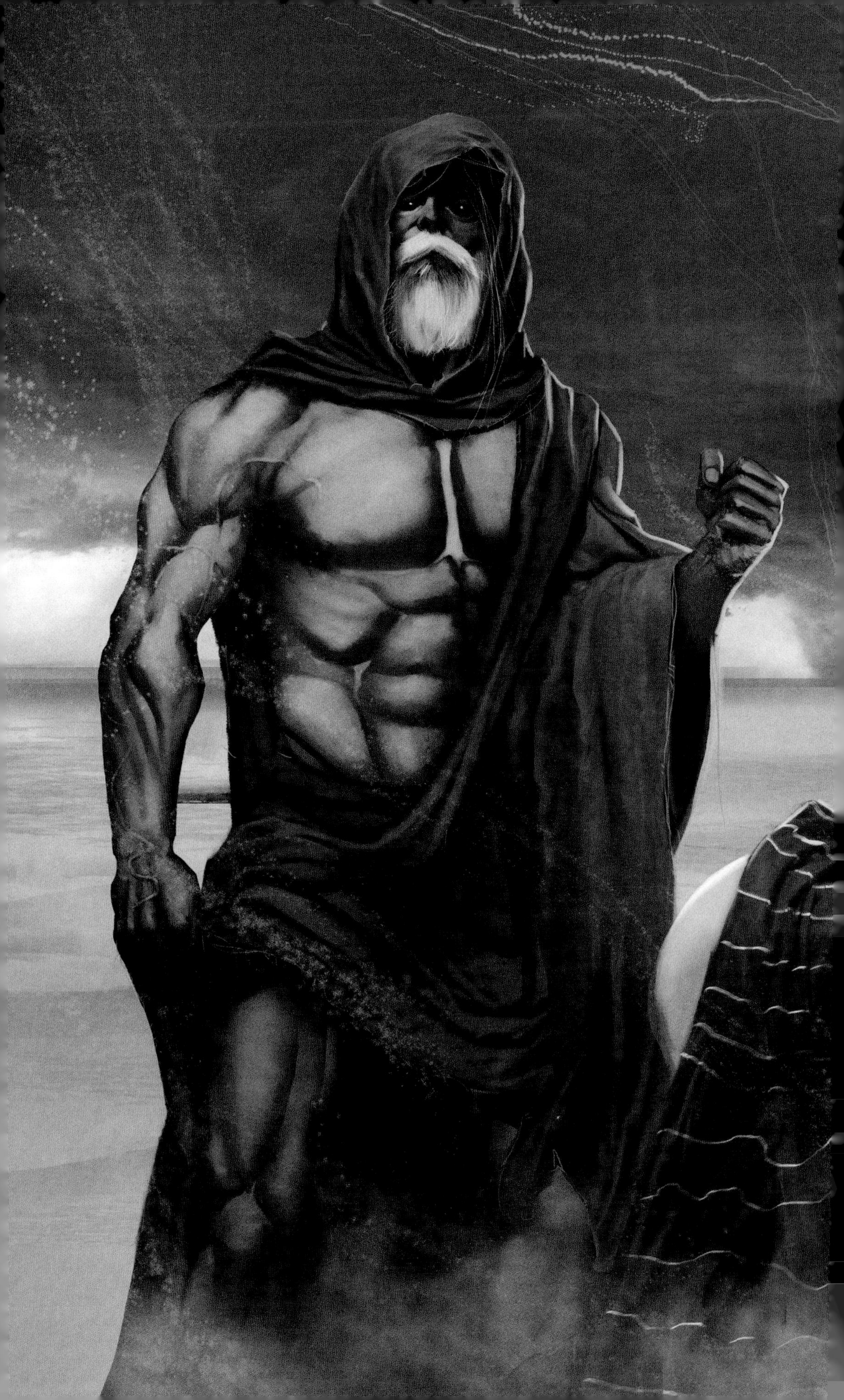

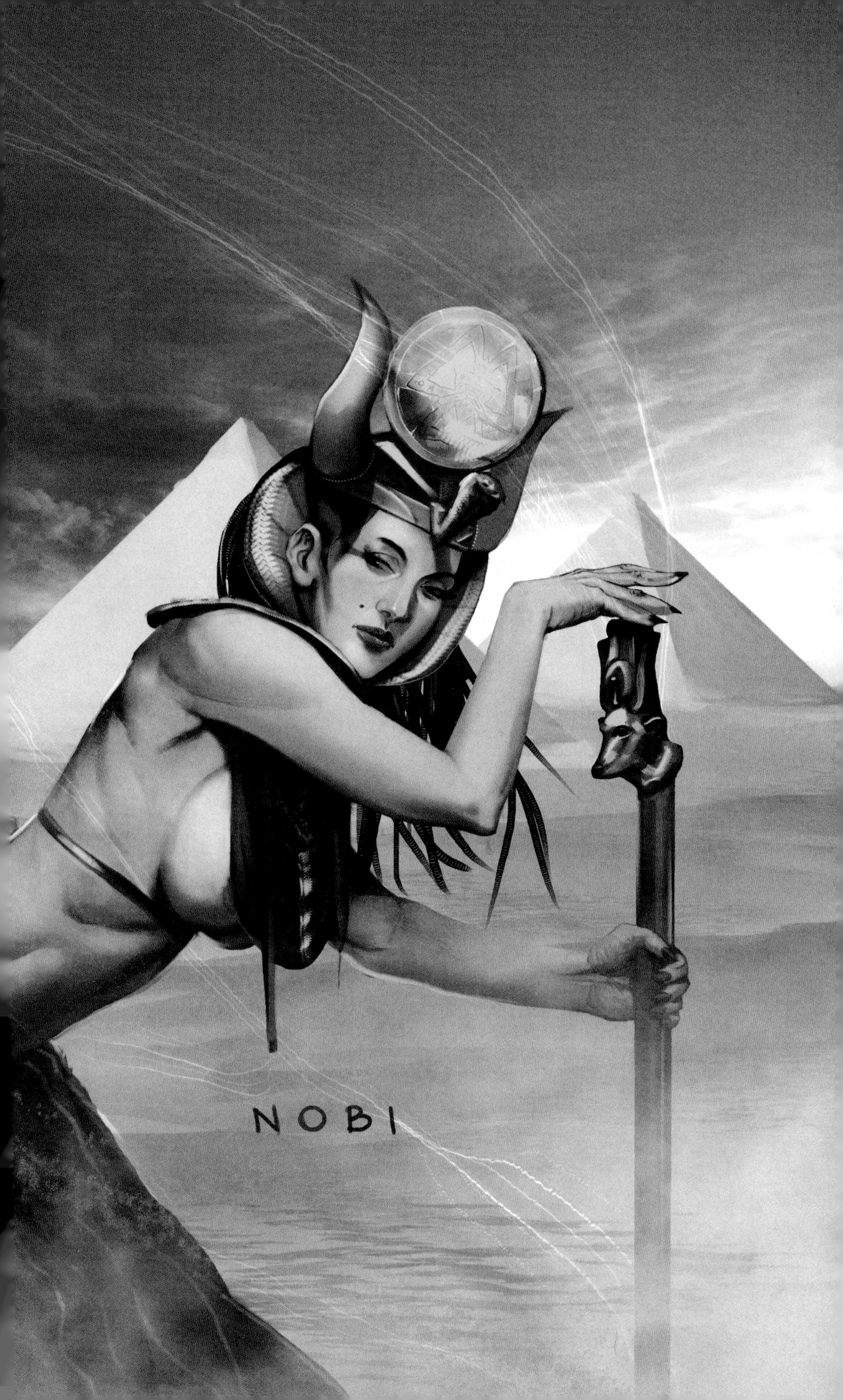
NOBI

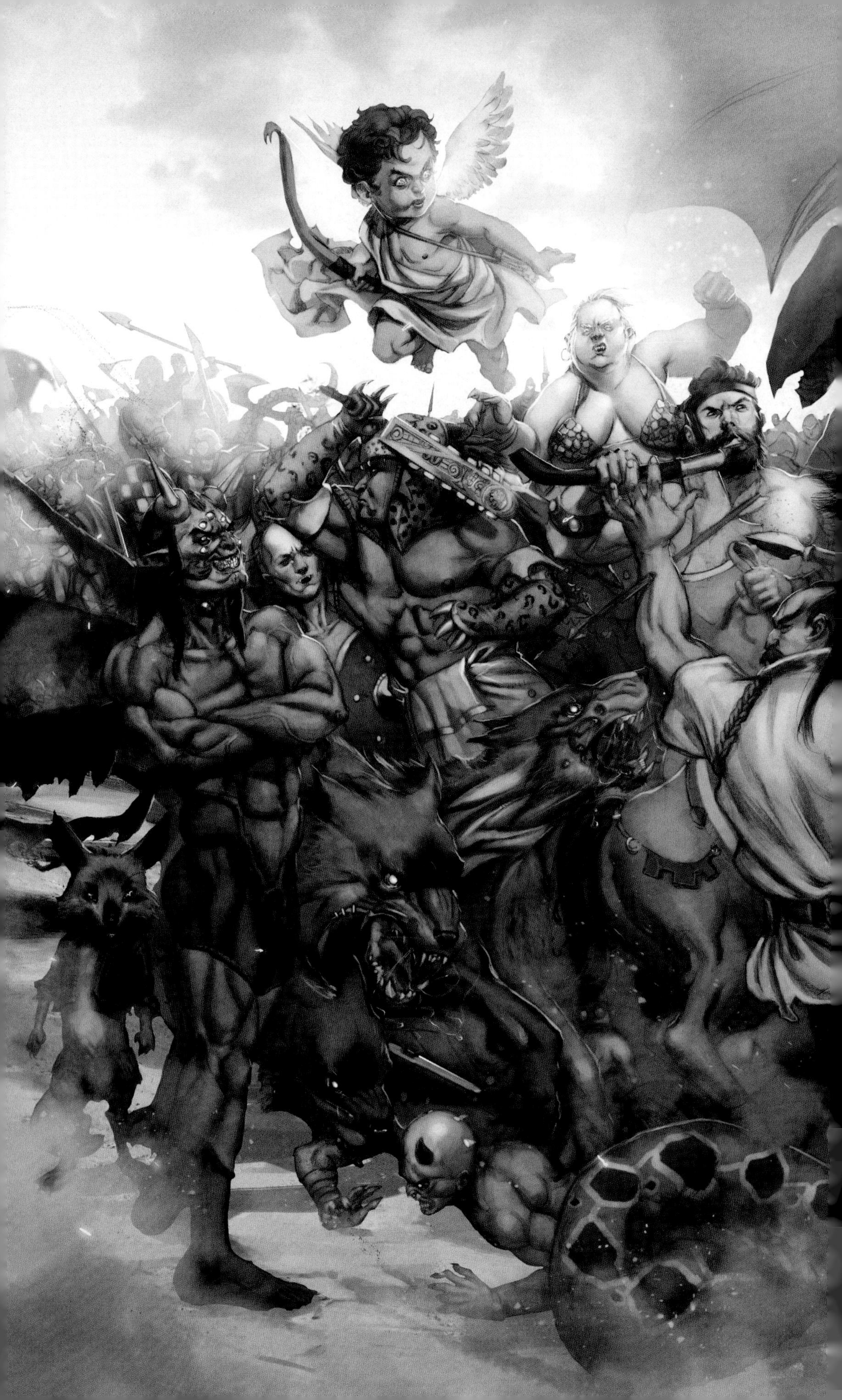

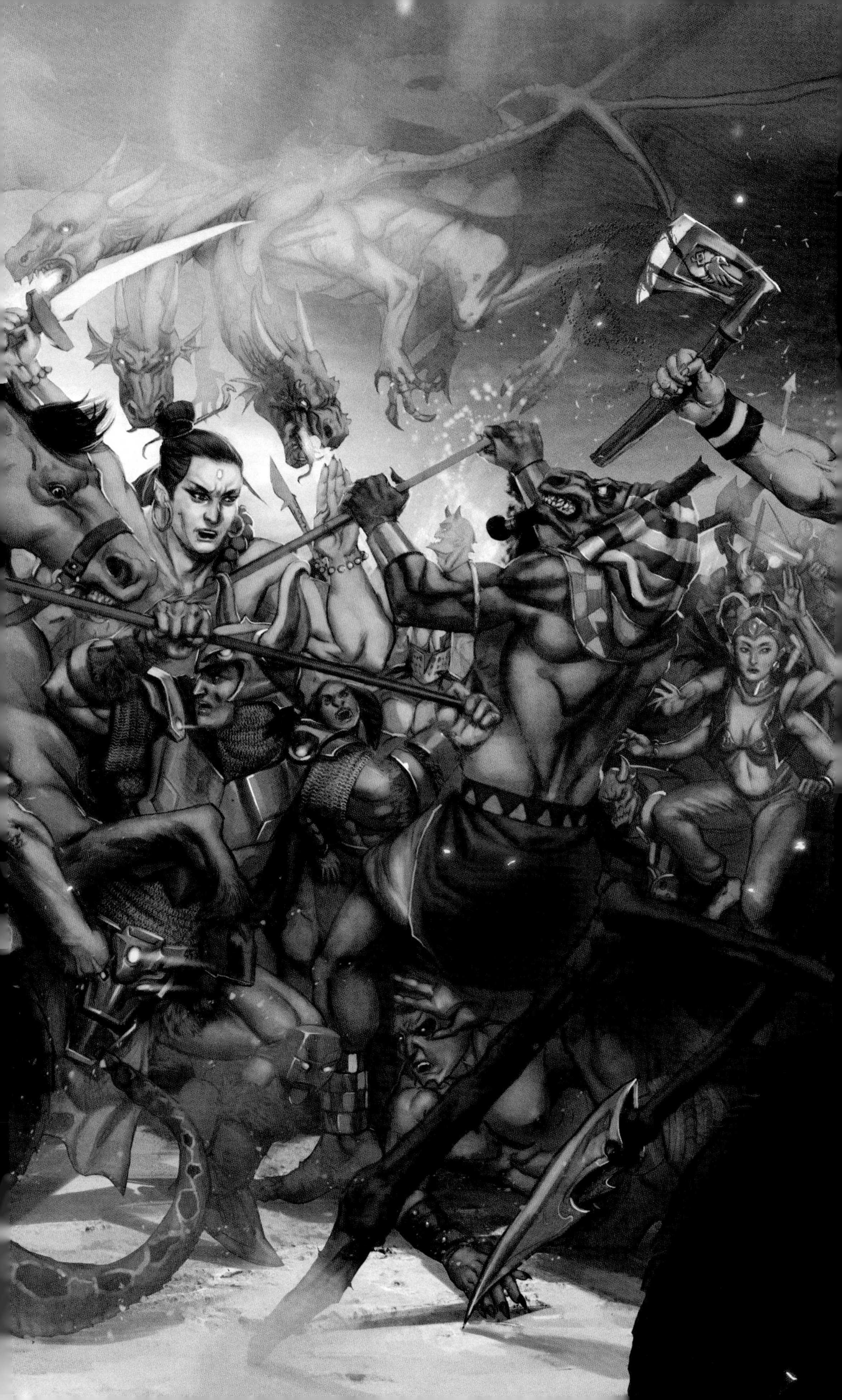

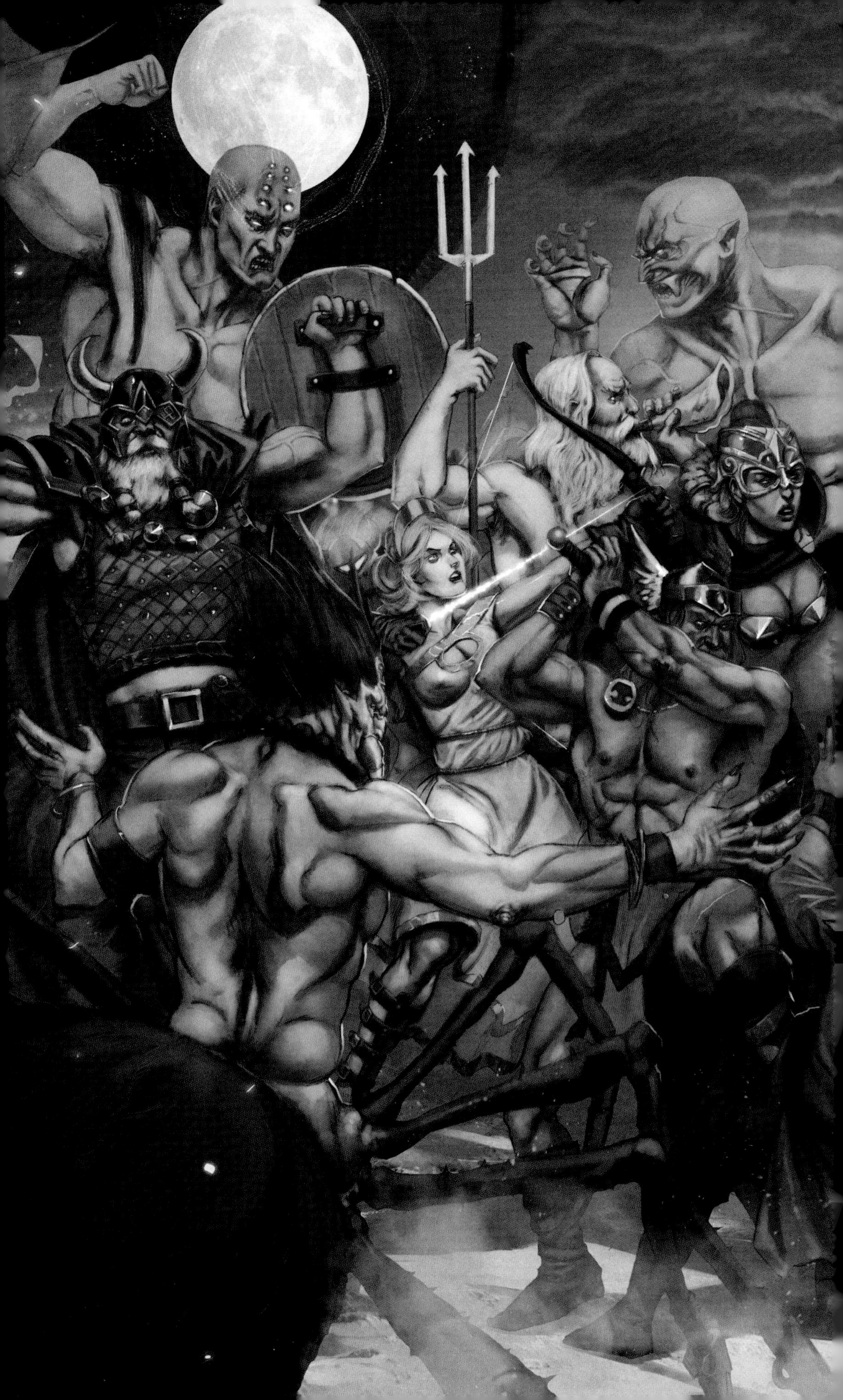

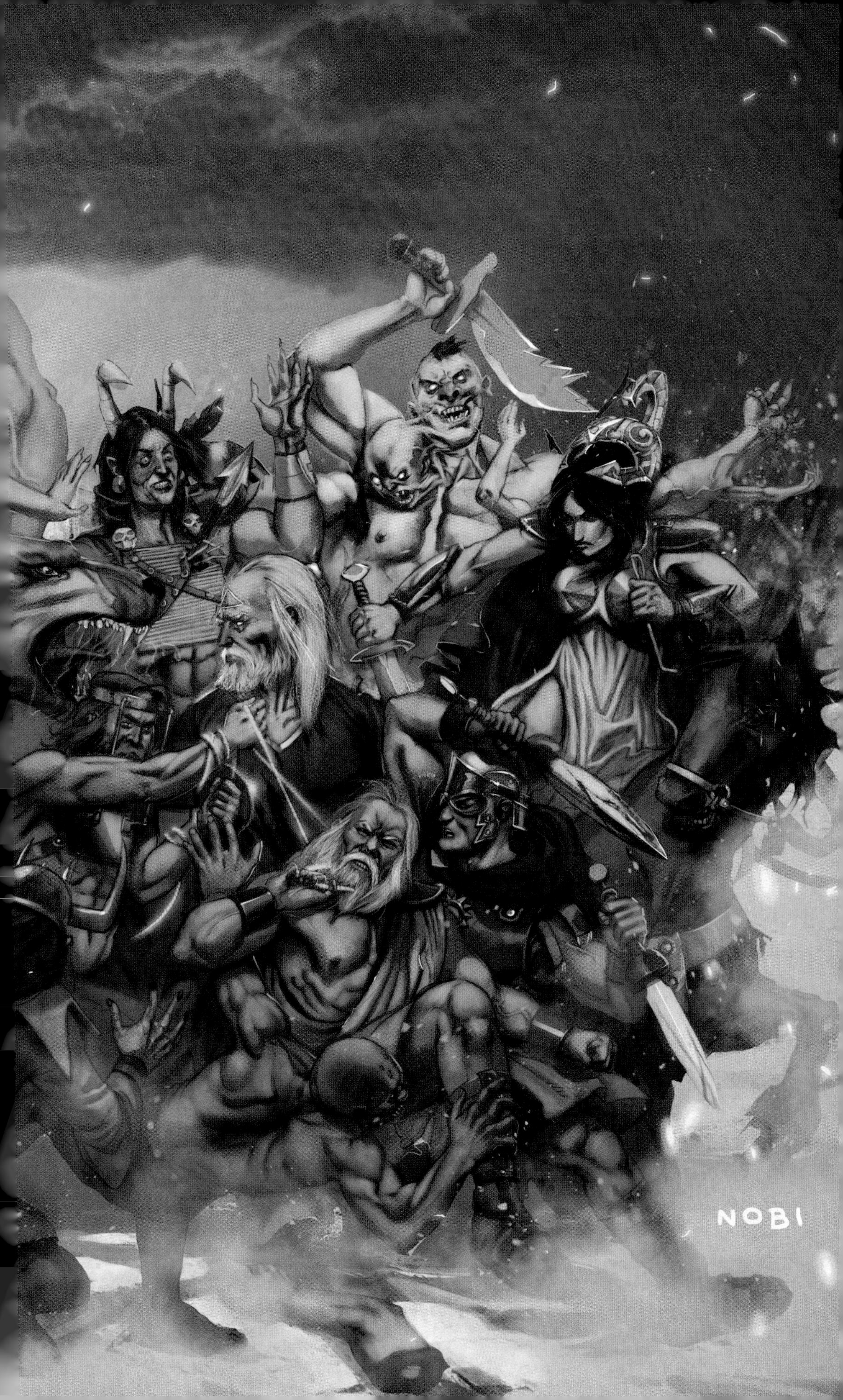
NOBI

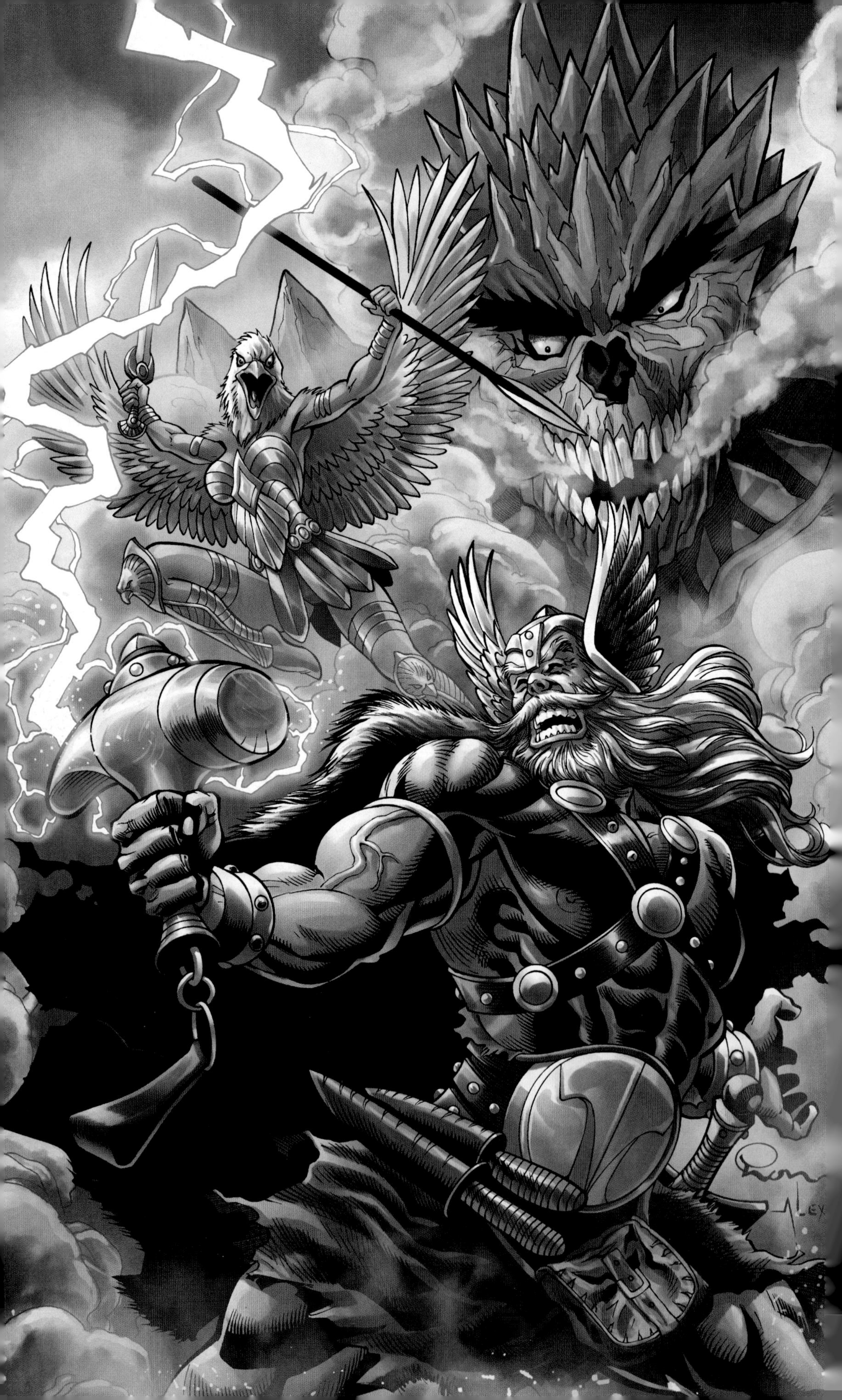